W9-AFL-799

"CO-OPERATION WITH LIKE-MINDED PEOPLES"

Recent Titles in
Contributions in American History

"CO-OPERATION WITH LIKE-MINDED PEOPLES"

British Influences
on American Security Policy,
1945–1949

RICHARD A. BEST, JR.

Contributions in American History, Number 116

Greenwood Press
New York • Westport, Connecticut • London

Wingate College Library

Library of Congress Cataloging-in-Publication Data

Best, Richard A.
  Co-operation with like-minded peoples.

  (Contributions in American history, ISSN 0084-9219 ;
no. 116)
  Bibliography: p.
  Includes index.
  1. United States—Foreign relations—1945-1953.
2. United States—Military relations—Great Britain.
3. Great Britain—Military relations—United States.
4. United States—Military policy.   5. United States—
National security.   6. Great Britain—Foreign relations
—1945-   . I. Title. II. Series.
E813.B46   1986   327.41073   85-27306
ISBN 0-313-24850-8 (lib. bdg. : alk. paper)

Copyright © 1986 by Richard A. Best, Jr.

All rights reserved. No portion of this book may be
reproduced, by any process or technique, without the
express written consent of the publisher.

Library of Congress Catalog Card Number: 85-27306
ISBN: 0-313-24850-8
ISSN: 0084-9219

First published in 1986

Greenwood Press, Inc.
88 Post Road West, Westport, Connecticut 06881

Printed in the United States of America

The paper used in this book complies with the
Permanent Paper Standard issued by the National
Information Standards Organization (Z39.48-1984)

10 9 8 7 6 5 4 3 2 1

FOR

MY MOTHER AND MY FATHER

CONTENTS

ACKNOWLEDGMENTS

The author is deeply grateful to Professor Thomas T. Helde of Georgetown University for his shrewd advice and kindly guidance in the preparation of the dissertation on which this study was based as well as for the example of his lifetime dedication to the study and teaching of the history of international relations.

Of the numerous librarians and archivists who provided professional assistance, I would like to mention several who were especially helpful. At the National Archives, Sally Marks and Kathy Nicastro of the Diplomatic and Legislative Records Branch made available the vast records of the Department of State with remarkable efficiency. In the Modern Military Headquarters Branch, John E. Taylor searched his now legendary mental file for pertinent materials and Wilbert B. Mahoney greatly assisted in locating and, in some instances, obtaining the release of key documents. At the Truman Library, Dennis Bilger provided valued advice and support. At the Naval Historical Center, Dean C. Allard gave me the benefit of his encyclopedic knowledge of modern naval history and Martha L. Crawley rapidly and intelligently guided me through the records of the postwar Navy.

In Britain the staff of the Public Record Office at Kew exceeded the traditonally high standards of the British civil service. The precisely ordered reports, minutes, recommendations and records of decisions provided insight into a decision-making process somewhat at variance with the more diffuse and less structured patterns customary in Washington.

In addition I would like to thank a number of private individuals who were particularly kind. Professor Donald Cameron Watt of the University of London graciously received me and gave me the benefit of his unrivaled insights into the conduct of British foreign policy. Keith Eiler readily gave me access to his notes on the career of Secretary of War Patterson. Professor Jon Wakelyn of Catholic University, an old friend, took an early interest in the publication of this study by the Greenwood Press. Professor James P. Shedel of Georgetown University supplied important assistance at a crucial juncture. Alison Luchs gave never-flagging encouragement.

ABBREVIATIONS

CAB	Cabinet Papers, United Kingdom
CCS	Combined Chiefs of Staff
COS	Chiefs of Staff, United Kingdom
DEFE	Defence Papers, United Kingdom, filed at PRO
FO	Foreign Office Papers, United Kingdom, filed at PRO
FRUS	*Foreign Relations of the United States* series
HSTL	Harry S. Truman Library, Independence, Missouri
JCS	Joint Chiefs of Staff, United States
LC	Library of Congress, Washington
NHC	Naval Historical Center, Washington
PRO	Public Record Office, Kew
RG	Record Group, National Archives

"CO-OPERATION WITH WITH LIKE-MINDED PEOPLES"

CHAPTER 1
INTRODUCTION

The historiography of the immediate postwar period from the Potsdam Conference in 1945 to the outbreak of the Korean War in 1950 has been dominated by analysis of the emerging competition between two superpowers, the United States and the Soviet Union. A large body of literature has dealt with this rivalry in terms of ideology, economic ambitions and atomic weaponry. The role of what was then the third world power, Great Britain, has been almost completely neglected, at least by American historians. The country which stood alone against Nazi Germany in 1940 and which fought with blood, toil, tears and sweat for almost six full years, longer than any other combatant country, receded out of the historiographical limelight with the coming of peace in 1945 and the defeat of Prime Minister Winston Churchill. According to the view apparently held by many American historians of the cold war, Britain contented itself with a distinctly subordinate position in international affairs, occasionally tugging at the coatsleeve of an all-powerful America to urge caution and restraint.

This fundamentally flawed stereotype obscures the fact that the British decisively shaped a historic transformation in world politics. Its widespread acceptance has gravely undermined our ability to comprehend the history of the crucial postwar period and the alliance system which emerged then and persists today. In reality,

Churchill's socialist successor, Clement Attlee, and Ernest Bevin, the trade unionist who followed Anthony Eden to the Foreign Office, successfully brought the United States into the European balance of power on the side of Britain and the other Western democracies, committed to defend the Western alliance should an attack be launched from the east. Although no statesman—not Castlereagh, Metternich, Bismarck, nor even Henry Kissinger—can systematically establish goals and priorities, allocate resources and meet deadlines with the efficiency of an engineer, Attlee and Bevin understood from the first the need for American involvement in Europe. They furthered it at every opportunity and secured its accomplishment during their terms in office. Few statesmen have achieved as much. As Alan Bullock has aptly suggested, to obtain American adherence to the North Atlantic alliance

in full reversal of the historical traditions of [American] foreign policy, was the peak of Bevin's achievement as Foreign Secretary, one which every one of his predecessors from Canning onwards would have recognized and one which, for over 30 years, has provided the security and confidence which Bevin sought for Western Europe.[1]

This Atlantic alliance is of course only one of the ties that has come to bind the United States and the West European countries together. Other links—trade, finance, culture, religion, politics and philosophy—exist and many antedate the post-World War II period. But it is NATO and the military strategy associated with it that created the European balance of military power that has provided the security underlying a period of economic and social progress unprecedented in world history. This study will focus on developments in the sphere of defense policy which led up to the military alliance codified in the April 1949 signing of the North Atlantic Treaty and the military strategies associated therewith. Although the British played a major role in the working out of the European Recovery Program and the beginning stages of European economic cooperation, London's decisive contribution to postwar history, and one which has received altogether inadequate attention by American historians, was in creating a European defense system with integral American involvement.

The United States did not, of course, passively allow itself to become gulled into globalism. Involvement was a conscious act of policymakers supported at crucial junctures by the Congress and the American people. Traditional American isolationism was discredited, considered to have contributed to the ambitions of the dictators in the 1930s. In framing U.S. policy in the immediate postwar years, American leaders responded to their own predispositions, the challenges of a militantly hostile Soviet policy, the demands of public opinion and their determination to prevent another war. An ideology of preparedness, the conviction that wars are invited by military weakness, led defense officials to seek far larger force structures than had ever before been considered necessary in peacetime. Public opinion was inevitably crucial in American democratic practice; Soviet policy in Eastern Europe and other adjacent areas made a profound popular impression which heavily influenced the evolution of American policy.

Yet this is not a history of the origins of the cold war or of Anglo-American relations per se, the "special relationship" of English-speaking peoples whose failure to materialize as an operative policy is often regretted in Britain.[2] Rather, it is an analysis of the calculations of policymakers working to promote and defend national interests. Before Pearl Harbor President Franklin D. Roosevelt and his advisers were moved, it is clear, less by a sympathy for a brave, stouthearted Britain under German siege than a realistic calculus of the peril to U.S. security interests if Britain, and especially the Royal Navy, fell into Hitler's hands. In the years 1945-1949 the United States came to accept a commitment to defend Western Europe primarily because key officials judged that American national interests demanded that Soviet power not be allowed to dominate all Eurasia, a likely eventuality absent a major U.S. role. Indeed, a few years after the end of the period under consideration here, Washington showed no inclination to let ties of sentiment and sympathy divert it from pursuit of its perceived interest when the United States and Britain (along with France and Israel) found themselves on opposite sides in the Suez crisis of 1956. The point is not that there were good and close Anglo-American relations in the years 1945-1949. Such did exist despite sharp differences in some areas; nevertheless it was the cooperative relationship in military policy which by then had been achieved which had decisive influence on the transformation of American and European politics. In large measure this was due to the exertions of British statesmen.

The higher echelons of American government in the late 1940s were filled by busy men facing a number of extraordinarily complex and controversial questions. It is impossible to isolate with finality the crucial influences on a particular set of decisions. Yet the American policymaking structure was a porous one, open to influence by political, commercial and diplomatic lobbies. The British used the opportunity to great effect.[3] American policymakers came, as a result of the influence of British colleagues, to share British conceptions of the importance of the European balance of power and prepared the way for formal peacetime alliance. Admittedly, the process of intellectual osmosis was a subtle one which can only be inferred as a principal influence involved in the transformation of American policy. There were, however, a number of discrete instances of British policy initiatives which did have clearly documentable results. The effort to establish the North Atlantic Treaty Organization in 1947-1948 was the most important. Neither aspect of British influence has been adequately noted; this study attempts to suggest a framework by which the imbalance may be eventually righted.

Inevitably, some considerations worked against British influence. The most important was the tradition established in the early years of the Republic and reflected in the Monroe Doctrine of avoiding commitments to or in the Old World—a tradition accepted by both conservative Republicans and liberal Democrats, exemplified by Senator Robert A. Taft on one hand and former Vice President Henry A. Wallace on the other. Elements of Anglophobia had not been completely eradicated by the experience of fighting together in two world wars. Widespread American opposition in principle, if not always in practice, to British colonialism gravely complicated British efforts to forge a common Anglo-American policy in the Middle East. Opposition in the United States to British policy in Palestine was a source of great friction. A complicating factor was the inevitable dissonance between a reformist Labour government in London and an enthusiastically capitalist regime in Washington.

These countervailing influences are important to bear in mind while looking at the postwar period. A particularly pernicious ramification, from the historian's point of view, was that Anglophobia made President Harry Truman most wary of revealing the extent of cooperation in defense matters with the British. It was kept as secret as possible because of political sensitivity; even the classified American documentary record which was released in the 1970s is meager in places, and the extent of collaboraton has to be pieced together or inferred with the help of British documents. More importantly, political realities further dictated that U.S. policy regarding the Soviet Union be cast in a uniquely American idiom which came eventually to center on a combative anticommunism which has obscured the realities of a policy based on a changed and broadened conception of national interest. As Robert Hathaway has written in connection with the Truman Doctrine of March 1947:

Ultimately, the shrill moralizing and uncompromising tone of much of America's foreign policy in the succeeding quarter-century must be attributed in part to the administration's determination to avoid any suggestion that the United States had simply stepped into Britain's shoes in the unsavory world of European power politics.[4]

The British had their own reasons, unrelated to self-effacing modesty, to allow the impression of America's initiative to persist. The Attlee government wished to avoid compromising its own socialist reputation by appearing to launch a cold war crusade. It also wished to avoid alienating the middle class, left-wing elements of the Labour party which have always been disposed to a certain degree of sympathy towards the Soviet experiment and suspicious of a Churchillian alliance with capitalist America. Moreover, the British government recognized that the effort to create an Atlantic alliance would be more successful in the United States if London's role went unremarked. As Foreign Secretary Ernest Bevin wrote in November 1948:

The conception of a North Atlantic Treaty has been widely canvassed in the United States, where it has been regarded as an American initiative. The circumstances that the idea originated in this country is not known except to a very narrow circle of officials who have been careful not to reveal it. There has been virtually no articulate opposition from the public, the press or Congress. If this state of affairs is to continue, there is much to be said for allowing the United States Government to continue to appear to be taking the initiative.[5]

What is most significant about the North Atlantic Treaty Organization is that it has not been merely a paper instrument, a pious declaration of intention unrelated to real-world concerns of defense policy, as has so often been the case with solemn covenants. Whatever may happen if war does come, NATO has since its early years encompassed a functioning military structure involving agreement on strategy, command, and disposition of forces in Europe even in peacetime to an extent unprecedented in history. The United States has from the first been closely involved and some estimates indicate that over 50 percent of American defense expenditures in recent years have been directed towards NATO-related missions.[6] This was by no means inevitable in 1947 when the effort to establish a Western alliance was launched. Many in the American defense community believed (and some still believe) that a capability to launch powerful nuclear strikes on the Soviet homeland was adequate in and of itself for deterrence against an attack on Western Europe and/or North America. Sole reliance on "strategic superiority" in hardware would have been much cheaper and such views were highly congenial to those within the Bureau of the Budget (the predecessor of today's Office of Management and Budget). But the British, and particularly Field Marshal Bernard L. Montgomery, then chief of the Imperial General Staff, disagreed. They argued that a viable defense in central Europe was possible. Attlee and Bevin also appreciated that French and West German security could be established only if British and especially American ground combat forces were deployed on their territory.

This strategy was proposed by the British in 1948; American and British military planners had previously concentrated on evacuation of occupation troops through Dunkirk once again or into an Iberian redoubt. Until this time, neither the United States nor Britain had been willing to face up to the political implications of a strategy based on leaving Western Europe to its own devices until a counterattack à la Normandy in 1944 could be mounted. A forward defense in Europe, a "continental commitment," not only ran counter to long tradition in both countries but would play havoc with attempts by both governments to balance budgets.

Obtaining the acceptance of this military policy by the United States proved even more difficult than obtaining ratification of the North Atlantic Treaty. Powerful influences were opposed to the permanent stationing of U.S. ground forces in Europe and they were not overcome in 1948 or 1949; in some measure they persist today. Nevertheless by the end of 1948, as a result of collaboration between British and American officials, including the occupation force commanders in Germany, a combined strategy was established which implicitly and inevitably required the presence of significant numbers of combat troops in Europe. Within three years much larger American ground combat forces had been sent to Germany, where they remain to this day.

In strictly military terms the results which have been achieved have never been wholly satisfactory; NATO's conventional forces would probably be unable to defeat a full-blown Soviet invasion. In a larger sense the perception of a determined and viable American commitment to the defense of Western Europe has nonetheless been sufficient to permit the reconstruction of free West European societies and has provided the necessary security for decades of economic development. By 1948 British and American officials came jointly to realize that the security of Western Europe in its fullest sense required significant defense capabilities that were in turn the prerequisite for economic and political development. They both came to accept that, after the destruction resulting from two world wars, participation in West European defenses by the United States was essential and that American political and diplomatic support, backing by the United Nations (which in the 1940s was taken more seriously than is now the case) or even vast quantities of economic assistance would be in and of themselves inadequate. It was this realization that lay at the heart of the creation of NATO, that was originally a British perception and that has been so often misconstrued by critics of the "militarization" of American foreign policy such as, on occasion, George Kennan and many less distinguished commentators. This commitment did not have its origins in blind phobias about communist encirclement nor in fixations about the efficacy of an "air atomic" strategy. It was a result of Anglo-American collaboration that was ultimately based on centuries of British efforts to maintain the European balance of power. It evolved in a long process of cooperation among like-minded peoples concerned to spare the world the ravages of further European conflict and the peoples of Western Europe the pervasive misery of famine, decay and despair in the years immediately following the collapse of the Thousand Year Reich.

To understand this process it is necessary first to review the different assumptions about the extent of national interests which prevailed in London and Washington during the war, and then to focus on developments in American defense policy during and immediately after World War II. Attention must be paid to the policies of the three major services as well as to the evolution of American foreign policy. Only when it became obvious that British power was inexorably in retraction, and that Soviet policies were threatening to interests that were now vital to the United States, did Washington accept defense responsibilities in the Mediterranean and in central Europe. At each step of the way the British encouraged greater American involvement; at each step the British provided essential support. By the end of 1947 cooperation both in practical matters of defense logistics and in the formulation of a combined policy for dealing with Moscow was sufficiently mature that Bevin could launch a major initiative for a Western alliance. The British took the initiative, but it was the United States which would have to supply the preponderance of resources; the American people would have to take on vast new responsibilities involving endless billions in expenditures and the permanent presence of U.S. troops in distant lands. There resulted a profound shift in American and European history, but it was based on cooperative endeavor, a fact which this study is directed at explaining.

NOTES

1. Alan Bullock, *Ernest Bevin: Foreign Secretary, 1945-1951* (London: Heinemann, 1983), p. 645.

2. Anglo-American relations in the post-World War II period have been cogently treated by Terry H. Anderson, *The United States, Great Britain, and the Cold War, 1944-1947* (Columbia, Mo.: University of Missouri Press, 1981); Robert M. Hathaway, *Ambiguous Partnership: Britain and*

America, 1944-1947 (New York: Columbia University Press, 1981); Donald Cameron Watt, *Succeeding John Bull: America in Britain's Place, 1900-1975* (Cambridge, England: Cambridge University Press, 1984); Elisabeth Barker, *The British between the Superpowers, 1945-50*, (Toronto: University of Toronto Press, 1983); William H. McNeill, *America, Britain and Russia: Their Co-operation and Conflict, 1941-1946* in *Survey of International Affairs, 1939-1946*, ed. Arnold Toynbee (London: Oxford University Press under the auspices of the Royal Institute of International Affairs, 1953).

3. The British did not neglect the need to influence American public opinion outside the Washington bureaucracy. See Caroline Antsey, "The Projection of British Socialism: Foreign Office Publicity and American Opinion, 1945-50," *Journal of Contemporary History* 19 (July 1984): 417-51.

4. Hathaway, *Ambiguous Partnership*, p. 303.

5. "North Atlantic Treaty and Western Union," 2 November 1948, C.P. (48) 249, CAB 129/30.

6. See, for instance, Richard Halloran, "Europe Called Main U.S. Arms Cost," *New York Times*, 20 July 1984.

CHAPTER 2
BRITAIN AND THE POSTWAR WORLD

In the aftermath of World War II the British attempted to pursue their traditional goals with vastly reduced resources in a world transformed by years of global conflict. The principal aim of British foreign policy has been accurately characterized as the maintenance of the European balance of power, to ensure that no one state dominated the Continent. In Sir Eyre Crowe's classic exposition of 1907, the only check on "a State at once militarily powerful, economically efficient, and ambitious to extend its frontiers or spread its influence" is the opposition by an equally formidable rival or combination of rivals. "The equilibrium established by such a grouping of forces is technically known as the balance of power, and it has become an historical truism to identify England's secular policy with the maintenance of this balance by throwing her weight now in this side and now in that, but ever on the side opposed to the political dictatorship of the strongest single State or group at a given time." Further, "The opposition into which England must be driven to any country aspiring to such a dictatorship assumes almost the form of a law of nature."[1] Having contested in turn the efforts by Spain, France and Germany to achieve European hegemony, after 1945 the British worked almost reflexively to assemble a grouping to counter the ambitions of a victorious and militant Russia. The effort to ensure a balance of power did not inherently preclude a policy based on conciliation or a willingness to meet what were seen as another state's legitimate security requirements. It did imply that Britain's own security interests required that efforts be undertaken to draw closer to friendly states. The British were well aware of the consequences of ignoring such considerations—the threat posed by Nazi Germany in the 1930s had been well understood, but the halfhearted effort to create an effective alliance in opposition to Hitler was a complete failure and the result was total war.

London's postwar policies continued to hinge on the need to maintain the European balance of power: to foster the revival of the West European democracies, to ensure that Germany could not again threaten the peace, to prevent one power—Russia—from dominating the entire Continent. Such ambitious intentions were not capable of realization by Britain acting independently. After six years of war, with her reserves dissipated, her factories in ruins and with occupation and peacekeeping duties around the world, the United Kingdom's position was incomparably weaker. All knowledgeable Britons understood this intellectually even if they had not made the psychological adjustment. The problem was to find a policy within British capabilities that would avoid a collapse of Western Europe that would pave the way for domination by the Soviet Union. This goal united the Tories and the overwhelming majority of the ruling Labour party. Even if many Labourites instinctively distrusted traditional British foreign policy, the leaders of the postwar government had served under Churchill during the war and intended to continue the main lines of British policy especially in regard to Western Europe.

THE SOVIET CHALLENGE

British concern about the implications of victorious Soviet power for the rest of Europe dated from the early days of the war. The Ribbentrop-Molotov pact of August 1939 had given an early indication of Soviet ambitions to push Russian borders westward. Moscow determinedly pursued the same goal in initial negotiations for an Anglo-Soviet pact in late 1941 and early 1942. The head of the Foreign Office's Central Department noted the obvious aims of Soviet policy in May 1942: "The whole of Eastern Europe, to be effected by the occupation of Finland, the Baltic states and Rumania, the closest possible association with Czechoslovakia and Yugoslavia, the crushing of Hungary and the encirclement of Poland.''[2] In and of themselves such Soviet ambitions did not directly conflict with British interests, and it was accepted that Moscow would have to be accommodated to an extent sufficient to ensure continued Soviet participation in the war (a concern stimulated by recurrent rumors of Soviet-German peace feelers). The British hoped through negotiations to gain a measure of leverage over the postwar settlement and acceptance of British interests in the West and in the Mediterranean. Preliminary discussions between London and Moscow, however, soon came into conflict with stern American disapproval of premature deals regarding boundary issues. American opposition to such arrangements derived from public dismay when World War I understandings had been revealed, from Roosevelt's wish not to incur opposition from various ethnic groups and a desire to avoid involving the United States in what was then perceived as a struggle between rival British and Russian imperialisms. For these reasons, Roosevelt and the State Department asked that any such discussions should be postponed. As a result, the Anglo-Soviet Treaty of May 1942 was silent on future transfers of territory and populations.

The British attempted to retain some influence over the future of Eastern Europe, particularly to secure the independence of Poland, for which ostensibly they had gone to war in 1939, and to ensure that Greece, which guarded the Eastern Mediterranean, would come in the postwar period under British and not Soviet influence. In the first years of the war, the Foreign Office considered the possibility of a series of alliances among the Eastern European states as a means to provide mutual support and as a form of *cordon sanitaire* against expansive Soviet influence. Various schemes were promoted for aligning Poland, Czechoslovakia and other states, but such efforts collapsed as a result of conflicts between the countries involved and as a result of predictable Soviet opposition, effectively exercised through the compliant Czech government in exile. Plans were laid for a Balkan federation involving Greece, Yugoslavia and Bulgaria but these too came to nought as a result of inherent contradictions and Soviet opposition.

Concerned about Moscow's ability to dominate the Eastern European governments, Eden attempted on several occasions to reach an understanding with the Soviets themselves that none of the great powers would make separate agreements with liberated countries, but a tentative arrangement in this direction was soon rendered inoperable by Soviet agreements with the Czech government in exile.

While these efforts reflected Foreign Office concerns in 1941-1943 for the future extent of Soviet power in Eastern Europe, they were not the principal preoccupation of the cabinet which was concentrating on the war effort. When, however, the Red Army began its offensives into eastern and central Europe in 1944, Churchill and Eden became directly interested in the approaching postwar situation in which Soviet influence was certain to be radically expanded. Eden recalled "a growing apprehension that Russia has vast aims and that these may include the domination of Eastern Europe and even the Mediterranean and the 'communising' of much that remains."[3] Churchill noted in May 1944 that "evidently we are approaching a showdown with the Russians about their Communist intrigues in Italy, Yugoslavia, and Greece. I think their attitude becomes more difficult every day."[4] The British were particularly concerned about future of Poland, whose fate the Soviets evidently intended to determine singlehandedly, without regard to the views of either the exile government in London or the British and the other Western powers.

Concern that the Soviets intended to settle Eastern European questions unilaterally led Churchill and Eden to propose a deal. In May 1944 Eden suggested to the Soviet ambassador in London that the British would accept a predominant Soviet role in Rumania if Moscow would recognize the predominant British interest in Greece. The Soviets parried with a request that Eden obtain Washington's acquiescence in the arrangement. Despite considerable diplomatic pressure, the State Department could be persuaded only to accept a temporary arrangement, but the Russians then backed off.[5]

The British did not let themselves be deterred by this failure. The following October Churchill ventured to Moscow to discuss Eastern European and other questions while Roosevelt remained in the

United States for the 1944 election campaign. On this occasion Churchill suggested to Soviet Premier Josef Stalin the famous percentages agreement, which would have recognized Soviet preponderance in Rumania and Bulgaria, equivalent British influence in Greece and an equal role in Yugoslavia and Hungary. Stalin appeared to accept the proposal. The State Department was adamantly opposed to such official delineations of spheres of influence, but Roosevelt refrained from repudiating the arrangement.[6] Although there was never a formal agreement, London and Moscow did in fact consolidate their positions in the countries which had been under discussion. Hungary tipped into the Soviet sphere, but the British proceeded shortly to establish a friendly government in liberated Greece without American support and despite strong opposition in broad circles of American public opinion.[7] The Soviets acted even more forcefully in Bulgaria and Rumania. Yugoslavia, under Marshal Josip Broz Tito's control after the war, sought its own path although it was assumed in the West at the time to be under Moscow's direct influence. Despite his background as a Communist guerilla leader, Tito would break with Stalin in 1948 and subsequently pursue a neutralist foreign policy. Thus, in a sense, Soviet and Western influence in Belgrade ultimately was even.

The approaching end of hostilities provoked great anxieties on the part of Churchill. He wrote at length of his concern for the implications of the Soviet role in liberating Berlin, the failure to live up to previous commitments regarding the composition of the new Polish government and Moscow's general high-handedness. He was, however, unable to persuade Roosevelt or Truman to take more assertive opposition to Soviet maneuvers, and left office in the summer of 1945 filled with a deep sense of foreboding.[8] As he advised the British ambassador in Washington in July 1945:

i have the impression that the Americans take a rosier view of European prospects than we do. They seem to think that, given the settlement of a few outstanding problems, and the enunciation of general political principles and desiderata Europe can safely be left to look after itself, and that it will soon settle down to peaceful and orderly development. Our view, on the contrary, is that unless we all work very hard the situation in Europe will deteriorate rapidly and dangerously.[9]

As the war in the European Theater was being victoriously concluded, the Chiefs of Staff were weighing postwar plans for the three services. There was considerable discussion regarding the need to base such planning on the assumption that Russia was in fact a likely military opponent. In early October 1944 the Chiefs of Staff had argued that it was their duty to consider the possibility that "Russia may start forth on the path to world domination, as other continental nations have done before her." Acknowledging that "no one will dispute for a moment the value of friendship with Russia or a successful world security organisation," they persisted in maintaining that the "examination of an unpleasant situation which may perhaps arise is in no way incompatible with the pursuit of a policy designed to prevent that situation arising."[10] Noting that only the Soviets among the European powers could pose a danger to Britain, the COS pressed for a thorough examination of the possibility that the Soviets would in fact emerge from the war as a potential enemy. While they recognized the importance of not antagonizing Russia and the fact that "the immediate object of a western European group must be to keep Germany down," they added: "We should not forget the more remote but more dangerous possibility of the use of German resources by a hostile Russia and we should consider whether any measures we were prepared to take now would assist in preventing such a contingency."[11]

In response to such arguments, Sir Orme Sargent, a senior official in the Foreign Office, argued that the possibility of a leak of such a study could seriously undermine British policy and generate suspicion and animosity on the part of the Soviets, leading to the very situation that it was desired to prevent. In a meeting between Eden and the COS it was concluded that there could be no easy solution to the problem and until such time as the cabinet could give firm directions, the COS should continue to work on their plans, taking "steps to restrict to the narrowest possible limits discussion and circulation of papers in which the hypothesis of Russia as a possible enemy was mentioned."[12]

Looming behind the Foreign Office's considerations of postwar planning was concern for the future of Germany. Here there were essentially two British aims: (a) to ensure that Germany would not again be able to threaten the peace of Europe, and (b) to protect Britain and the rest of Europe against ruin by the deadweight of a prostrate German economy. Britain, alone or in combination with France or the other West European countries, would not be able to keep Germany under control and President Roosevelt had made clear his determination not to keep American troops in Europe for more than two years after the end of the war. Thus, for the Foreign Office, the need for cooperation with the Soviet Union was based on the two countries' mutual interest in overseeing German postwar development. It did not result from a pious conviction that Soviet power was benign, but rather was a logical and inescapable necessity in the view of the Foreign Office. The need to encourage an atmosphere conducive to such cooperation goes far to explain the antipathy of Foreign Office officials to the Chiefs' tendency to base their plans on the worst-case assumption that Russia was the next enemy. The Foreign Office had a realistic expectation of leaks and an understanding of the ease with which Stalin's paranoia could be fanned.

All recognized that the attempt to find a locus of cooperation with Moscow in Germany could not be divorced from considerations of postwar balance of power. The British focused on two general lines of defense policy to achieve a viable balance. The effort to create a grouping of West European states was favored by the Foreign Office. As a counterweight to the prospect of Soviet predominance in Eastern Europe, Foreign Office officials gave extensive consideration to the possibility of forming a group of Western democracies under British leadership. Duff Cooper, who had resigned as first lord of the admiralty in 1938 in protest against the appeasement of Germany, was in 1944 serving as the British representative to the French National Committee in Algiers. Remembering the fatal absence of Anglo-French joint planning in the prewar period, in July 1944 Cooper proposed a program for regional cooperation in Western Europe.

Cooper's proposal inevitably raised concerns. He had argued that ''Russia, when Germany was eliminated, would present the greatest political menace to the peace of the Continent.'' In response, he suggested, Britain should form an alliance, not with Poland or Czechoslovakia for whom Britain could not possibly provide protection, but with France and the smaller Western powers—Holland, Belgium, Portugal and Italy. Cooper considered that these countries would follow the British lead if an appropriate policy were energetically pursued. He had, he later recalled, "a vision of such an alliance gradually leading to a federation of the western seaboard of Europe together with the principal Powers of the Mediterranean."[13] While Eden was receptive to this suggestion, he and the Foreign Office staff were very conscious of the need to avoid the appearance of launching an anti-Soviet coalition which would complicate relations with Moscow and generate opposition by the American State Department.

The question of an arrangement of Western European states was reviewed in a series of memoranda by Gladwyn Jebb, a senior Foreign Office official. In Jebb's view, the first goal was to secure the capability to resist future aggression by a resurgent Germany by stationing forces "according to some plan, and for ensuring that the arms and equipment of the whole group were of uniform pattern."[14] In view of the likelihood that Moscow would view such an arrangement as a potential anti-Soviet bloc, Jebb suggested linking it officially with the nascent world organization, which was intended to harmonize the policies of the Big Three.

Discussions on the question of a western regional defense arrangement were not pushed forward, however, in part because of concentration on planning for the establishment of the United Nations. The fact that American opinion and State Department policymakers continued to be firmly opposed to blocs or spheres of influence also induced caution. Nevertheless, provisions were made at the Dumbarton Oaks Conference in August 1944 for the possibility of regional security arrangements in coordination with the future world organization. Both American and Soviet diplomats were apprised of London's thinking in regard to a form of Western European association and neither raised objections. The British of course presented their concept as comparable to American plans for a Western Hemisphere defense arrangement and Soviet links with the Czech government.

Although no negotiations with the West Europeans were to be undertaken in 1944, the British took out further insurance against the possibility of leakage of their intentions. The ambassador in Moscow, Sir Archibald Clark Kerr, was instructed in November 1944 to brief the Soviet foreign ministry further on various proposals that had been made regarding Britain's relations with the West European governments. Soviet Foreign Minister Vyacheslav M. Molotov was told that the British "put the World Organisation first on our list of desiderata, and, in any case, we proposed to rely on the Anglo-Soviet alliance for the purpose of holding Germany down.'' Clark Kerr reported that Molotov appeared interested in the information for he "had clearly been watching the press closely and had probably attached undue importance to the reports about a western *bloc*."[15]

Churchill was sympathetic to the need for a revival of the West Europeans, particularly the French. At Yalta, he insisted that France be given a zone of occupation in Germany. Britain, he argued, could not bear the burden of its occupation zone alone for an extended period, especially in view of the likelihood that, as Roosevelt had indicated, American forces would be withdrawn within two years.[16] Yet he was not prepared to commit inevitably limited British forces to the defense of the weak West European countries. Moreover, he was by no means persuaded of the usefulness of a formal West European bloc. As he indicated in a memorandum to Eden in November 1944,

The Belgians are extremely weak, and their behaviour before the war was shocking. The Dutch were entirely selfish and fought only when they were attacked, and then only for a few hours. Denmark is helpless and defenceless, and Norway practically so. That England should undertake to defend these countries, together with any help they may afford, before the French have the second [largest] Army in Europe, seems to me contrary to all wisdom and even common prudence.[17]

The prime minister's primary postwar goal was a permanent security relationship with the United States. As he told a group of senior American officials at a luncheon in 1943:

He could see small hope for the world unless the United States and the British Commonwealth worked together in what he would call fraternal association. He believed that this could take a form which would confer on each advantages without sacrifice. He would like the citizens of each without losing their present nationality to be able to come and settle and trade with freedom and equal rights in the territories of the other.[18]

He felt that alliances with the smaller European states were only half-measures at best and a potential source of complication in the relationship that he was carefully cultivating with Roosevelt.

Churchill's emphasis on ties to Washington was wholly shared by the Chiefs of Staff, who saw Anglo-American cooperation as the essential element of British defense policy. As a June 1945 assessment prepared for the Chiefs of Staff concluded, "A united British Empire would by itself be unable to secure its world wide interests against Soviet aggression without the help of powerful Allies. It is vital to ensure the full and early support in war of the U.S.A."[19]

LABOUR IN POWER

The coming to power of the Labour government in July 1945 did not fundamentally affect the conduct of British foreign policy.[20] Senior cabinet members, especially Prime Minister Clement Attlee and Foreign Secretary Ernest Bevin, had been part of Churchill's coalition government and had shaped and supported its decisions. The need to avoid Russian domination of the Continent and to promote the resuscitation of the West European countries was clearly recognized from the first days of the new government. The need for American support, especially in the form of a new loan to replace lend-lease assistance which had been discontinued, and for ongoing cooperation in atomic energy was clearly recognized. A Labour government inevitably had different emphases than one headed by Winston Churchill, but Attlee's cabinet continued to share the traditional British concern for the balance of European power even if they were prepared to jettison the bulk of the British Empire. No attempt was made to revive the pacifist traditions of the Labour party in the 1930s or to retreat into a neutralist isolationism. Although Attlee was not given to the rhetorical expression of English-speaking solidarity with which Churchill endeavored to sway American opinion, he supported the continuation of Anglo-American defense cooperation, realizing the great benefits it provided to the British even if he was at times skeptical of some of the Chiefs of Staff's more expansive plans. In an August 1945 message Attlee urged Truman to continue postwar defense cooperation on defense research and development and made the same request in his November 1945 visit to the White House.[21]

The arrival of Ernest Bevin at the Foreign Office represented the beginning of one of the most creative periods in the history of British foreign policy.[22] Bevin, who came from the lowest stratum of

English society, worked his way up by a combination of natural ability and iron will to the leadership of the trade union movement and a position of great influence in the Labour party. As minister of labour during the war he had presided over the mobilization of the manpower resources of the entire nation for the struggle against Germany; without compulsion, he led the country to a more extensive and efficient commitment of the economy to the war effort than was achieved in any other country. Seeking appointment to the Treasury in order that he could continue his life's work of improving the employment and living conditions of the British workers, Bevin was appointed instead to the Foreign Office, despite his lack of the educational (and social) background customarily considered prerequisite for the job. Bevin did, however, have long experience in issues of international trade and economics, believing that expanded commerce was essential for the health of the British economy and the welfare of British workers. He also shared the general concern that a Russian-dominated continent would be fatal to British interests, but, unlike Attlee, he had a strong conviction that Britain's economic health and security were involved in the defense of her traditional position in the Middle East. He gave decisive weight to the position of the Chiefs of Staff in their argument that British forces should be retained in the area, although in the end the best he could do was to delay a British pullback while drawing the United States into the area. Bevin's power in the Labour government came from his prestige among the trade unionists. His ability to influence the prime minister derived from complete personal loyalty, as was displayed in his refusal to become involved in an effort launched by Stafford Cripps, then president of the Board of Trade, to replace Attlee in September 1947.[23] Above all, there was the sheer force of Bevin's personality, the strength of purpose of a man who had risen from the bottom to the top of a class-ridden society, whose "instinctive reaction to opposition had been to flatten it."[24] A more critical observer, Alan Taylor, has stated that "Bevin often bullied for a good cause; he was a bully all the same."[25]

At the Foreign Office Bevin picked up the threads of West European security arrangements earlier promoted by Duff Cooper and Gladwyn Jebb. As the historian John Baylis has written, "By late 1944 and early 1945 . . . [there was] a general acceptance in the

Foreign Office of the advantages of a Western European security group and a recognition of the need for a more positive approach by Britain to the establishment of such a group."[26] Bevin very early in his tenure at the Foreign Office expressed his interest in the revival of the West European economies and in renewing British ties to France with "a view to using their friendship as the foundation for greater collaboration between the states of Western Europe as a whole."[27] Unfortunately, relations with the French were not subject to immediate improvement. The causes were varied: de Gaulle's difficult personality and his resentment over wartime slights, the offense given by British opposition to the return of Syria and Lebanon to French control in the summer of 1945, and a deteriorating political situation in Paris which led to de Gaulle's resignation in January 1946.[28] In 1946, while the British government devoted much of its energies towards keeping afloat its occupation zone in Germany and attempting to establish some sort of working relationship with the Soviet Union, the French government remained politically paralyzed as the Communists, Gaullists and others contended for power. French policy in Germany remained vengeful, and Paris resisted cooperation with any of the other powers including Britain.

Only at the end of 1946, with a Socialist government headed by Léon Blum temporarily in office, was there a possibility of improving Franco-British relations. Duff Cooper, now ambassador in Paris, seized the opportunity to resurrect his earlier proposals for a security arrangement. He shifted discussions regarding an increase in the allotment of coal going from the British zone of Germany to France into talks for an Anglo-French alliance. Bevin was receptive and negotiations were pursued during a visit by Blum to London in January 1947.

The Treaty of Dunkirk signed by Bevin and Georges Bidault, the new French foreign minister, on 4 March 1947, was specifically directed towards the possibility of renewed German aggression but, as Duff Cooper certainly intended, it had a greater function. It was a logical culmination of the wartime proposals for a European security group.[29] While the historian Sean Greenwood is correct in arguing that the treaty was intended in part to stabilize the fluid internal politics of France at a difficult point, it is also obvious that the Dunkirk accord was intended to inaugurate a climate of closer

Anglo-French cooperation on a variety of European questions—political, economic and eventually military.[30] Alexander Cadogan, the British representative to the United Nations, suggested that, "if Russia chooses to regard it [the Dunkirk treaty] as an insurance against herself, and if the cap fits, let her wear it."[31]

The military implications of the treaty were not immediately felt (except perhaps in Attlee's pressure on the Chiefs of Staff to discontinue planning to evacuate British and American troops from the Continent).[32] The Chiefs of Staff conditioned their approval of the treaty on the understanding that it would not impair efforts to improve Anglo-American defense cooperation. They continued to regard collaboration with the Americans as the "keystone on which our major strategy and planning are based, and consider that any risk of impairing those relations would be too great a price to pay for such a treaty."[33] The British realized that they were in no way able to contemplate providing the extensive military assistance which French rearmament would clearly require. Nor did they want the Americans to believe that an Anglo-French security arrangement would be adequate to balance Soviet strength. Nevertheless the treaty had major military implications; it committed Britain to precisely the sort of continued involvement in European defenses which had been assiduously avoided in the interwar years. It was manifestly a prelude to a wider grouping. A few weeks subsequent to its signing—and after the disappointing results of the Moscow meeting of the Council of Foreign Ministers—Bevin determined that "the time has come when we should start to bind our friends in Western Europe more closely to our side and if any of them are anxious to conclude alliances with us it would be a mistake to oppose their wishes."[34]

While pursuing ties to the French and other West Europeans, from the beginning Bevin accepted the need for close Anglo-American relations. He faced not inconsiderable difficulties. Both Truman and Secretary of State James F. Byrnes were initially put off by his seeming stubbornness at their first meeting at Postdam, and U.S. policy in the second half of 1945 was still influenced by a presumed need to avoid involvement in a potential conflict between Britain and the Soviet Union.[35]

As would often be the case, the Soviets provided crucial inducements for Anglo-American cooperation. At the London meeting of

the Council of Foreign Ministers held in September and early
October 1945, Bevin and Byrnes were both put on the defensive by
Molotov's intransigent efforts to exclude the French from discussions of major issues. The conference degenerated into squabbling
over issues relating to Eastern Europe, especially the composition
of the Bulgarian and Rumanian governments, Japanese matters and
Soviet efforts to play a major role in Italy's former North African
colonies (today's Libya) and the Dodecanese islands.

For the British delegation the Mediterranean questions were
crucial. Bevin was adamant that the Russians not gain territory in
the Mediterranean which would allow them to threaten British lines
of communication. He preferred British supervision of the territories which had been liberated by British arms and only with reluctance did he go along with American plans for creating U.N. trust-
eeships for Italy's former colonies.[36] Molotov's abrasive tactics,
probably dictated by domestic political considerations in Moscow,
gave an aura of solidarity to the positions taken by Byrnes and
Bevin, which had not been coordinated beforehand.[37]

The implicit Anglo-American solidarity which existed at the
London meeting did not deter Byrnes from subsequently proposing
that the foreign ministers of the Big Three meet together in Moscow
in late December 1945 to try to salvage a degree of great power
cooperation. Bevin, furious at the hasty calling of a conference
without prior coordination,[38] was further dismayed to see Byrnes
cut a deal with the Russians over Eastern European and Japanese
questions while brushing aside his concerns over Soviet pressure on
Iran and Turkey where long-standing British, but not American,
interests were at stake. As Bullock writes, Bevin "returned from
Moscow with the impression that Byrnes still thought of bringing
off a settlement with the Soviet Union which would allow the
Americans to withdraw from Europe and in effect leave the British
to get on with the Russians as best they could."[39]

The Moscow Conference was both the nadir of Anglo-American
postwar relations and the end of an era in American diplomacy. In
late 1945 American public opinion was becoming increasingly skeptical of Soviet ambitions; President Truman sensed this and warned
Byrnes upon his return from Moscow against trusting or appearing
to trust the Soviets. Republican criticism of the Democratic administration's handling of foreign policy was growing. This domestic

discontent provided an opportunity for the British—Bevin himself, defense officials and, most noticeably at the time, the former prime minister at a speech in Fulton, Missouri—to encourage a change in American policy.[40]

During the long series of conferences in 1946 and 1947 Bevin and Byrnes (and subsequently Byrnes's successor, George Marshall) came to work together, not without disagreements, but increasingly on terms of cordial familiarity that would be impossible to establish with Molotov. Bevin gradually won the confidence and respect, if not always the affection, of the Americans. His determination to maintain the closest possible ties to Washington was sufficiently strong for him to overcome his strong resentment of American policy regarding Palestine as well as what he considered onerous loan terms. British and American diplomats came gradually to perceive and eventually act upon a common interest in preventing the economic collapse of Europe, the disintegration of West German society and ultimately the achievement of predominant European power by the Soviet Union and its Communist allies.

MECHANISMS OF ANGLO-AMERICAN DEFENSE COOPERATION

The influence of the British upon American policy derived as much from the influence of defense officials as from the Foreign Office; in many respects it was greater and certainly more pervasive. British and American officers had worked together during the war as if they were nationals of the same country; there had grown up bonds of familiarity and friendship based on shared experience in fighting the common foe. On neither side of the Atlantic was there a readiness after the war to let this relationship wane, but for the British the determination to continue defense cooperation was a matter of national policy accepted throughout the foreign policy and defense establishments and, on the whole, by the leaders of the Labour government.[41]

During the war Anglo-American cooperation had been institutionalized through an elaborate system of combined organizations which had been created to manage the war effort. The Combined Chiefs of Staff—the U.S. Joint Chiefs of Staff and senior British counterparts stationed in Washington—provided, under the guidance of Roosevelt and Churchill, supreme direction for Allied commands throughout the world. The British sent Field Marshal Sir John Dill to Washington to serve as their senior member of the CCS. Upon his death in late 1944, he was succeeded by Field Marshal Sir Henry Maitland Wilson, who remained until March 1947.[42] The British prime minister and the Chiefs of Staff saw these instrumentalities as providing a way to perpetuate Anglo-American defense cooperation after the end of the war against Germany and Japan. In September 1943 at a speech at Harvard University, Churchill had praised the CCS machinery:

This is a wonderful system. There was nothing like it in the last war. There never has been anything like it between two allies.

Now in my opinion it would be a most foolish and improvident act on the part of our two Governments, or either of them, to break up this smooth-running and immensely powerful machinery the moment the war is over. For our own safety, as well as for the security of the rest of the world, we are bound to keep it working and in running order after the war—probably for a good many years.[43]

The instrumentalities of cooperation—and there was a host of committees operating under the CCS—were not abolished after the end of hostilities in 1945. A need existed for continued cooperation in winding down various combined enterprises, training programs, and so forth. The CCS also continued to command Allied forces in Italy, in Southeast Asia, and along the volatile border between Italy and Yugoslavia. Nevertheless, on the American side at least there was no clear conception of what the future role, if any, of the CCS should be.

At Potsdam the British Chiefs of Staff had tabled a memorandum which formally suggested that

some machinery for the continuation of joint and combined United States/ British collaboration is desirable . . . it may be to the great advantage of both the United States and ourselves that some machinery should exist for the mutual exchange of information. Some measure of uniformity in the design of weapons and in training may also be mutually beneficial.[44]

At the CCS meeting of 19 July 1945 at Potsdam the record indicates that the proposal was only noted since, as the American side explained, "the United States Chiefs of Staff were not in a position to discuss at this date the post-war relationship between the respective military staffs."[45] Truman was later reported to have felt then that "it was undesirable to bring up the question of military alliance with the British until our relations with our allies become sufficiently stabilized to warrant consideration of a permanent relationship between military commands."[46] Although the Americans clearly did not then want to commit themselves to any formal agreement to continue official collaboration, it is evident that senior officials appreciated the need for some measure of postwar defense cooperation with the British. General George C. Marshall, the army chief of staff, had a private talk with Field Marshal Sir Alan Brooke, his British counterpart, and advised him that

> he personally felt that all possible steps should be taken to ensure that some similar organisation to the C.C.S. should be kept alive after the war. Only by so doing would the lessons which have been learnt during the war and the experience which had been gained during it be perpetuated. U.S. and British staffs had worked together at all levels and much had been gained as a result. He recalled the state of affairs which occurred after the First World War. No exchange of information or liaison at a staff level had been arranged for. It was consequently found to be almost impossible for British and U.S. officers to get together and discuss matters which did arise after that war.[47]

Marshall's views were similar to those held by other senior American military and naval leaders, particularly those who had worked closely with the British. The CCS was allowed to continue for the time being but there was uncertainty about its future role and it was divorced from the American postwar planning process.[48]

Much of the official liaison between the British and American military forces was conducted under the auspices of the British Joint Staff Mission in Washington. British officers assigned to the CCS were also part of the BJSM. The BJSM consisted of representatives of the several services and supply organizations who worked directly with their American counterparts to provide support to the war effort particularly in such areas as equipment design and coordination of tactics. The BJSM, which also continued in existence after the war, sponsored continuing technical liaison between the respective services. It allowed for an extensive exchange of information which would have been difficult to achieve if the British were represented in Washington only by service attachés.

As the war was drawing to a close, British officials responsible for the work of the CCS and the BJSM had begun to plan for the future. It was obvious that the vast wartime staffs (the British at one point had over 4,000 representatives in Washington) would be reduced. The BJSM established an ad hoc committee in September 1945 to study the question and report back to the Chiefs of Staff in London. The committee recommended that some eighty-six officers should be retained to provide liaison for cooperation in training, communications, intelligence, tactics and research and development.[49]

Personnel were required for coordinating remaining CCS functions, particularly the Allied command in Italy, which was not disbanded until 1947. These were finite responsibilities which did not require constant high-level attention. The British COS had, however, other and more ambitious reasons for keeping the CCS in existence. They calculated that

(a) Any form of post-war military collaboration presupposes the impossibility of war between the United States and Britain;

(b) Anglo-American military co-operation is the best possible deterrent to and guarantee against aggression;

(c) The C.C.S. is both the symbol and instrument of that military cooperation.

In view of the Americans' unwillingness at Potsdam to take an official position on the continuation of the CCS, the British COS realized that "it would be bad tactics to raise the matter with the Americans at this stage." Wilson and a much reduced BJSM remained in Washington without a formal decision as to the future of the organization.[50]

The British Chiefs of Staff, supported by their political masters, were making every effort to retain much of the intimate working relationship between senior military commanders that had characterized the wartime experience. The British had a real need for technical exchange, but also kept larger strategic issues much in mind. The CCS was seen as a way to influence the thinking of American

military officials and perhaps to promote joint strategic planning in
the future. British officialdom had concluded that

> it would be very much to the British advantage to maintain the C.C.S. or-
> ganisation for as long a period as possible after the war . . . it was always
> conceivable that some boorish act on the part of Russia might jerk Ameri-
> can opinion into postponing its dissolution much longer than was
> expected.[51]

The influence of British defense officials on their American
counterparts cannot be accurately measured, but it is clear that by
1945 many senior officers were beginning to share their British colleagues' concerns about Soviet policies and were becoming persuaded of the need for Anglo-American combined policies. Marshall for instance told Wilson in November 1945 that the JCS
"thought that everything possible had been done to co-operate with
the Russians and that now it was better to face facts and get down
to work with people who are really willing to co-operate."[52]

General Dwight D. Eisenhower, who relieved Marshall as army
chief of staff in early 1946, shared this attitude. As supreme allied
commander, Eisenhower had worked closely with his British associates and with Prime Minister Churchill. Much of the credit for
harmonious working of the Supreme Allied Expeditionary Force
has been credited to Eisenhower's tact and diplomacy, amply
required for handling of such difficult personalities as Generals
George S. Patton and Bernard L. Montgomery. Eisenhower was
now disposed to work quietly but consistently for closer relations
with the British military. He told Field Marshal Wilson in early
January 1946 that he and his JCS colleagues "all felt the time was
approaching when we should both clear our minds on the policy we
were going to adopt in all fields of mutual collaboration and work
out the detailed methods by which it should be put into effect."[53]
Although Admiral Ernest J. King, the chief of naval operations,
has often been characterized as an Anglophobe because of his abrasive insistence on the priority of the Pacific Theater during the war,
he too favored close cooperation with the British. In June 1945
Admiral Sir James Somerville, who was attached to the BJSM, reported to London his informal discussions with King and Navy
Secretary Forrestal. Both indicated to him that they were in favor

of continuing close Anglo-American cooperation after the end of hostilities.[54] King's successor as chief of naval operations, Admiral Chester W. Nimitz, also supported close consultation with British naval leaders; by the summer of 1946 he was advocating a "coordinated naval policy with appropriate members of the British Commonwealth of Nations."[55] Air Force officers in both countries had carefully coordinated air strategy and tactics during the war, often together in opposition to the ground and naval leaders of their respective countries. Senior RAF officers coaxed their American counterparts in the most effective arguments for establishing an independent U.S. Air Force.[56]

For many senior American military and naval officers the desire for cooperation reflected more than the search for allies in the face of growing hostility to the Soviet Union. Shared experience in World War II had produced a common outlook which antedated hostility towards Russia. Naturally the British made every effort to put their views across, but it was more the case that American officers had come to accept certain assumptions about the importance of the Western democracies working together in international affairs to prevent a repetition of the pattern of events of the 1930s. In March 1946 Wilson and the JCS had contended that

it was not a question of producing arguments to persuade each other that [continuing cooperation] was the right answer as we are all completely of one mind. The problem is a far more difficult one in as much as we must produce arguments which will persuade our Heads of State that we have a good case that they in turn can explain to the world.[57]

From these shared assumptions flowed a willingness to cooperate with the British in maintaining the European balance of power and, in years to come, to assume peacekeeping duties which the British could no longer shoulder. The precise extent of British influence on changing American views can never be determined, but the symbiotic relationship which existed between British and American officers at the highest levels during and immediately after World War II undoubtedly contributed to an American willingness to accept responsibilities clearly congruent with Western interests as the British conceived them.

Despite the predilection for cooperation among senior American officers and their tacit willingness to continue the CCS, British officials were concerned that without some formal charter the process of collaboration would slowly atrophy or become centered on essentially routine housekeeping functions. By the end of 1945 Field Marshal Wilson had become convinced that a decision about the future status of the CCS could not "to my mind be much longer delayed."[58] He arranged with Eisenhower to hold an informal and off-the-record talk in early January with senior American officers. The meeting may have been characterized as informal, but Wilson coordinated his preparations with the COS in London. His comments were prudently diffident. He intended to note that it was unthinkable that there should ever be "grave misunderstandings between our two countries" and that arrangements between the two countries must not "prejudice the part we must both play in making the United Nations Organisation an effective power in the world." He would then turn to his main purposes in the discussion: first, collaboration in the development of new and improved weapons and techniques, and second, the "exchange of views on the lessons of the war and the possible development therefrom of tactical or operational doctrines." In regard to the former, he would advocate the continuing exchange without restriction of "all the scientific and technical information at the disposal of each of our countries." He intended to note that this practice had been observed since 1941, that Attlee had discussed it with Truman and that the president was understood "to be well disposed to the idea." He would explain that liaison would be conducted with a small staff of some twenty-five British officers in Washington with occasional visits by specialists. Other contacts would be maintained by American staffs in London. Concerning collaboration in tactical and operational doctrine, he would suggest that the two countries

should try to deduce together what lessons should be drawn from the war and exchange ideas on the best way to handle the weapons and forces we create. I am thinking here in terms of the exchange of ideas on such things as communication procedure, signal books, tactical methods in all three services, the technique of amphib[i]ous operations and air cooperation with ground and sea forces.

In regard to what Wilson termed "the field of policy," he did not propose to introduce the subject himself but thought it inevitable that the American officers would raise the question of the future of the CCS. His proposed presentation was somewhat coy, as if he were going to make every effort to avoid being overly eager. "What our Chiefs of Staff would really like is to feel that they will always be free to discuss military policy and plans with you; and that sufficient of the existing machinery will always be retained to enable this to be done." He intended to suggest that there was still enough work in clearing up the loose ends of the war to keep a number of senior British officers in Washington, allowing collaboration to continue for the time being, and "we rather feel that this is a question that can be left over for a while."[59]

With concurrence from London, Wilson duly made his pitch at a luncheon meeting on 8 February 1946 with Eisenhower, Nimitz and Admiral William D. Leahy, who chaired the U.S. Joint Chiefs of Staff. A background paper for Eisenhower, drafted by the Army staff, reviewed very briefly the history of the CCS. It noted that, of eight CCS committees still technically in existence, only the Combined Communications Board and the Combined Meteorological Committee had much to do, and the combined field commands no longer existed except for the headquarters in Italy. The memorandum acknowledged the continuing value of the CCS for "close understanding and ready resolution of problems," but pointed to a major drawback to its continued functioning: "The continuation of the CCS might be considered as a military alliance by certain other nations regardless of the extent of the military collaboration involved."[60]

According to Wilson the meeting provided "a very good informal discussion." He indicated that the American officers stated that "they wanted collaboration to continue in peace on exactly the same scale as it had in war and in the same fields (i.e., exchange of views on policy, together with collaboration in the technical, scientific, tactical doctrine, intelligence and training fields)." As Wilson had predicted, they did turn to the question of national policy, but the Americans suggested, no doubt to the field marshal's consternation, that

it would be impossible for the United States administration to recognise officially a special degree of United States/British collaboration. So much now has been said about [the] UNO and the need for collaboration with everyone on an equal footing, that the American people simply would not understand discrimination in our favour.[61]

The way around the dilemma, as suggested by the Americans, was for the CCS machinery to "go underground." They indicated that this might be done through the service attachés or perhaps through a combined Anglo-American board which could be set up ostensibly to deduce lessons from the conduct of the war. The American chiefs also proposed the option of continuing work under the auspices of the Permanent Joint Board on Defense, U.S.-Canada.[62]

American officials readily appreciated the need for continued working-level cooperation between U.S. and British staffs on such matters as equipment, tactics and communications. They also considered that "the key to the duration of the CCS lies in the Russian attitude." Cooperation would be essential if any conflict should arise in the Mediterranean region. They were nonetheless sensitive to the fact that a continuing CCS showed a lack of confidence in the U.N. and they were reluctant to endorse explicitly the British goal "to formalize this [CCS] arrangement so that it operates during peacetime as almost a military alliance, [which] would be to give it a stature which might make it utilizable by the British as a political instrument or political threat in their international dealings with third parties."[63] The Americans preferred, in effect, to return to the situation which prevailed in the months immediately before Pearl Harbor, when extensive collaboration and combined planning were secretly undertaken on the president's verbal authority.

This proposal was not well received by the British; there were, they considered, limits as to what could be accomplished on an "underground" basis due to the sheer difficulties involved in doing business. More importantly, one of the major benefits in British eyes of continued Anglo-American collaboration was the healthy impact such combined endeavors might have on the policies of other states. It was of course doubtful that such relationships could have been in any event kept secret from Moscow because of the regular reports then being sent to the Soviets by Donald Maclean, a member of the British Embassy in Washington regularly involved in discussions relating to Anglo-American defense cooperation.[64]

Wilson agreed to establish a combined committee to study the future of the CCS. The committee drew up a draft memorandum for the president and prime minister that recommended abolishing the organization and providing less formal means of continued co-operation. In early March, however, Wilson learned that Leahy had also come to have doubts about the wisdom of "going underground." He was now, Wilson reported, inclined to "let things drift on and [he felt] that there was no need to put anything up to the Heads of Government until our open collaboration was seriously challenged." Leahy was undoubtedly reflecting the president's desires at a time of increasing Soviet-American hostility.[65] Truman said the same month at a press conference that the CCS would continue at least until the war "is officially ended" and the organization's future would be settled "when the time comes."[66]

The CCS did not in fact ever receive a serious challenge. Contingency announcements for its demise were prepared but did not have to be used. The question of its continuing role arose again both in 1947 and 1948. Only in 1949, after the creation of NATO, was the CCS abolished. The CCS was no longer the command center for worldwide Anglo-American planning and operations that it had been during the war. Its significance lay in the fact that its continued presence in Washington accorded British officials ready access to the highest echelons of the American defense establishment. It also provided a means by which combined planning for specific operations could be quietly undertaken in the first postwar years.

In essence the Americans considered that interservice collaboration was acceptable and useful, but cooperation on larger questions of defense strategy had to be handled on an ad hoc basis when crises arose. In any event, it was not possible to proceed further on major issues of combined defense strategy as long as no consensus existed on American military policy. Wilson's position was not filled when he departed Washington in 1947, but the senior member of the BJSM became the primary British point of contact with the JCS. The BJSM even managed to secure office space in the Pentagon. Wilson nonetheless considered that his mission to Washington had been successful:

During the war years we had got to appreciate each other's value and to understand our different ways and customs; after two years of post-war experience there existed a genuine feeling that by standing together we formed a bulwark for the maintenance of peace and that our two nations, having the same interests and ideals, should carry forward that spirit of cooperation which in times of stress had allowed our respective combat services to work as one team; it would be of inestimable value in facing problems that lie ahead.[67]

Considerable ad hoc liaison did in fact occur and served to impress upon senior American officials the compelling need for the two countries to work together. As will be discussed in Chapter Four, American and British officers gave considerable study in 1946 to combined plans for the evacuation of the occupation forces in central Europe in the event of a surprise Soviet attack. But in 1946 and 1947 it was the possibility of conflict with Tito which induced combined actions. As a result of the presence of American and British troops near the bitterly contested city of Trieste on the Italian-Yugoslav border, there had to be a certain amount of contact between planners as to how to deal with emergencies. The need for agreed-upon plans was particularly acute in the summer of 1946 when it was feared that Tito might seek a military settlement of the question. Admiral Nimitz in particular was concerned with the need to bring British officers into contingency planning in view of his belief that any naval combat operations in the Mediterranean would inevitably involve the Royal Navy. In June 1946 he wrote to Eisenhower and Leahy suggesting that the Joint Planners study the problem and that, because of the dangers of "leaks and serious embarrassment," this should be done by informal arrangements with the British rather than through the official CCS machinery.[68] The desire for secrecy in regard to contacts with the British was overriding. As one Army document stated:

The Chiefs and the Chiefs of Plans of the three Services were to be kept informed [of such Anglo-American planning] but . . . if any questions came up officially, or from civilians, they would know nothing about it and lay any blame on the Planners for unilateral action . . . no papers were to be processed through the JCS Secretariat or through the JPS [Joint Planning Staff] Secretariat.[69]

The question of combined planning did not concern only uniformed officers. Forrestal's diary noted a conversation with Nimitz and Eisenhower on 21 August 1946 in regard to the command situation in the event of war, presumably over Trieste, in which American forces would undoubtedly be fighting alongside the British. The navy secretary noted that

Eisenhower's view was that the land commander in Europe would be an American with the British Commander . . . retaining his present job as Commander at the head of the Adriatic. Nimitz said he thought the British would not agree to an American Commander of the Mediterranean and that he would not insist upon it.[70]

In a meeting between the JCS and British Army and Navy representatives on 30 August 1946, it was agreed that there should be a meeting of planners from the two countries in Washington to deal with an emergency if one arose. Wilson had earlier reported to London that the American chiefs desired an informal luncheon with him to exchange "preliminary thoughts . . . on the possible repercussions and actions to be taken in the event of an attack against Allied forces in Venezia Giulia."[71] Although it proved possible to defuse the Trieste crisis largely by diplomatic means, the incident underscored the need for U.S. planners to seek coordination with the British in regard to European crises. Further it demonstrated that it was possible to use the World War II channels in Washington to coordinate a combined response to a postwar crisis. The sense, if not the formality, of an Anglo-American alliance persisted.

The question of cooperation between the two countries continued to receive high-level attention in the second half of 1946. September 1946 saw the visit of Field Marshal Montgomery, now chief of the Imperial General Staff, to the United States and Canada. Montgomery sought to shore up channels for cooperation among the three English-speaking countries. He noted in his memoirs that in a talk with President Truman he had suggested that the American and British military staffs should begin discussions "covering the whole field of defense" and that the president had replied, "That's O.K. by me, go right ahead."[72] The following day Montgomery and the JCS (Leahy, Eisenhower, Nimitz and General Carl Spaatz, the head of the Army Air Forces) lunched onboard the S.S. *Sequoia* en route Mount Vernon and discussed the general question of cooperation. Leahy noted that "discussion was devoted to parallel actions that may be possible for the British and American forces in Europe in the event of a sudden attack by Soviet or Yugoslav armies."[73] Montgomery wrote of his talks, "And so ended a remarkably successful visit—successful beyond my wildest dreams. It had been established that the continued functioning of the machinery of the Combined Chiefs of Staff was accepted without question by the President and the American Chiefs of Staff."[74]

The following month Eisenhower himself made a trip to Europe which included a stop in London. On 10 October 1946 he met with the British Chiefs of Staff. An aide-mémoire prepared by the British after the meeting noted that discussions ranged broadly, based on the assumption that in any future global war the United States and the British Commonwealth would "be in together" and that "our first aims should therefore be to hold (a) places vital to our war-making capacity and (b) those places from which we could hit back." The participants agreed, according to the British record, that these areas included the United Kingdom base, the Eastern Mediterranean base, and the Continent. In regard to holding the line on the Continent, the participants considered that prior planning-level discussions had reached "unduly pessimistic" conclusions and that planners should be instructed to count on being able to hold "a bridgehead on the Continent" at least for evacuation purposes. It was further agreed that "in the event of a serious threat developing in the Central Mediterranean, the United States forces in Italy would retire south and not attempt to join the forces in the American Zone in Germany." Eisenhower, the aide-mémoire indicated, agreed to "do everything possible to maintain up to strength the American division in Italy." Further, he suggested, "United States naval forces would be available to assist British naval forces in the control of the Mediterranean."[75]

When a copy of the aide-mémoire was forwarded to Eisenhower in Washington, the chief of staff was careful to reply that "it accords with my understanding of the informal views expressed" and emphasized that he had enjoyed "my informal meeting." As the editors of the Eisenhower papers state, "The Chief of Staff's emphasis on the informal nature of the meeting was no doubt a reflection of how politically sensitive the issue was—in the United

States, Great Britain, and possibly in the United Nations." Nonetheless Eisenhower saw to it that the "Army Planner is undertaking a study of [a] course of action in Europe in case of an emergency, which takes into account the possibility that it may prove practicable to hold a bridgehead."[76]

This flurry of activity among senior officers and their staffs died out with the abatement of the Trieste crisis in late 1946 and the signing of the Italian peace treaty in February 1947. In some respects the tense weeks in the late summer and early autumn of 1946 were a final spasm of World War II; American and British military responsibilities in Italy were part of the wartime missions established by the CCS. The settlement of Italy's border with Yugoslavia was not a new responsibility taken on by the Truman administration. In other respects, however, the closer Anglo-American cooperation engendered by the Trieste crisis served as a precedent for future combined planning against Soviet or Communist expansionism. The senior officers of both the United States and the United Kingdom realized that in any confrontation with the Soviets or their protégés, they would need to work together as a matter of military necessity.

Only a limited amount of combined planning for contingency operations apparently continued into 1947. In addition to American hesitations about public alliances, the British government was also seeking to avoid damaging leaks at a time when the left wing of the governing Labour party was particularly critical of any Anglo-American tendency to "gang up" on the Soviet Union. The British COS were also engaged in extensive discussion of their future defense policies and the large forces being retained in the Mediterranean were coming under close scrutiny and high-level opposition. In addition, the Foreign Office was preparing a determined effort to reach an agreement with the Soviets in regard to the future of Germany. All in all it was a time when zeal for new initiatives seemed inappropriate.

Despite the hiatus in operational planning, cooperation between the British and American services in scientific and technical areas proceeded apace. With the continued presence of the BJSM in Washington, it was possible to coordinate matters relating to equipment and tactics which could make operational coordination possible once the political decision was made.

During 1946 and 1947 much effort was expended in providing for the exchange of classified materials between the United States, Britain and certain Commonwealth countries. There was relatively little reluctance on the part of American officials to exchange information with the British and the Canadians, who were both prepared to share their data with the Americans on a free and open basis. The problem was with another member of the British Commonwealth—Australia, because of what were considered lax security practices. Eventually it was possible to work out an agreement and on 27 February 1946 the president approved a "Basic Policy Governing the Disclosure of Classified Information to Foreign Governments."[77] The new policy in essence provided for free exchanges between the United States and Britain, with responsibility for implementation assigned to the military services. Other agreements were made to promote standardization of military equipment, although this effort was never very successful in view of the concerns of national industries to protect their markets.

Anglo-American cooperation in regard to the development of nuclear weapons reflected all the difficulties and inconsistencies in the overall relationship during the period. Much of the initial work on the atomic bomb had been undertaken by scientists in Britain and the two countries had worked closely together during the war. At the Quebec Conference in August 1943 Roosevelt and Churchill agreed that the two countries would never use the atomic bomb against each other, that they would use it against third countries only with each other's consent, that atomic energy information would not be disseminated to third countries without mutual consent and that arrangements would be made for future collaboration. At Hyde Park in September 1944 Churchill and Roosevelt signed another agreement pledging that cooperation would continue after the war. Attlee renewed the effort to continue cooperation in his meetings with Canadian Prime Minister Mackenzie King and Truman in Washington in November 1945 and the three leaders signed a memorandum calling for full cooperation in the field of atomic energy.

The vicissitudes of American politics, however, undid this pledge of cooperation. The need to pass the McMahon Act of August 1946, which established the Atomic Energy Commission as well as civilian control of atomic energy, was overwhelming. The legisla-

tion, as enacted, included limitations on dissemination of information relating to atomic energy to other countries that were at variance with Roosevelt's agreements with the British prime minister.
Although the British protested against the legislation, the administration considered that it was too important to risk even for the
sake of living up to previous agreements.[78]

The British, having no choice but to accept this setback, went to
work to enlarge upon what cooperation with the United States remained possible and pressed ahead with their own effort to build a
British bomb. There was, however, a genuine need for the two
countries to cooperate in obtaining critical supplies of uranium at
a time when the element was not being produced in significant
quantities in the United States. The British retained a right to share
in the uranium available, particularly from mines in the Belgian
Congo. American authorities hoped to obtain access to a large
share of this supply. Thus London was able to induce Washington
to reassess the need for closer cooperation. In January 1948 the two
countries signed an informal modus vivendi by which each agreed
to support the other's atomic energy program, to initiate cooperation with Commonwealth countries and to permit the United States
to have access to large supplies of uranium. An earlier agreement
that the British could veto American use of atomic weapons was
officially voided. The modus vivendi was a strange document,
never actually signed or ratified, which reflected the needs of both
governments to work together more closely without raising clouds
of publicity on an extremely sensitive and controversial issue.[79]

British defense policy was itself undergoing a period of uncertainty in the first postwar years. It was a period of military re-
trenchment when much of the attention of defense officials was
given over to interservice rivalries and to struggles to maintain adequate levels of funding, and to complete complex postwar reorgani-
zations. The British COS were trying to maintain a position in the
Mediterranean and the Middle East at a time when their supply
base in Egypt, long the lynchpin of their operational capabilities in
the area, was jeopardized by the rising clamor of Egyptian nation-
alists who wanted all foreigners out of the country. The granting of
independence to India also raised many difficult questions for
defense planners.[80] In the event of a Soviet invasion of Western
Europe, British planners saw no way to provide an adequate resis-

tance; the tendency was to think in terms of maintaining the security of the British Isles and the North Atlantic as well as the Mediterranean Sea through which American aid would, it was hoped, be delivered.

Ernest Bevin's great achievement was to draw together the two strains in British security policy—cooperation with the West Europeans and cooperation with the United States—into one coherent policy. He launched the critical initiative which brought Britain, the United States and Western Europe together in a security alliance which he saw as the most effective way to maintain the European balance of power and the peace of the world. This signal accomplishment was possible, however, only because of the long process of cooperation among the like-minded peoples of the British and American governments, military and civilian alike.

NOTES

1. Eyre Crowe, "Memorandum on the Present State of British Relations with France and Germany," 1 January 1907, Great Britain, Foreign Office, *British Documents on the Origins of the War, 1898-1914*, ed. G. P. Gooch and Harold Temperley, 3 (London: His Majesty's Stationery Office, 1928): Appendix A, 403. The importance of the concept of the balance of power, long derided by American political oratory (including that of President Roosevelt and especially Secretary of State Cordell Hull) would soon gain new respectability in the United States. In late 1947, James Forrestal, by then secretary of defense, noting George Marshall's dislike of the term, argued that "there was no reason why he should not use it because that was precisely what we were now compelled to reestablish." Diary entry for 19 December 1947, Forrestal Papers, NHC.

2. Quoted in Victor Rothwell, *Britain and the Cold War, 1941-1947* (London: Jonathan Cape, 1982), p. 98.

3. Anthony Eden, Earl of Avon, *The Memoirs of Anthony Eden, Earl of Avon: The Reckoning* (Boston: Houghton Mifflin, 1965), p. 509.

4. Quoted in Winston S. Churchill, *The Second World War*, 6, *Triumph and Tragedy* (Boston: Houghton Mifflin Co., 1953): 73.

5. See Introduction to *The Foreign Office and the Kremlin: British Documents on Anglo-Soviet Relations, 1941-45*, ed. Graham Ross (Cambridge, England: Cambridge University Press, 1984), pp. 43-44.

6. The "percentages agreement" is discussed by Albert Resis, "The Churchill-Stalin Secret 'Percentages' Agreement on the Balkans, Moscow, October 1944," *American Historical Review* 83 (April 1978): 368-87;

Llewellyn Woodward, *British Foreign Policy in the Second World War*, 5 (London: Her Majesty's Stationery Office, 1976): 184. Churchill's own account is in *Triumph and Tragedy*, pp. 226-28. The American reaction is discussed by Eduard Mark, "American Policy toward Eastern Europe and the Origins of the Cold War, 1941-1946: An Alternative Interpretation," *Journal of American History* 68 (September 1981): 324-25; Joseph M. Siracusa, "The Night Stalin and Churchill Divided Europe: The View from Washington," *Review of Politics* 43 (July 1981): 381-409.

7. See Hathaway, *Ambiguous Partnership*, pp. 90-100; Anderson, *United States, Great Britain, and the Cold War*, pp. 21-24.

8. Churchill, *Triumph and Tragedy*, pp. 329-676 passim.

9. Churchill to Halifax, 6 July 1945, *Documents on British Policy Overseas*, ed. Rohan Butler and M. E. Pelly, Series 1, 1 (London: Her Majesty's Stationery Office, 1984): 3.

10. Woodward, *British Foreign Policy*, 5: 207-8.

11. Ibid., 5: 190.

12. Ibid., 5: 210.

13. Alfred Duff Cooper, Viscount Norwich, *Old Men Forget: The Autobiography of Duff Cooper, Viscount Norwich* (London: Readers Union, Rupert Hart-Davis, 1955), pp. 338-39.

14. Woodward, *British Foreign Policy*, 5: 184.

15. Ibid., 5: 197.

16. See Minutes of the Second Plenary Meeting, 5 February 1945, *FRUS, Malta and Yalta*, pp. 616-17.

17. Quoted in Woodward, *British Foreign Policy*, 5: 194.

18. Memorandum by the British Embassy, 22 May 1943, *FRUS, Washington and Quebec*, p. 171.

19. "The Security of the British Empire," 29 June 1945, Post-Hostilities Papers (45) 29 (O) (Final), CAB 81/46.

20. Recent studies of Attlee's premiership include Kenneth O. Morgan, *Labour in Power, 1945-1951* (Oxford: Clarendon Press, 1984); Kenneth Harris, *Attlee* (London: Weidenfeld and Nicolson, 1982).

21. Attlee to Truman, 16 August 1945, *Map Room Messages of President Truman (1945-1946)* (Frederick, Md.: University Publications of America, 1980), reel 1; Note by the Secretary, 22 November 1945, COS (45) 670 (O), 22 November 1945, CAB 80/98. However, the senior British military representative in Washington was cautioned that Attlee "intended to cover such matters as the attendance of U.S. officers at the I.D.C. [Imperial Defence College] etc. and the continuance of close collaboration between the staffs [of the two countries] but his conversation would not justify a demand for new departures in defence collaboration." COS to Wilson, 5 December 1945, COS (W) 196, CAB 105/65. For Attlee's views on defense questions in general see the important article by Raymond

Smith and John Zametica, "The Cold Warrior: Clement Attlee Reconsidered, 1945-7," *International Affairs* 61 (Spring 1985): 237-52. Perhaps influenced by his own skepticism of the continued importance of the Eastern Mediterranean and by domestic political considerations, Attlee was often less enthusiastic than either Bevin or the COS about comprehensive planning with the Americans particularly outside the areas of atomic weaponry and West European security. He did not, however, thwart Foreign Office and COS efforts to work ever more closely with Washington.

22. For a discussion of the impact of Bevin's forceful personality on the processes and conduct of British foreign policy, see, in addition to Bullock, George Mallaby, *Each in His Office: Studies of Men in Power* (London: Leo Cooper, 1972); Piers Dixon, *Double Diploma: The Life of Sir Pierson Dixon, Don and Diplomat* (London: Hutchinson, 1968); Roderick Barclay, *Ernest Bevin and the Foreign Office, 1932-1969* (London: published by the author, 1975). Dean Acheson, *Sketches from Life of Men I Have Known* (New York: Harper and Brothers, 1961), pp. 1-29; Avi Shlaim, Peter Jones and Keith Sainsbury, *British Foreign Secretaries Since 1945* (Newton Abbot, England: David and Charles, 1977), pp. 27-37.

23. See Bullock, *Bevin*, pp. 455-56.

24. Ibid., p. 83.

25. A. J. P. Taylor, review of *The Life and Times of Ernest Bevin*, vol. 2, *Minister of Labour*, by Alan Bullock, in *The Observer*, 16 April 1967, p. 27.

26. John Baylis, "British Wartime Thinking About a Post-war European Security Group," *Review of International Studies* 9 (October 1983): 279.

27. Sean Greenwood, "Ernest Bevin, France and 'Western Union': August 1945-February 1946," *European History Quarterly* 14 (July 1983): 320.

28. See John Wilson Young, "The Foreign Office and the Departure of General de Gaulle, June 1945-January 1946," *Historical Journal* 25 (March 1982): 209-16; for the crisis in the Levant, see William Roger Louis, *The British Empire in the Middle East, 1945-1951: Arab Nationalism, the United States, and Postwar Imperialism* (Oxford: Clarendon Press, 1984), pp. 147-72.

29. See Cooper, *Old Men Forget*, pp. 351-65.

30. Sean Greenwood, "Return to Dunkirk: The Origins of the Anglo-French Treaty of March 1947," *Journal of Strategic Studies* 6 (December 1983): 49-65.

31. Minute by H. A. Rumbold, 16 March 1946, FO 371/59953. Bevin's own goal was to avoid "anything which might give either isolationist opinion in America or the Soviet Government an opportunity of claiming

that a Four Power Treaty to guard against German infringements of the military clauses of the Peace Settlement was superfluous and that American intervention in the matter was therefore unnecessary." "Anglo-French Alliance," 26 February 1947, C.P. (47) 64, CAB 129/17. Discussions in the spring of 1947 for a renewal of the 1942 Anglo-Soviet Treaty collapsed because the British were unwilling to jeopardize movements towards a larger Western bloc. See Rothwell, *Britain and the Cold War*, pp. 275-76.

32. See below, pp. 90-91.

33. Waterfield to Harvey, 10 February 1947, FO 371/67671. See also John Baylis, "Britain and the Dunkirk Treaty: The Origins of NATO," *Journal of Strategic Studies* 5 (June 1982): 243. In the event, American approval of the Dunkirk Treaty was privately forthcoming; see Department of State to American Embassy London, 23 January 1947, RG 59, 741.51/1-1647.

34. Quoted in Sargent to Hollis, 16 May 1947, FO 371/67724.

35. See Eben A. Ayers, diary entry of 7 August 1945, Eben A. Ayers Papers, HSTL; William D. Leahy, *I Was There: The Personal Story of the Chief of Staff to Presidents Roosevelt and Truman Based on His Notes and Diaries Made at the Time* (New York: Whittlesey House, McGraw-Hill, 1950), p. 420.

36. See Bullock, *Bevin*, pp. 129-30; 132-33.

37. See William O. McCagg, *Stalin Embattled, 1943-1948* (Detroit, Mich.: Wayne State University Press, 1978), p. 208.

38. Winant to Byrnes, 26 November 1945, *FRUS* 1945, 2: 581-86.

39. Bullock, *Bevin*, p. 216.

40. See below, pp. 115-16.

41. See below, Chapter Four.

42. For the establishment of the CCS, see Ray S. Cline, *Washington Command Post: The Operations Division* (Washington: Office of the Chief of Military History, Department of the Army, 1951), especially pp. 98-104; see also Hathaway, *Ambiguous Partnership*, pp. 264-72, and Sally Lister Parker, "Attendant Lords: A Study of the British Joint Staff Mission in Washington, 1941-1945" (Ph.D. dissertation, University of Maryland, 1984).

43. *Winston S. Churchill: His Complete Speeches 1897-1963*, ed. Robert Rhodes James, 7 (New York: Chelsea House Publishers in association with R. R. Bowker Co., 1974): 6825.

44. Memorandum by the British Chiefs of Staff, 15 July 1945, *FRUS, Potsdam*, 1: 825.

45. Meeting of the Combined Chiefs of Staff, 19 July 1945, and Memorandum by the United States Chiefs of Staff, 19 July 1945, *FRUS, Potsdam*, 2: 113, 1202.

46. Memorandum for the Chief of Staff, 8 February 1946, RG 319, P & O 334 (Section I) (Cases 1-27).

47. "Joint Staff Mission Report," [30 October 1945], CAB 122/1579.

48. See Wilson to Ismay, 31 August 1945, PREM 8/120.

49. "British Post-war Service Representatives in the United States," 23 October 1945, CAB 139/1384. Continued cooperation in defense research and development was a matter of special interest for the British. Attlee proposed continued cooperation in a personal message to Truman in August 1945. Although the president was unwilling to make an official commitment, most cooperative efforts in this area, especially between the armies and navies, apparently continued (as will be noted, Atomic energy was a special case.) See Attlee to Truman, 16 August 1945, and Truman to Attlee, 18 August 1945, *Map Room Messages of President Truman (1945-1946)*, reel 1; British Joint Staff Mission Report, "Collaboration with the United States in the Technical and Scientific Fields," 9 April 1946, COS (46) 110 (O), CAB 80/101.

50. COS (45) 235th Meeting, 27 September 1945, CAB 79/39.

51. "Joint Staff Mission Report," [30 October 1945], CAB 122/1579.

52. Wilson to COS, 27 November 1945, CAB 105/188.

53. Wilson to COS, 8 January 1946, CAB 105/188.

54. COS (45) 158th Meeting, 21 June 1945, CAB 79/35.

55. Nimitz to Forrestal, 23 July 1946, enclosed in Forrestal to the President, 25 July 1946, Clifford Papers, Box 15, Folder: Russia (folder 5), HSTL.

56. The close ties between British and American airmen are reflected in the papers of General Carl Spaatz, who became commanding general of the Army Air Forces in March 1946 and, subsequently, the first chief of staff of the independent United States Air Force. Upon assuming the latter position, he wrote to British Air Marshal Sir Hugh Sanders: "It is almost impossible to say what a help to us the precedent set by the RAF has been. In the recent gaining of our parity with the other two services, the background of your own struggle for the organization of the RAF was an immeasurable aid." Spaatz to Sanders, 19 September 1947, File: Britain (2), Box 257, Spaatz Papers, LC. See also the comments of Spaatz' predecessor as head of the Army Air Forces, H. H. Arnold, in his memoirs, *Global Mission* (New York: Harper, 1949), p. 607.

57. Wilson to COS, 16 March 1946, CAB 105/52.

58. Wilson to COS, 8 January 1946, CAB 105/188.

59. Wilson to COS, 11 January 1946, CAB 105/51.

60. Lincoln to Eisenhower, 8 February 1946, RG 319, P & O 334 (Section I (Cases 1-27). See Eisenhower to Nimitz, 29 June 1946, *The Papers of Dwight David Eisenhower*, ed. Louis Galambos, 7 (Baltimore, Md.: Johns

Hopkins University Press, 1978): 1157-59. Leahy noted simply in his diary that "at a closed meeting of the Combined Chiefs of Staff, discussed with our British colleagues possible methods of maintaining close military relations during the peace that is approaching." Leahy, diary entry for 8 February 1946, Leahy Papers, LC.

61. Wilson to COS, 9 February 1946, CAB 105/51. Wilson believed that opposition to closer Anglo-American defense cooperation centered in parts of the State Department; see Wilson to COS, 16 March 1946, CAB 105/52.

62. The Permanent Joint Board on Defense, U.S.-Canada was set up in 1940 to provide a venue for military cooperation between the two North American countries. It was not disbanded after the end of the war and continued to serve as a forum for discussing North American security concerns. Canadian officials shared American suspicions of Soviet intentions but impressed upon their U.S. counterparts their view that any conflict with the Soviets would be more likely to occur in Europe than as a result of an over-the-North Pole surprise attack. See my "Approach to Alliance: British and American Defense Strategies, 1945-1948" (Ph.D. dissertation, Georgetown University, 1983), pp. 59-71.

63. G. A. L[incoln], Memorandum for the record, 12 February 1946; Lincoln, Memorandum for the record, 14 March 1946; unsigned memorandum for General Hull, 25 April 1946, all in RG 319, ABC 381 United Nations (1-23-42), section 9.

64. On Maclean, see Daniel Yergin, *Shattered Peace: The Origins of the Cold War and the National Security State* (Boston: Houghton Mifflin, Sentry Edition, 1978), p. 482 n. 55; Patrick Seale and Maureen McConville, *Philby: The Long Road to Moscow* (Hammondsworth, England: Penguin Books, 1978), p. 237. There were in addition occasional references in the press to the continued functioning of the CCS; see Arthur Krock, "In the Nation," *New York Times*, 7 March 1946; Joseph Alsop, "Our New Entente with Britain," *Washington Post*, 16 March 1947 and "Mr. Truman's Balloon," *Time*, 18 March 1946. Indeed, Field Marshal Montgomery, probably intentionally, may have provided Stalin with grounds for suspicion of Anglo-American military cooperation in his January 1947 interview with the Soviet leader; see Bernard L. Montgomery, *The Memoirs of Field-Marshal Montgomery* (Cleveland: World Publishing Co., 1958), pp. 401-4.

65. Wilson to COS, 8 March 1946 (FMW 244), CAB 105/188. Leahy advised Wilson, however, in the wake of the controversy over Churchill's Fulton speech that the JCS would not have the support of the State Department in "raising the issue of permanent military collaboration." JSM to COS, 16 March 1946, JSM 204, CAB 105/51.

66. The President's News Conference of 8 March 1946, United States, *Public Papers of the Presidents of the United States, Harry S. Truman,*

1946 (Washington: Government Printing Office, 1962), p. 146. Truman reiterated the same point later in the year; *Public Papers of the Presidents, Truman, 1946*, pp. 428, 514. Hathaway oddly argues that "working without the knowledge of their civilian heads, even contrary to the desires of these superiors, a small group of officers took it upon themselves to enter into arrangements with the British which had the effect of tying their two countries together far closer than all but a few imagined." *Ambiguous Partnership*, pp. 263-64. While Truman may not have wanted the political liability of institutionalizing permanent military cooperation with the British, he (along with the civilian service secretaries and Secretaries of State Byrnes, Marshall and Acheson) were all well aware of and participated in the continuing arrangements for cooperating with the British and the Canadians. See Montgomery, *Memoirs*, p. 395. Attlee reported his November 1945 conversation with Truman (quoted in "Collaboration with the United States on Research and Development," COS (45) 670 (O), 22 November 1945, CAB 80/98) in which he referred to "the matter of postwar co-operation in defence resources stressing the point of the great advantage of our keeping in line with regard to equipment and weapons and also having a common defence doctrine. I expanded these points at some length, and the President entirely agreed with me." Similar views are reflected in the account of the 28 October 1946 conversation between Truman and Canadian Prime Minister Mackenzie King on the value of continuing U.S., U.K., and Canadian defense cooperation: "The President and the Prime Minister discussed the closest possible cooperation in defense matters in the interest of efficiency and economy. Under this heading was included full exchange of military information, not only between the United States and Canada but also with the United Kingdom. It was agreed by both that the closest cooperation was necessary." Memorandum by Parsons, 31 October 1946, *FRUS* 1946, 5: 62; see also the account in *The Mackenzie King Record*, ed. J. W. Pickersgill and D. F. Forster, 3 (Toronto: University of Toronto Press, 1970): 362. Continuing U.S.-Canadian cooperation was publicly announced in February 1947; "U.S.-Canadian Permanent Joint Board on Defense to Continue Collaboration for Security Purposes," *Department of State Bulletin* 16 (23 February 1947): 361.

67. Henry Maitland Wilson, *Eight Years Overseas, 1939-1947* (London: Hutchinson [1950]), p. 265. The Foreword to Wilson's book was written by Dwight David Eisenhower.

68. Nimitz to Eisenhower and Leahy, undated [June 1946], quoted in Eisenhower, *Papers*, 7: 1157 n.2.

69. OSP to Lincoln, 3 July 1946, RG 319, ABC 381 USSR (3-2-46), section 2, quoted in Eisenhower, *Papers*, 7: 1157-58 n.4.

70. Forrestal, diary entry of 21 August 1946, Forrestal Papers, NHC.

71. Wilson to COS, 23 August 1946, CAB 105/188.

72. Montgomery, *Memoirs*, p. 395.

73. Leahy, diary entry for 16 September 1946, Leahy Papers, LC.

74. Montgomery, *Memoirs*, p. 396.

75. Ismay to Eisenhower, 10 October 1946, RG 319, P & O 091 Great Britain (October-November 1946).

76. Eisenhower, *Papers*, 8: 1345 n.3; Memorandum by G. A. L[incoln], 4 November 1946, RG 319, P & O 091 Great Britain (October-November 1946).

77. See RG 353, Records of the State-War-Navy Coordination Committee, File: 206/9.

78. Hathaway, *Ambiguous Partnership*, pp. 212-16, 260-63.

79. The history of Anglo-American cooperation and noncooperation on matters relating to atomic energy is treated by Margaret Gowing, *Independence and Deterrence: Britain and Atomic Energy, 1945-1952*, 1, *Policy Making* (London: Macmillan, 1974); Richard G. Hewlett, Oscar E. Anderson and Francis Duncan, *A History of the Atomic Energy Commission*, 2 vols. (University Park, Pa.: Pennsylvania State University Press, 1962, 1969), especially 2: 261-84.

80. See Anita Inder Singh, "Imperial Defence and the Transfer of Power in India, 1946-1947," *International History Review* 4 (November 1982): 568-88.

CHAPTER 3

AMERICAN STRATEGIES FOR POSTWAR DEFENSE

It has often been pointed out that the United States faced the post-war world with unprecedented power and influence. Unlike the other major powers involved in the global conflict, it had suffered neither invasion nor intensive bombing of its home territory. American casualties were far fewer than the millions lost by Russia, Germany and Japan. The U.S. economy was not only intact, but was vastly strengthened by wartime expenditures and by taking advantage of the commercial opportunities presented by the absence or weakness of former trade competitors.

The U.S. government had not been idle in laying plans for the postwar period. State Department and Treasury officials had given careful attention to the problems of the postwar economy and moved determinedly to implement a program of free trade, currency stabilization and international banking mechanisms designed to prevent the recurring trade wars, high tariffs and depressions which had hurt American business and contributed to the international instability and economic weakness in the interwar years. New York was supplanting London as the center of world trade and banking; the dollar was becoming the central international currency, replacing the pound. The plans laid by American officials before and during the war led directly to the policies followed by the government in the postwar years. The new international economic order, inaugurated at Bretton Woods in 1944, was effectively implemented and became within a few years an accomplished goal of American policy.[1]

American planning for postwar defense policy was another matter. The monumental defense budgets and the dispersal of U.S. forces around the globe that have characterized most of the years since V-E Day were envisioned neither by President Franklin D. Roosevelt nor by senior officials of the War and Navy Departments. The defense policies that have come to seem permanent fixtures of American life did not logically progress from the wartime plans for the postwar future. Such planning as had been undertaken, while it inevitably received less high-level attention than plans for imminent military operations, did not envision the decline of British power, nor was it based on the assumption that the goal of postwar policy was the prevention of a Soviet-dominated Eurasia. Notwithstanding the self-confidence of victorious soldiers, sailors and airmen and the emerging antipathy towards the Soviet Union, American postwar defense planning was not designed to lay the groundwork for the defense policies that have been subsequently characteristic.

The emphasis of recent historical scholarship in the United States has been on the development of what has been described by Michael Sherry as an "ideology of preparedness." According to this view, American defense officials saw the military weakness of the United States in the 1930s as having encouraged aggression in Europe and the Far East, resulting in the surprise attack on Pearl Harbor in 1941. In the future, defense officials argued, potential aggression—particularly by surprise attacks with weapons of mass destruction—could be deterred by "unprecedented forces-in-being to ward off the coming blitzkrieg. If attack were to come without warning, the war machine had to be ever ready."[2] Thus there would be a continued need for extensive military forces requiring, in turn, the militarization of the American economy. Up to a point, there is validity to this thesis. American defense officials were, not illogically, convinced of the value of maintaining strong ground, air and sea forces. Having suffered at the hands of the tightfisted Congresses of the 1930s, they truly believed that the price of parsimony had been paid in blood from Iwo Jima to the Ardennes. They were determined to retain sufficiently powerful defense forces in the postwar period, supported by universal military training (UMT), to prevent the recurrence of such circumstances. This is clear from the record.

On the other hand, this concept has major limitations in explaining the course of American defense policy in the first two postwar years. It is quite possible to move from the ideology of preparedness to a few characteristically truculent statements by President Truman and other administration officials, and thence to a discussion of the expansive American expenditures and commitments of the 1950s and 1960s, without accounting for the evolution of policy in the mid- and late 1940s. It is, however, misleading to suggest that, emerging from their World War II experiences, American defense officials were determined to be the world's policemen, believing "virtually every development in the world . . . to be potentially crucial. An adverse turn of events anywhere endangers the United States."[3] Inherent in such a view has been an overemphasis on the role of nuclear weaponry within American national security policy —the presumption that mere possession of such weapons would give the United States the power to impose its will on other states. This view has also ignored the extent to which American policy-makers presupposed a continuing strong British presence in Europe and the Middle East.

While there was indeed an ideology of preparedness shared by American defense officials by 1945, it was circumscribed by a number of factors—principally the determination of the American public to bring the boys home (exceeded only by the boys' determination to get home) and the continuing resistance of the Truman administration and the Congresses of the period to large defense expenditures. The postwar Congresses were now prepared to vote much larger sums to maintain America's defenses, but they were also committed to reducing government expenditures and lowering taxes. The services could hardly expect wartime levels of appropriations and they had to bear their share of government reductions. In fact, reductions in defense spending severely limited American military capabilities in the years 1945-1950 and undercut efforts to maintain preparedness.[4]

Another factor which has been much less well understood is the inherent regionalism which characterized American planning for postwar security. The United States ended the war intending to withdraw its occupation forces from Europe in a year or two and planning to devote its energies to a defense structure for the Western Hemisphere and towards maintaining some sort of hegemony in the Pacific. This regional focus represented clear continuity with prewar planning, not an intention to create a global Pax Americana single-handedly maintained by the force of American arms.

The evolution of American defense planning for the postwar period was heavily influenced by President Roosevelt. His role was clearly decisive on central issues even if the processes of his analysis and the means of policy implementation which he employed remained as obscure to his officials then as they often still do to historians. An instinctive politician, he planned and acted on the basis of his understanding of the interests of the country and what public opinion would tolerate. In earlier years, he had campaigned on the basis of Wilsonian internationalism and the League of Nations only to be repudiated at the polls. In later successful elections and during his White House years, FDR took more account of isolationist sentiment and the currents of Anglophobia which influenced an electorate not psychologically prepared for constant global involvement. While he had early recognized the dangers that aggression by the several dictatorships posed to world peace and American interests, his response was tentative and cautious. Roosevelt's policies, because of the absence of political consensus in the nation, were often carried forward under conditions of tight secrecy. After war in Europe broke out in 1939, he moved the United States into furtive cooperation with Great Britain and towards firmer opposition to Japanese expansion in the Pacific. As scholars such as James Leutze and David Reynolds have demonstrated, American policy in this period, however fluctuating, was not based on sentiment or affection, but on Roosevelt's shrewd calculations of national interest and an awareness of the dangers to U.S. security if Britain should fall and especially if Hitler should gain control of the Royal Navy.[5] After war came, the forces of isolationism and Anglophobia were quiescent but tended to express themselves in support of a "Pacific first" strategy. The persisting public disinclination to defend the British Empire—whether in Burma or the Eastern Mediterranean—was a political fact of life that could not be ignored by any astute American politician.

Such influences affected U.S. defense planning for the postwar period. It could not be built on a policy of global intervention or on the permanent entanglement in European affairs that had been anathematized by President Washington in his Farewell Address. The complete shape of Roosevelt's conception of postwar policy can never be known; in all probability he had not rigorously thought through the implications of what was likely to be a continuing decline of British power (a decline which in many ways the United States was helping to further). Nor did he assess the implications of the fact that the Soviet Union would clearly emerge from the war as Europe's foremost power. While FDR promoted the cause of international cooperation, he had known at first hand the limitations of the League of Nations and of the difficulties in persuading all countries to implement policies of collective security, embargoes and nonintervention.

Roosevelt's hope for future peace appears to have been based instead on an anticipation of cooperation among the great powers —the Soviet Union, Great Britain, the United States and, at his insistence, China. To the extent that conflicts would emerge in Europe and the Middle East they would be matters to be settled by Britain and Russia. That these two countries could achieve a stable balance became increasingly unlikely, but Roosevelt does not appear to have resolved the implications of this situation for American interests. FDR was undoubtedly uncertain as to a realistic American role; he may have been hoping that a period of delay might remove a then intractable problem or, with his health failing, he may have simply lacked the energy to devote to the central question of the postwar period. In any event, from late 1942 on he had encouraged a process of postwar defense planning which was not based on the likelihood of Soviet-American hostility, but upon cooperation among the United States, Great Britain and the Soviet Union.

Roosevelt began with an emphasis on the importance of the continuing peacekeeping role of the major powers, expressed in terms of the "Four Policemen." He intended that the United States, Britain, Russia and China would cooperate in enforcing the peace in a disarmed world by inspecting all other countries and threatening to quarantine any who were secretly arming and, if necessary, to bomb them into compliance. The concept, while never fully and publicly articulated, was mentioned by Roosevelt on a number of occasions to public and private figures alike, including Soviet Foreign Minister Molotov, Stalin, British Foreign Secretary Anthony Eden, former Senator George Norris, and others.[6]

The concept of the Four Policemen which Roosevelt discussed in vague terms in 1942 and 1943 eventually evolved into the United Nations Security Council.[7] The basis of the concept, and indeed of the United Nations Charter, was that the great powers, the permanent members of the Security Council, would cooperate in resolving disputes; no means was provided to coerce a great power against its will.

In addition, Roosevelt envisioned that the world would be divided into zones in which each of the great powers or policemen would have, or share, peacekeeping responsibilities. The United States would have the Western Hemisphere and the Far East; Russia and China would control Asia; Britain and Russia would keep the peace in the Mediterranean, Europe and the Indian Ocean area. This variation on the concept of a global allocation of spheres of influence is reflected in Roosevelt's comments to Stalin at Tehran.[8] In April 1944 Admiral Ernest J. King, the chief of naval operations and commander in chief, U.S. fleet, advised the secretary of the navy that

yesterday while at luncheon with the President, he brought up the subject of postwar security force[s] and expressed certain views in regard thereto—chiefly that he inclined to "regional responsibilities" on the part of the great powers, the "regions" correspond generally to the current "theaters of strategic responsibility" in which the United States is responsible for the conduct of the war effort in the Pacific Theater (generally east of the Longitude of Singapore).[9]

This was of course geopolitics at its most sweeping and grandiose, but the regional concept of America's defense responsibilities reflected continuity with the prewar practice (with some expansion into the Western Pacific). It was consistent with political realities as Roosevelt, a shrewd judge of public opinion, assessed them and it coincided with a belief, not yet undermined, that Britain would continue to be a major power in the postwar period. The President remained skeptical that the United States would maintain troops in Europe beyond a year or so of occupation duties. As one historian has written, "From the beginning of the war, the President's cardinal aim in the European theater was to avoid American embroilment in the tangled and melancholy political affairs of Central and Eastern Europe."[10] In discussions of plans for conquered Germany with the Joint Chiefs of Staff en route to the conferences at Cairo and Tehran, the President envisioned an American occupation force of about one million men for a period of one to two years; above all, "We should not get roped into accepting any European sphere of influence."[11] This was made clear to America's wartime allies; he wrote to Churchill in February 1944: " 'Do please don't' ask me to keep any American forces in France. I just cannot do it! I would have to bring them all back home."[12] At the Tehran Conference he made the point explicit to Stalin and reiterated it at Yalta.[13]

The regional basis of postwar defense planning can be clearly seen in the extended and complicated process by which defense planners established priorities for acquiring base rights and the subsequent efforts of the State Department to negotiate with other countries for such rights.[14] The planning which lay behind the search for bases—both for the Navy and the Army Air Forces— clearly indicates that Roosevelt's concept of regional responsibilities reflected not merely casual ruminations over cocktails, but the basis of U.S. plans for its postwar defense policy.

The search for postwar bases, as Elliot Converse has recently demonstrated in a path-breaking study, involved a multiplicity of commercial, military and diplomatic factors and a variety of interested parties—military and civilian, government and private, U.S. and foreign.[15] Nevertheless it is significant that until 1946 bases were sought for Western Hemisphere defenses and to maintain American power in the Pacific, with some attention to bases to support transit flights between theaters of operation on different continents. This is reflected in JCS, Navy and Army Air Forces studies of base requirements.

The president launched the effort in December 1942 in a request to the JCS to prepare a study of worldwide locations for air facilities for an International Police Force (although, as Converse has noted, he may also have been interested in seeking airfields for postwar commercial aviation.)[16] The task was delegated to the

Joint Strategic Survey Committee composed of Lt. General
Stanley D. Embick, Vice Admiral Russell Willson and, for the
Army Air Forces, Major General Muir S. Fairchild. Embick, who
was called back from retirement to serve on the JSSC, was a
"continentalist" with strong convictions that the United States
should avoid involvement in overseas affairs in general and European entanglements in particular. He distrusted the aims of British
policy and was determined to see that American forces were not
employed in defense of British imperial goals.[17] The March 1943
JSSC report on base requirements clearly reflected the regional
concept of postwar American security; in the Western Atlantic the
United States would retain rights to bases in areas leased from
Britain in 1941 (as part of the Destroyers for Bases agreement) and
other bases in the Caribbean and on the northwest coast of Brazil.
In the Pacific the United States would need a chain of fortified
bases from Hawaii to the Philippines and the Bonins, along with
other sites south of the thirtieth parallel. The Army Air Forces
considered that bases in the Atlantic, particularly in Greenland,
Iceland, the Azores, Dakar and Ascension Island, were necessary
to support air routes to occupation zones in Europe and to extend
the perimeters of hemisphere defense. This view was strongly contested by Admiral King who shared the distrust of many naval
officers for expansive air force plans. As a result the JCS held the
study in abeyance until the president asked for it the following
October. In the meantime the service staffs reassessed their postwar
base requirements.[18]

As part of the same process, the Navy's General Board also
looked at the postwar base problem. The board, composed of
senior and retired officers, had served the Navy since 1900 as a
source of strategic guidance and policy planning; its influence had
sharply declined in recent years, but it seemed to be the appropriate
body to investigate a problem not immediately related to the pressing combat operations which absorbed the time of most staff
officers in Washington. The board's March 1943 report, signed by
Admiral Thomas C. Hart, who would later become a U.S. senator,
called for effective cooperation between Britain, Russia and the
United States "for the specific post-war purpose of keeping good
order over such portions of the world as involve any danger of out-
breaks that might menace the general peace." It noted that only the

United States and Britain had significant naval forces and urged that the two naval powers hold conversations "looking for a division of responsibility for maintaining order over the water areas of the world." The American Navy would, according to the proposal, be responsible for the Pacific and for the sea areas west of longitude twenty-five west in the Atlantic, while the British would take over the Eastern Atlantic, the Mediterranean and the Indian Ocean. The board appended a list of bases oriented to the Pacific and the Caribbean which would be needed to support the U.S. Navy's future responsibilities.[19]

Some months later General H. H. Arnold, the head of the Army Air Forces, directed that a staff study be undertaken regarding needs for airbases. The response prepared by the Air Staff, although reflecting the preparedness ideology, foreswore any attempt at air domination of the world. It was also based on the assumption that the Big Four "would divide the world into spheres of influence after the war to keep the peace."[20] As described by Converse,

In the AAF blueprint, the United States' enormous "sphere of responsibility" included the entire Western Hemisphere and nearly all of the Pacific. The bases "essential" for the defense of the United States, its territories and the Western Hemisphere defined a giant perimeter running on the west from extreme northwestern Alaska, southwest through Attu in the Aleutian Islands, Paramashiru in the Kuriles, the Bonin Islands, to the Philippines; thence eastward through the South Pacific (via New Britain, the Solomon Islands, Suva Island, Samoa, Tahiti, the Marquesas, Clipperton and the Galapagos) to the west coast of South America, and around the northern rim of that continent to the northeast Brazilian coast. From there, the United States' eastern defense line ran to Ascension Island in the South Atlantic, north along the west coast of Africa through the Azores and Iceland. The northern boundary extended from Iceland through Greenland and across Canada to Alaska.[21]

When in October 1943 the president asked for the results of the JCS base study that he had requested, Embick and his JSSC colleagues drew together their previous proposal, shelved since the preceding March, coordinated it with the Army Air Forces and General Board studies and forwarded it to the JCS. It was discussed with the president en route to the Cairo and Tehran Confer-

ences. With minor revisions the report (designated JCS 570/2) was
approved and the following January the State Department was
asked that "as a matter of high priority" negotiations be opened
with governments concerned to secure bases and base rights as
indicated in the JCS study.[22]

JCS 570 became the "base bible" until the end of the war, the
master document which established presidentially approved postwar base requirements. It specifically assumed that "U.S. interests
will be primarily the Western Hemisphere, and the Central Pacific
to the Far East." It envisioned a ring of bases from which U.S.
aircraft could intercept hostile attacks and launch rapid counter-
attacks. As Converse points out, "The military planners selected
bases not with any particular enemy in mind, but saw them rather
as defining a protective ring or perimeter around the country."[23]
Some attention was given to bases in the far West Pacific, an area
postulated as under United States responsibility for peacekeeping
but not apparently of direct security concern. There was still dis-
agreement on bases in Greenland, Iceland, the Azores and West
Africa with the JSSC being opposed (undoubtedly as a result of
Embick's determination to avoid anything approaching European
involvement) and the JCS and the President inserting them, reflecting a more expansive view of hemispheric and Atlantic Ocean
defense requirements.[24] No bases were suggested for Europe, the
Mediterranean or the Indian Ocean areas.

The principles underlying JCS 570 were directly related to the
services' separate postwar planning documents. Navy planning was
based on the assumption that command of the sea would be maintained by the U.S. "in the western part of the North and South
Atlantic Oceans including the approaches thereto, and in the entire
Pacific Ocean including the approaches thereto."[25] Army Air
Forces plans for a seventy-group and 400,000-man structure were
based on the assumption that missions in Europe would be
minimal, related only to occupation duties, and that "strategic
coverage" would be maintained in the Western Hemisphere and the
Pacific.[26] In November 1944 General Carl Spaatz, the commanding
general of the U.S. Strategic Air Forces in Europe, was expressly
advised by General Arnold that "since it is the expressed policy of
the United States to withdraw from Europe as soon as practicable,
leaving possibly a token force in Germany to carry out our armis-

tice decisions, I believe that planning for post-war air bases in Europe is inadvisable."[27] Base requirements were primarily the concerns of the Navy and the Army Air Forces. The ground Army was less concerned with base requirements, and in any event it was concentrating on plans for occupation duties for Germany and Japan and for universal military training.

In the final year of the war the State Department moved with no great urgency to negotiate base rights with foreign countries, although agreement with Brazil was reached.[28] Talks with Australia, New Zealand, the native leaders in the Philippines, Iceland, Denmark (regarding Greenland) and Portugal (regarding the Azores) were postponed until after the end of hostilities. State Department officials naturally understood how difficult it was going to be to persuade sovereign states to allow the United States to establish peacetime bases, especially since in some cases the JCS desired "exclusive" rights allowing only U.S. forces, not even those of the host country, to use the facilities. The base rights question did not receive much high-level attention until mid-1945 when it came under the purview of the State-War-Navy Coordinating Committee (SWNCC), an interagency group which included the State Department and the JCS but also the civilian service secretaries (who had been jealous of the heretofore exclusive input by the JCS).[29]

Despite the fact that postwar planning envisioned a perimeter around the United States, the planners did face the reality of potential threats to North American security. Although hostility between the United States and Britain was ruled out, there was a lingering, almost reflexive concern about a rejuvenated Germany or Japan.[30] This latter fear was indicated in tentative plans to station aircraft in Europe to attack Germany should that country again pose a threat to the peace, but such plans never received Washington's blessings.[31] The Navy's absorption with the Pacific, which persisted into early 1946, also reflected that service's concern to contain potential Japanese power.

Defense planners were aware that when Germany and Japan were under occupation (and assuming continuing friendly ties with the British Commonwealth) the only country with the capability of posing a significant military threat to North America was the Soviet Union. This threat did not exist in 1945 and its potential realization

influenced American defense planning in 1945 only to the extent
that the Army Air Forces reemphasized the need for perimeter
bases in the north—Newfoundland, Greenland, Iceland—arguing
that the greatest threat to North America could come only from
that direction.[32] In addition, it is significant that even Navy
Secretary James V. Forrestal, one of the first officials in Washington to give serious thought to the implications of Soviet power
for U.S. interests, did not in 1945 attempt to reorient Navy planning on the assumption that the Soviet Union was a potential
enemy.[33] In June 1945 Forrestal advised a joint session of the
Senate and House Comittees on Naval Affairs that

it should be emphasized that we seek naval superiority, not throughout the
world, but only in the ocean areas which are approaches to our homeland.
In all probability these areas are . . . the North and South Atlantic Oceans
or anywhere in the Pacific Ocean, including the approaches thereto. More
specifically the pivotal areas are: The North Atlantic approaches to North
America; the Middle Atlantic between the bulges of South America and
Africa; the eastern and southern approaches to the Caribbean; the waters
contiguous to Japan and to the Philippines; the Alaskan and Arctic sea-air
approaches to North America; the Pacific approaches to the Panama
Canal.[34]

In September 1945 Admiral King indicated to the House Committee on Naval Affairs that he considered the western part of the
North and South Atlantic Oceans and the entire Pacific Ocean as
areas over which the United States "must retain and maintain
undisputed control."[35]

The regionalism inherent in American defense planning for the
postwar period is consistent with the conduct of American policy in
1944 and 1945 regarding the future of Europe. The United States
was committed to the unconditional defeat of Germany and
intended to play a major role in the occupation of that country for
only one to two years. Otherwise Washington did not plan a continuing military presence in Europe; it was assumed that future
security matters could be handled through the United Nations or,
somehow, by Britain and the Soviet Union working together. In
considering the disposition of the ships of the Italian fleet, U.S.
Navy officials were quite prepared to defer to the Royal Navy since
"theirs is the primary strategic responsibility in the Mediterranean."[36]

In the last months of the war, American officials were well aware of the likelihood that Britain would follow her balance of power tradition and build up a coalition against the Soviet Union. It was, they argued, clearly in the American interest to avoid any such "ganging up," to use the phrase of the day. A September 1944 study by the Office of Strategic Services suggested that "the general recognition of any identity of interest between the United States and Great Britain is not likely to be widespread in America, and any attempt on Britain's part to harness America's strength to British interests is foredoomed to failure."[37] American diplomacy was directed towards avoiding involvement in an Anglo-Soviet struggle for power and would encourage accommodation between the two old rivals.[38] American officials turned a deaf ear to Churchill's pleas to have Western forces remain in Czechoslovakia and there was strong opposition to any American involvement in British efforts to ensure a pro-Western regime in Greece in December 1944 and London's meddling in domestic Italian politics.[39] Similarly, when Britain and the Soviet Union found themselves at loggerheads over the latter's demands in March 1945 that Turkey grant Moscow bases in the Straits and cede back two districts in eastern Turkey, the United States temporized, refusing to join Britain in opposing the Soviet démarche.[40] Both Roosevelt and Truman in their meetings with the Russians attempted to avoid giving the impression that there was an Anglo-American bloc although one suspects that the shared language, culture, institutions and intimacy of working relationships in the military area might have suggested otherwise even to a figure less inclined to paranoia than Stalin. Nonetheless, one cannot speak of an Anglo-American postwar policy in mid-1945; Truman was sincere when he remarked in June 1945 to Joseph Davies, the former ambassador to Moscow, that "he was not in 'cahoots' with either [Britain or the Soviet Union]. It was necessary for all three to cooperate if we were to have Peace."[41]

By the end of the Second World War there was an American postwar defense policy that is clearly reflected in the planning of the services and in the conduct of American diplomacy. It was illustrated in President Truman's comment to Admiral Leahy in September 1945 that "the future foreign interests of the United States will be in the Western Hemisphere and in the Pacific (Eastern

Asia)."[42] That policy was based on the maintenance of powerful defenses and the ability to protect the Western Hemisphere and the Pacific against aggression from any quarter. It had several sources: lessons learned from the history of the interwar period, from the perception of a need for preparedness and also from a continuing intention to avoid European entanglements. There were a number of major ongoing disputes with Moscow, but Soviet cooperation had been earnestly desired by American defense officials in the final struggle against Japan and no fundamental conflicts of strategic interest between Washington and Moscow were believed to exist. The Soviet problem, to the extent that one existed, was diplomatic and not military.

This view is somewhat at variance with the one set forth by a number of historians of American national security policy. Citing the subsequent extension of U.S. defense interests throughout the world, the great advances in military technology achieved in the United States during the war and the pride, even the boastfulness, of defense officials in the days of victory, they have argued that by the end of the war the United States had adopted a policy of "global deterrence," a concept of national security which justified "nuclear deterrence, global intervention, peacetime conscription, and the spinning of an intricate web of relationships among the military and those institutions—industry, science, education, labor—which supported or profited from preparedness."[43]

In the aftermath of victory in global war, American defense officials, uniformed and civilian alike, did emphasize the continuing need for military strength, and they did warn their countrymen that a concept of Fortress America protected by vast oceans and the British Navy was no longer credible. The Army Air Forces in particular pressed for a strategy based on the capability for massive retaliatory bombing. But when one looks at the state of the planning process and the defense budgets which would be increasingly cut in the next few years, it is evident that such statements did not automatically constitute a policy of global involvement. Historians writing in the aftermath of the rhetoric of the Kennedy administration and the Vietnam War have not always sufficiently appreciated the limitations, uncertainties and complexities of U.S. defense policy in the early post-World War II years. There was a strong tendency, which has never completely died out, to focus on developing a sufficiently strong capability for retaliation to deter an attack on North America. This was consistent with the inherent regionalism of postwar defense planning and with the ideology of preparedness. It cannot, however, explain the global deployment of American forces. An essential element, almost always missing, is the role of Britain which in 1945 maintained large forces throughout the world—and was conceded by both the United States and the Soviet Union to have the responsibilities of a great power. The United States eventually did assume many of Britain's traditional responsibilities in Europe, the Mediterranean and the Middle East; but this did not occur in 1945, and its eventual occurrence cannot be adequately explained as merely the unfolding of an American ideology of preparedness.

NOTES

1. See Harley Notter, *Postwar Foreign Policy Preparation, 1939-1945* (Washington: Deparment of State, 1949); Richard N. Gardner, *Sterling-Dollar Diplomacy: The Origins and the Prospects of Our International Economic Order*, new expanded ed. (New York: McGraw-Hill, 1969); Hathaway, *Ambiguous Partnership*, pp. 70-88, 182-201, 230-38; Robert A. Pollard, "Economic Security and the Origins of the Cold War: Bretton Woods, the Marshall Plan, and American Rearmament, 1944-50," *Diplomatic History* 9 (Summer 1985): 271-89.

2. Michael S. Sherry, *Preparing for the Next War: American Plans for Postwar Defense, 1941-45* (New Haven, Conn.: Yale University Press, 1977), p. 235.

3. Yergin, *Shattered Peace*, p. 196.

4. See below, pp. 69-71.

5. See James R. Leutze, *Bargaining for Supremacy: Anglo-American Naval Collaboration, 1937-1941* (Chapel Hill, N.C.: University of North Carolina Press, 1977); David Reynolds, *The Creation of the Anglo-American Alliance, 1937-1941: A Study in Competititve Co-operation* (Chapel Hill, N.C.: University of North Carolina Press, 1981).

6. Roosevelt's concept of the Four Policemen is best explained by Robert A. Divine, *Roosevelt and World War II* (Baltimre, Md.: Johns Hopkins Press, 1969), pp. 58-65. Divine based his account in part on evidence from Memorandum of conference by Cross, 29 May 1942, *FRUS 1942*, 3: 568-69; Memorandum of conference by Hopkins, 29 May 1942, *FRUS 1942*, 3: 572-73; Roosevelt-Stalin Meeting, 29 November 1943, *FRUS, Cairo and Tehran*, pp. 529-33; Roosevelt to Norris, 21 September

1943, in *F.D.R.: His Personal Letters*, ed. Elliot H. Roosevelt, 2 (New York: Duell, Sloan and Pearce, 1950), 1445-47; Memorandum of conversation, 27 March 1943, *FRUS* 1943, 3:38. See also Divine's *Second Chance: The Triumph of Internationalism in America during World War II* (New York: Atheneum, 1967), especially pp. 157-60; Forrest Davis, "Roosevelt's World Blueprint," *Saturday Evening Post* 215 (10 April 1943): 20 + ; Eden, *The Reckoning*, p. 437; Willard Range, *Franklin D. Roosevelt's World Order* (Athens, Ga.: University of Georgia Press, 1959), pp. 172-76.

7. See Ruth B. Russell, assisted by Jeanette E. Multher, *A History of the United Nations Charter: The Role of the United States, 1940-1945.* (Washington: The Brookings Institution, 1958), pp. 228-29, 646-57.

8. *FRUS, Cairo and Tehran*, pp. 530-32. Similar comments were made to the president's aide, William D. Hassett, who reported them in his *Off the Record with F.D.R., 1942-1945* (New Brunswick, N.J.: Rutgers University Press, 1958), pp. 166-67.

9. Memorandum to the Secretary of the Navy, 13 April 1944, Double Zero Files 1941-1946, Box 37, File 18 SECNAV, NHC.

10. William R. Emerson, "F.D.R. (1941-1945)," in *The Ultimate Decision: The President as Commander in Chief*, ed. Ernest R. May (New York: George Braziller, 1960), p. 168.

11. Quoted in Maurice Matloff, *Strategic Planning for Coalition Warfare, 1943-1944* (Washington: Office of the Chief of Military History, Department of the Army, 1959), p. 342.

12. Roosevelt to Churchill, 29 February 1944, *Roosevelt and Churchill: Their Secret Wartime Correspondence*, ed. Francis L. Loewenheim, Harold D. Langley and Manfred Jonas (New York: Saturday Review Press/E. P. Dutton, 1975), p. 457.

13. Roosevelt-Stalin Meeting, 29 November 1943, *FRUS, Cairo and Tehran*, p. 531; Second Plenary Meeting, 5 February 1945, *FRUS, Malta and Yalta*, p. 617.

14. Only some of the bases desired lay on foreign territory to which access would have to be arranged diplomatically; other sites were located on U.S. territory, islands captured from the Japanese, or on land transferred to the United States by special arrangements.

15. Elliott Vanveltner Converse III, "United States Plans for A Postwar Overseas Military Base System, 1942-1948," (Ph.D. dissertation, Princeton University, 1984).

16. Converse, "United States Plans," p. 11; for the controversy over commercial aviation, see John Andrew Miller, "Air Diplomacy: The Chicago Civil Aviation Conference of 1944 in Anglo-American Wartime Relations and Postwar Planning," (Ph.D. dissertation, Yale University, 1971).

17. See Mark A. Stoler, "From Continentalism to Globalism: General

Stanley D. Embick, the Joint Strategic Survey Committee, and the Military View of American National Policy during the Second World War," *Diplomatic History* 6 (Summer 1982): 303-21.

18. See Converse, "United States Plans," pp. 17-20.

19. Chairman, General Board to Secretary of the Navy, 20 March 1943 (G.B. No. 450), Records of the General Board, Navy and Old Army Branch, National Archives. A discussion of this and related General Board reports is found in William Roger Louis, *Imperialism at Bay: The United States and The Decolonization of the British Empire, 1941-1945* (New York: Oxford University Press, 1978), pp. 262-68. The Navy's plans, writes Louis, constituted "a blueprint for transforming most of the Pacific into an American lake" (p. 267).

20. CG, USAAF to JCS [9 October 1943], RG 218, CCS 360 (12-9-42), section 2, quoted in Converse, "United States Plans," p. 36.

21. Converse, "United States Plans," pp. 36-37.

22. Roosevelt to Hull, 7 January 1944, *FRUS* 1944, 7: 546-47. Maps illustrating the administration's priorities for base access and indeed the regional focus of its postwar policies were enclosed in a 1 February 1944 letter from Roosevelt to Hull, RG 59, 811.24500/1-744.

23. Converse, "United States Plans," p. 54.

24. Ibid., pp. 51, 54.

25. COMINCH and CNO to SECNAV, ser 0604, 3 March 1945, File: Basic Post-War Plan No. 1A, RG 80, SECNAV/CNO Central Correspondence File, 1945, Confidential, File: A16-3. This delimitation endured into 1946; see CNO to Distribution List, 21 March 1946, ser 051P001, File: Basic Postwar Plan No. 2, Development Plan—Atlantic and Pacific Bases, RG 80, SECNAV/CNO Central Correspondence File, 1946, Confidential, File: A16-3.

26. See Herman S. Wolk, *Planning and Organizing the Postwar Air Force, 1943-1947* (Washington: Office of Air Force History, United States Air Force, 1984), p. 75; Perry McCoy Smith, *The Air Force Plans for Peace, 1943-1945* (Baltimore, Md.: Johns Hopkins Press, 1970), p. 58; Converse, "United States Plans," pp. 70-73.

27. Arnold to Spaatz, 8 November 1944, File: Post Hostilities, Box: 188, Spaatz Papers, LC.

28. See Frank D. McCann, Jr., *The Brazilian-American Alliance, 1937-1945* (Princeton, N.J.: Princeton University Press, 1973), pp. 339-41.

29. See Converse, "United States Plans," pp. 113-15.

30. See Smith, *Air Force Plans*, p. 53.

31. See Converse, "United States Plans," pp. 173-74.

32. Ibid., p. 37.

33. Ibid., pp. 77-79.

34. Quoted in Vincent Davis, *Postwar Defense Policy and the U.S.*

Navy, 1943-1946 (Chapel Hill, N.C.: University of North Carolina Press, 1966), pp. 159-60.

35. "Hearings on House Concurrent Resolution 80, Composition of the Postwar Navy, 19 September 1945," in United States, Congress, House, Committee on Naval Affairs, *Hearings on Sundry Legislation Affecting the Naval Establishment, 1945*, 79th Cong., 1st sess., p. 1186.

36. COMINCH and CNO to Commander, U.S. Naval Forces Europe, 22 September 1945, RG 353, Records of the State-War-Navy Coordinating Committee, File: 155/2.

37. "Britain's Security Interests in the Post-War World," 15 September 1944, RG 59, Office of Strategic Services, Research and Analysis Branch, Report No. 2218.

38. See Briefing Book and Excerpt from a Letter from the JCS, 16 [May] 1944, *FRUS, Potsdam*, 1: 256-66.

39. See Herbert Feis, *Between War and Peace: The Potsdam Conference* (Princeton, N.J.: Princeton University Press, 1960), pp. 18-20.

40. See Department of State to British Embassy, 23 June 1945, *FRUS, Potsdam*, 1: 1027-28. A briefing paper prepared for the president on this issue noted two U.S. interests involved in the Straits question: preventing the Dardanelles from becoming an area of international dispute and ensuring the unrestricted use of the Straits for peaceful commerce. (Memorandum Regarding the Montreux Convention, 30 June 1945, *FRUS, Potsdam*, 1: 1014). No American strategic interests were considered to be involved nor was it suggested that the U.S. should support traditional British interests.

41. Journal entry, 13 June 1945, Joseph E. Davies Papers, LC.

42. Quoted in diary entry for 12 September 1945, Leahy Papers, LC.

43. Sherry, *Preparing for the Next War*, p. 238.

CHAPTER 4
THE AMERICAN
SERVICES AND
POSTWAR REALITIES

Postwar American defense planning emerged in an atmosphere marked not only by uncertain foreign policy objectives but also by bitter interservice rivalry, largely generated by tight limits on defense spending between 1946 and 1951. The eventual acceptance of new international commitments was not matched by increased appropriations until the 1950s; defense officials conceived war plans for which no resources were available, nor was it likely that they would soon be made available. Considerable jockeying, particularly between the Navy and the Army Air Forces, which would become the independent Air Force in 1947, occurred in regard to the assignment of roles and missions which would guarantee organizational survival. As Robert Donovan has written, "the Pentagon was turned into a pressure cooker when, after the war, Truman embarked upon a course of severely restricting military spending in an effort to restore a normal peacetime economy."[1]

There was to be no early relief to the budgetary crunch. Although no attempt was made to return to prewar levels of defense spending ($1.4 billion in FY 1939; $1.8 billion in FY 1940), a consensus emerged that postwar defense budgets should be held to a level approximately 30 percent of the level of total federal expenditures which ranged in these years between $30 and 40 billion. It was widely believed that such a level was the maximum that could be afforded without generating massive distortions in the national economy.

Furthermore, no political constituency existed for major increases in defense spending. Congressional Republicans, although easily converted to a strong anticommunist stance, were determined to cut back on New Deal programs and to reduce spending and taxes. As Susan Hartmann has written, "Most Republican legislators . . . were simultaneously politically interventionist and economically isolationist. They were loudly anticommunist and urged the Administration to take a stronger stand against Russia, but were extremely hesitant when it came to spending money abroad."[2] GOP majorities in both houses of Congress attempted in 1947 to reduce federal taxes, only to be thwarted by a presidential veto. Truman would propose his own tax credit plan in the following year to be accompanied by a modified excess profits tax, but the Eightieth Congress was determined to go further and passed, over his veto, a general reduction in individual income tax rates and an increase in individual exemptions. In 1949 Republicans and conservative Democrats rejected an effort by the administration to increase taxes.[3] The administration was determined to preserve some New Deal programs that Republicans wanted to axe, but on the whole Truman and his economic advisers, especially James E. Webb, director of the Bureau of the Budget from 1946 to 1949, were "hard money" men, opposed to deficit spending and well aware of congressional and public opposition to higher taxes even for defense. The result was that defense budgets had to be held at roughly the same levels throughout the period. Only the outbreak of the Korean War changed the political climate.

The discrepancy between what military officials felt they required and the amounts actually provided was understood at the time. Decisions to limit defense expenditures were based on assessments of political realities and on the firmly held belief that greater spending would choke an economy still on the mend from wartime dislocations and that overspending could reduce the nation's overall productive capacity, thus playing into the hands of the Soviets.[4] Many officials also hoped that once the Europeans were back on their feet as a result of American economic and perhaps military assistance, there would be no need for an American defense commitment to the Western Europeans, at least not one which required the stationing of large numbers of ground forces abroad.

These factors remained unchanged even during several years of intense international crises. In 1949-1950, however, certain of the president's aides, especially Leon Keyserling, who would shortly become chairman of the Council of Economic Advisers, came around to the view that government spending at much higher levels could eventually generate increased revenues without doing permanent damage to the nation's economic life. The fact that administration economists became persuaded that higher defense expenditures were possible enabled Truman to seek and obtain vastly increased military appropriations after 1950, not only to support the Korean War but also to fund a major expansion in both strategic and conventional forces.[5]

Despite the economists' willingness to shift their allegiance from hard money to an acceptance of deficit spending, it was not really they who determined the nature of defense programs after 1949. The groundwork was built by Defense officials working in cooperation with the State Department and with British colleagues who analyzed the requirements of Western defense and believed that American forces would be required in Europe if an adequate deterrent against Soviet expansionism were to be maintained. As Warner Schilling has written, "Motivation will turn on people's sense of need, purpose, and accomplishment, and of all the simplifying assumptions behind [the rationale that the country could afford heavier defense expenditures], the most vital was . . . that the country had been politically persuaded that higher defense expenditures were worth the costs involved."[6] Pervasive hostility to the Soviet Union combined with analysis of the needs of Western defense ultimately persuaded the administration and the Congress that the funds would have to be found if Western security were to be protected; the economists demonstrated how the monies could be obtained.

The process by which officials in the United States came to recognize the inadequacy of a defense policy based on protection of the Western Hemisphere and the Pacific evolved from the early months of 1946, about the time of Churchill's Iron Curtain speech and a toughening of the State Department's stance on a number of issues in dispute with the Soviet Union. It was in large measure an independent process in each of the three services. Senior officials in each service came separately, for differing reasons, to accept the need for increased American involvement in Europe and the Mediterranean. In each of these cases, senior Defense officials like their State Department colleagues, were influenced by British counterparts in Washington as part of the CCS/BJSM structure, in London and in various places in Europe and the Eastern Mediterranean where U.S. and British forces were deployed together or in close proximity to each other. The precise extent of British influence cannot be gauged, but it is clear that there was an emerging consensus that the need to maintain the European balance of power was a vital American interest and that Anglo-American defense cooperation was the only way to accomplish it. The years 1946-1947 saw a gradual metamorphosis in the policies of the three services (and, as will be discussed in the following chapter, in American foreign policy as well). Although the formalization of the metamorphosis would occur only after the beginning of the Berlin crisis of 1948-1949, and much higher levels of defense spending would be voted only in the 1950s, it was in this earlier period that American national security officials (along with key wielders of influence outside the executive branch) were converted, and the principles previously governing American defense policy were undermined.

THE ARMY AIR FORCES

The Army Air Forces (AAF) emerged from World War II with an impressive reputation for having contributed mightily to the defeat of Germany and for dramatically ending the war in the Pacific with atomic explosives over two Japanese cities. Airmen believed that they were now justified in assuming the Navy's traditional position as the nation's "first line of defense." The arrival of the age of long-range bombers and unmanned missiles meant in their view that the United States must hereafter base its defense policy on air forces in being, capable of instant retaliation against any country attempting another Pearl Harbor.

The airmen's goals were not, however, to be quickly realized. The administration and the Congress were determined to reduce spending. The Army ground forces and the Navy, especially the latter, did not endorse Air Force ambitions at the expense of their own desiderata. In addition, Air Force planning and its implementation were hampered by a confused and rapidly changing organizational structure which did not begin to be resolved until the creation of an independent service. Finally, the basic uncertainties of the aims of overall American policy precluded an early or easy resolution of the related planning dilemmas.

The fundamental aim of Air Force planners was the establishment of a seventy-group Air Force based on twenty-five Very Heavy Bomber (VHB) groups and twenty-five fighter groups. The origins of the seventy-group structure, a force of some 12,000 aircraft, ultimately derived from personnel levels dictated by the War Department's postwar planning efforts in 1945. It was based on requirements to provide strategic coverage of the Western Hemisphere and the Pacific. The seventy-group force structure became a touchstone of Air Force planners and was endorsed by congressional studies and outside airpower advocates including the Air Policy Commission (the Finletter Commission) established by President Truman in the summer of 1947 to sort out the nation's airpower requirements. As it turned out, despite intensive lobbying and expanding defense commitments, the resources for seventy groups were not to become available until the time of the Korean War.[7] In December 1946, as General Spaatz, then the commanding general of the AAF, would later recall, only fifty-five groups were extant and only two of them were capable of operating effectively.[8]

A long-standing rivalry with the Navy over roles and missions intensified, particularly over the strategic bombing mission which was now coming to lie at the heart of the nation's defense strategy. It soon spilled over into Congress and the press. As competition for limited funds became ever more severe towards the end of the decade, the Navy instigated congressional investigations of alleged irregularities in bomber procurement and Air Force publicists launched vicious attacks on the Navy and the Marine Corps. The acrimony contributed in large measure to a dismissal of a chief of naval operations, a resignation in protest of a secretary of the navy, and perhaps to the suicide of the first secrtary of defense and the sudden dismissal of his successor. Even in the first year after V-J Day, the conflicting goals of the Air Force and the Navy tended to distort planning in the effort to establish priorities for base requirements.[9] Air Force claims for the effectiveness of an air atomic strategy became exaggerated; belief in the sufficiency of a large bomber force became a dogma of airpower advocates in the struggle with the Navy and hampered realistic planning and effective operational training.

Revamping the AAF's wartime structure to meet postwar conditions was a major undertaking resulting in incessant reorganization, constant relocation of command headquarters and operating bases and rapid turnover of personnel. The effort to establish the Air Force as an independent service inevitably occupied the time of senior officers. The departure of the skilled personnel of World War II left the newly independent service in 1947 with a large number of inexperienced enlisted men, many of whom could not even be adequately housed, dispersed in isolated bases both in the United States and abroad.

Air Force strategy was significantly reflected in the effort to acquire overseas bases, which had been scarcely begun by mid-1945 when it became obvious that previously agreed-upon priorities were no longer realistic. New requirements were negotiated by the various bureaucracies in several fora—the JCS, the State-War-Navy Coordinating Committee (SWNCC), the Committee of Three (the regular meetings of the secretaries of state, war and navy which began in 1944) and eventually the National Security Council which was created in 1947. State Department diplomats undertook negotiations with the potential host countries with occasional assistance and/or interference from the Pentagon.

The process was in large measure responsive to the Air Force requirements, inasmuch as most of the bases desired by the Navy were already under U.S. control.[10] Attention continued to focus on Iceland, Greenland (which was under Danish sovereignty), and the Portuguese islands of the Azores which lay along the most direct air route from North America to the Mediterranean.

On 23 October 1945, after extensive interservice discussions, the JCS approved JCS 570/40, "Over-All Examination of U.S. Requirements for Military Bases and Rights."[11] The list of bases for which negotiations would be required was subsequently forwarded to the SWNCC as SWNCC 38/25. After a certain amount of bureaucratic wrangling due to Navy reluctance to see major emphasis placed on North Atlantic bases intended for Air Force use, agreement was reached on a document listing primary base areas "essential to the security of the United States, its possessions, the Western Hemisphere, and the Philippines": the Azores, the Ryukyus, Iceland, the Panama Canal Zone, the Hawaiian Islands, the Marianas, the Philippines, the Southwestern Alaska-Aleutian area, Newfoundland and Puerto Rico-Virgin Islands. Even though the Navy remained most concerned with the Pacific, as Elliot Converse notes,

The choice of primary base areas demonstrates the swing of the strategic pendulum from the Pacific orientation of earlier plans [i.e. JCS 570/2 of November 1943] to a greater concentration on the Atlantic. But the strategic shift went beyond equal division between east and west; fully half of the primary bases focused American power astride the northern approaches to the United States and its possessions."[12]

Brigadier General George A. Lincoln, the Army's deputy director of plans, advised his JCS counterparts with customary concision: "We should give the weight of our attention to the north as any future threat would be most likely to come from the northeast or the northwest and not from the south."[13]

When the JCS transmitted this list to the SWNCC,[14] they listed those areas to which base rights had to be acquired by new negotiations with foreign governments, and where access was considered essential.[15] Early in January 1946 the JCS also forwarded to SWNCC a list of an additional twenty air fields where landing rights were described as needed for transit between the U.S. and the Western Pacific and between North Africa, India and the Philippines. These routes were sought to facilitate transfers of personnel and supplies to, from and between U.S. occupation zones in Europe and Asia. The rights desired were of a much more limited character than was the case with the bases listed previously, but they were nonetheless seen by the Joint Staff Planners as bases in being "in the event future world conditions again require U.S. military operations in those areas as were required in World War II."[16] An anomaly was the U.S. base at Dhahran in Saudi Arabia, which, while useful for supporting transport flights between Europe/North Africa and the Far East, was built shortly after the end of the war primarily to assure U.S. commercial access to that country and its resources.[17] Despite the emphasis on the North

Atlantic, neither JCS 570/40 nor the January 1946 listing of transit fields included facilities on the European continent. Converse notes correctly that "in late 1945, the long history of American aversion to permanent involvement in Europe still enveloped military planners."[18]

In dealing with the complicated question of base requirements and related negotiations, it is important to realize that the North Atlantic bases were required not only for potential use in war, but also for current support of flights between North America and U.S. occupation zones in Europe. This requirement was in fact the main factor which drove the State Department's negotiating efforts in the years 1945-1949. Bases for wartime missions were not the primary goal of negotiations. John Hickerson, a key State Department official, explained the importance of Iceland in May 1946:

The requirement for retention and use of facilities in Iceland to support the military line of communication to Europe will exist so long as U.S. occupational forces in Germany and Italy are required. Without Iceland, the North Atlantic air route will become unreliable and unsafe as a regular route for ferrying short-range tactical aircraft to reinforce occupational forces. Also, without Iceland, the capacity of this military air transport route will be reduced by 20 percent on east-bound trips and 60 percent west-bound. Also, because of the tenuous position of U.S. rights and because of the distances on the Azores and South Atlantic routes, all military flights across the Atlantic, except by 4-engine aircraft with reduced loads, would be made exceedingly difficult and flights by single-engined aircraft would have to be suspended.[19]

To the extent that the occupation of Germany came to acquire a semipermanent aspect in the following years, Iceland and Greenland (which provided backup airfields and weather stations) continued to be needed; as long as it was necessary to supply American forces in Italy, access to the Azores would be a decided asset.

Beyond these considerations, from the autumn of 1945 these bases had come to have a greater importance. In their 7 November 1945 memorandum, the JCS had noted that

the comprehensive base system which will result from obtaining the desired rights is not only an inescapable requirement for United States security in the event of a failure of the United Nations Organization to preserve world

peace, but the provision of this system of bases will contribute materially to
the effectiveness of that organization in maintaining peace throughout the
world.[20]

Behind this somewhat elliptical comment was an emerging perception that the United States had to face the necessity of considering
defense planning "in the event of a failure of the United Nations
Organization to preserve world peace." Serious concern about
Soviet actions and long-range intentions had been evident in Joint
Staff and SWNCC documents during late 1945 and early 1946. In
October 1945 a JCS paper cautioned about the "undefined character of Russian aspirations, the background of mutual suspicion
existing between the Soviet Union and the rest of the world, and the
lack of a common basis of information and understanding with
Russia."[21] Reflecting Air Force views, the Joint Staff went on to
warn of new weaponry which would require keeping an unnamed
enemy at the maximum possible distance from vital United States
installations. This would in turn require

forces and installations disposed in an outer perimeter from which to
reconnoiter and survey possible enemy actions, to intercept his attacking
forces and missiles, to deny him use of such bases, and to launch counter-
actions which alone can reach a decision satisfactory to us.[22]

JCS requirements for bases had been duly approved by SWNCC
in the same month, but prompt action by the State Department
negotiators was not to be forthcoming. During the winter of
1945-1946 concern with Soviet policy was constantly growing in
Washington along with clear recognition that no threat could be
expected from occupied Japan and Germany. The need for Pacific
bases in particular appeared less and less obvious. In addition
Secretary of State Byrnes was becoming increasingly aware of the
diplomatic difficulties in obtaining military base rights, even from
Great Britain. The end of the war had encouraged forces of nationalism which were inevitably hostile to bases even of friendly powers.
Finally, the service secretaries, and especially Forrestal, had
become involved in the question of base negotiations, previously
the preserve of the JCS.[23]

In February 1946, Forrestal indicated his belief that base requirements were excessive, and that the JCS were "all over the map" on

the question and should be made to "come down to earth."[24] His request for a reassessment led to SWNCC 38/35, "Overall Examination of U.S. Requirements for Military Rights." This study, completed on 5 June 1946, reaffirmed and strengthened the shift away from the Pacific, listing six required bases of which four were in the Atlantic area, namely Iceland, the Azores, Greenland and Casablanca/Port Lyautey; several formerly important Pacific sites were dropped entirely.[25] A later revision, SWNCC 38/46, undertaken in 1947, would further emphasize the shift towards the North Atlantic.[26]

The State Department subsequently undertook negotiations with Iceland, Denmark and Portugal. After a maximum effort by U.S. diplomats, an agreement was signed with the Icelandic government in October 1946 which allowed use of Keflavik airport by American transport aircraft. While negotiations with Denmark dragged on, a 1941 arrangement with the Danish government in exile was allowed to remain in force, allowing the United States use of radar and emergency landing facilities in Greenland. Talks with the Portuguese government produced an interim agreement in May 1946 for U.S. and British use of Lagens airport; a follow-up agreement was reached in February 1948. In all of these cases the U.S. received diplomatic support from Britain despite initial reluctance in London to set a precedent which could be of use to Moscow elsewhere. Attlee determined that "the desirability of getting the United States committed in the Eastern Atlantic outweighed any possible repercussions."[27] Arrangements with the French for limited use of Port Lyautey were quietly conducted on a navy-to-navy basis and an agreement was signed in September 1947.[28]

Despite the limited nature of the agreements reached, the emphasis on Greenland, Iceland and the Azores continued. The newly established National Security Council at its second meeting in November 1947 forwarded to the President a report concluding that "it is difficult to conceive of a war in the next 15 to 20 years in which Greenland, Iceland, and the Azores would not be of extreme importance to the war effort." Variously the bases were needed for "offensive operations, as bases forming a part of the defense system about the U.S., as areas to be denied to the enemy, and as bases for staging of air transport and combat aircraft." For offensive operations Iceland was considered close to the industrial heartland of our only conceivable enemy; its logistic support is feasible; its weather and terrain is suitable for air operations; it is reasonably defensible. For offensive purposes Iceland is of greater potential value to the U.S. than any other area short of England and the Afro-Eurasian land mass.

Greenland, despite "logistics and weather handicaps," presents "a prospect for VHB [Very Heavy Bomber] bases even closer to the industrial heartland of the potential enemy." While the Azores bases were of minor importance in offensive operations, their utility lay in their potential role as a staging base for the transport and combat aircraft; they were "the most vital spot in the world in this respect, exclusive of the war zone and the U.S. proper. These islands are the key to our primary air lines of communication." All three would be "of considerable importance to both the U.S. and possible enemies as naval bases and for the conduct of antisubmarine operations."[29]

The arrangements that were actually worked out with Iceland, Denmark and Portugal were not designed to provide support for offensive operations, and none of the three countries had an interest in antagonizing the Soviet Union. As a result it was clear, even in 1946, that in the final analysis the overseas bases which could most easily be utilized by American bombers if a war with the Soviet Union should suddenly break out were those in Britain. Arrangements were quietly worked out in 1946 between General Spaatz and Air Marshal Arthur Tedder, the chief of the RAF's Air Staff, that four East Anglian bases would be prepared to support nuclear capable B-29s in case of an emergency.[30] This arrangement preceded development of joint war plans; when, however, the plans were developed in 1947-1948, they included strategic attacks by aircraft flying from British bases.[31] In the midst of the 1948 Berlin crisis, B-29s were deployed to British bases in a dramatic move to underscore the American commitment to maintaining its position in the former German capital.[32]

War plans under preparation in 1947 and 1948 envisioned attacks on key Soviet targets not only from airfields in the United Kingdom but also from bases in the Middle East from which bombers could attack major Soviet targets that lay beyond the range of British-based aircraft. SWNCC 38/46 had not addressed the need for such bases. This incongruity may have resulted, as Converse suggests, from a case of the right hand of the Joint Staff not knowing what the left hand was doing;[33] more likely, it reflected a then raging interservice feud over the need for a Mediterranean strategy that would include shore facilities in North Africa whose protection the Navy hoped and the Air Force feared would justify additional funds for aircraft carriers.[34]

North African bases were always a special problem because of the colonial relationships involved. The Navy obtained access to Port Lyautey by working quietly with French naval officials and maintaining good relations with the local population. Access to Egyptian and Suez Canal Zone facilities was complicated by the long-festering Anglo-Egyptian dispute into which the State Department was very reluctant to be drawn.[35] Beginning in the early fall of 1947 attention switched to Wheelus Field near Tripoli in what later became the independent country of Libya. There an American airfield, constructed during World War II at a cost of $7 million, had recently been declared surplus. Arrangements were quickly made with the British, who were exercising temporary control of the former Italian territories, to reopen the facility. The first U.S. fighter aircraft deployed briefly to Wheelus in December 1947 and were followed by a visit some months later by B-29s. Eventually Wheelus would become an essential element of Strategic Air Command operations.[36]

Although originally intended as only part of the occupation force, U.S. air forces in Germany came to play an important actual and symbolic role in subsequent American policies designed to deter Soviet aggression in central Europe. The aircraft and Air Force personnel assigned to U.S. Forces in the European Theater were designated United States Air Forces in Europe (USAFE). USAFE, which had a personnel strength of 315,000 in August 1945, was reduced along with other parts of the occupation force; by December 1945 there were only some 64,000 airmen and a year later only 33,00 remained. The principal USAFE mission was to provide transport and to assist in salvage and property removal functions. The demands of these missions naturally declined; by December 1947 only 21,000 Air Force personnel remained in Germany.[37]

Changes occurring in 1946 and 1947 in American policy towards the Soviet Union had only a marginal impact on USAFE. After the attacks on two American C-47 transports in August 1946 by Yugoslavia, Assistant Secretary of the Army for Air Stuart Symington sought a demonstration flight of B-29s along the Yugoslav border, but it was three months later that B-29s first appeared in Europe when six bombers were sent to Germany to demonstrate American concern and capabilities.[38]

B-29s continued to appear in Europe as a result of the decision of the Strategic Air Command, a principal component of the AAF and subsequently of the independent Air Force, to retain centralized control of its aircraft while rotating them periodically from their home bases in the United States to forward bases overseas. The policy served to provide realistic training and ensured that pilots were familiar with overseas facilities.[39] Regular deployments to Europe and Japan began in July 1947. The bombers deployed to Germany initially operated from the American base at Giebelstadt but later shifted to Fuerstenfeldbruck where the base was expanded to better accommodate the B-29 squadron. Permission was also obtained from the RAF to use landing and gunnery ranges in the British zone of Germany, and training flights were made to Dhahran in Saudi Arabia and to Wheelus Field. Conditions for the operations were not ideal given the need to obtain permission to overfly European countries. At one point in 1947 the Air Force's Strategic Air Command (SAC) desired to cancel the European deployments, but they were continued in large measure because senior officials had become convinced of the salutary political effect.[40]

Although the beginning of B-29 deployments gave USAFE at least embryonic involvement in vital strategic missions, personnel strengths in Germany continued to decline. In February 1947, the USAFE Commander, General Idwal H. Edwards, proposed to reduce his troop levels to 7,500 by early 1948 by removing all combat units and providing only for communications, air transportation and combat support functions. Approval was obtained for reductions to an 8,000-12,000 troop level. This effort was largely dictated by budgetary pressures which required worldwide troop reductions, but there was also some concern that airbases in Germany would be in an extremely exposed position in the event of hostilities.[41]

In September 1947 another plan was proposed which would have brought troop levels down to under 10,000 by mid-1948, envisioning the reduction of USAFE to a small headquarters element of less than 3,000 troops. This plan was disapproved by Air Force Vice Chief of Staff General Hoyt S. Vandenberg in November 1947. Like his civilian superiors, Vandenberg had become convinced of the psychological necessity of retaining a significant Air Force presence in Europe.[42] Troop levels nonetheless continued to be reduced until the spring of 1948.

During a period of constantly rising tension between the United States and the Soviet Union and at a time when Washington was moving much closer towards involvement in the struggle against Communist insurgents in Greece, the numbers of Air Force personnel in the European Theater were being constantly reduced. Even the training visits by B-29s could not obscure the fact that the American Air Force presence in central Europe was declining in strength.

Despite reductions in personnel, Air Force officials were attempting to enhance U.S. combat capabilities in Europe. This new activism was highlighted by the arrival in October 1947 of Lt. General Curtis E. LeMay as head of USAFE. LeMay, who had previously directed bombing operations in both the European and Pacific Theaters during the war, would later go on to head the Strategic Air Command and to serve as Air Force chief of staff. Bringing considerable reserves of energy and initiative to his European post, he displayed a willingness to short-circuit official channels. In his not immodest memoirs, he recalled that when he arrived in Germany his initial impression was that "USAFE would be stupid to get mixed up in anything bigger than a cat-fight at a pet show."[43] LeMay moved quickly to improve the training and readiness of the forces he had available, and worked surreptitiously with French and Belgian officials to establish supply depots outside Germany: "What this amounted to, in effect, was that we had our own private little NATO buzzing along, there in West Germany and France and Belgium, before the North Atlantic Treaty Organization ever existed."[44] LeMay found his efforts justified when he was assigned responsibility for the Berlin airlift the following summer.

The second half of 1947 thus saw a fundamental ambiguity in Air Force planning for the European Theater. On one hand troop strengths were declining along with numbers of combat aircraft; simultaneously, the most powerful long-range bombers were being deployed to Germany for training flights and to demonstrate American concern with Soviet policies. Much of the impetus for the latter policy, it should be noted, came from the State Department and civilian officials in the Pentagon. These men valued the psychological impact of B-29 deployments at least as much as the actual augmentation of combat capabilities. The main thrust of strategic planning within the Air Force rested, however, not on deployments to vulnerable airfields in central Europe but on plans for long range air strikes from more secure airbases in the Pacific, the North Atlantic and the Middle East. The acquisition of such bases could not, however, be achieved without consideration by the United States of the security needs of host countries. The requirement to obtain reliable access for facilities overseas directly implied a need to protect key base areas and thus a security relationship with the host countries. American security, even if it was centered only on an air-atomic strategy, required U.S. involvement in the defense of certain European countries. Thus, in the process of negotiating an Atlantic treaty in 1948, Washington pressed for the inclusion of essential North Atlantic islands.

THE GROUND FORCES

In the first postwar years the ground forces of the U.S. Army underwent a rapid process of demobilization which virtually eliminated their combat capabilities. Large numbers of experienced soldiers were released in a short period of time and a much smaller number of green recruits—some with only two months basic training—served in the continental United States and as members of the occupation forces in Europe and the Far East. It was a period of exceptional military weakness and there would be no significant personnel augmentation until after the outbreak of the Korean War in 1950.

U.S. occupation forces in Europe served to ensure that Germany would remain demilitarized. Their presence both reflected and demonstrated Washington's determination to retain a major role in the settlement of the delicate and vital questions relating to the future of Germany. These troops performed many of the essentially civilian functions of governmental administration. They had no substantial military capability; it was recognized that in the event of hostilities with the Soviet Union the best that could be hoped for would be an orderly evacuation of U.S. forces from the continent à la Dunkirk in 1940. U.S. planners came to realize that any involvement of these troops in combat, even in full retreat, would require as a matter of military necessity close cooperation with the British, and to a certain extent the French, both of whom also had occupation forces in Germany. Combined plans undertaken in 1946 for the evacuation of the Continent laid the basis for future defense cooperation which would become formally institutionalized in 1948-1949.

The first priority of the American people after the victories of 1945 was to bring the troops home to civilian life. The process of demobilization, based primarily on an individual's length of service, quickly became a political imperative for the Truman administration as servicemen joined protest demonstrations and members of Congress demanded immediate action. The net effect of the process was to release the more experienced enlisted men and replace them with recruits fresh from basic training. As an official historian has written, "By the Fall and Winter of 1945-1946 the armies and air forces that had been victorious in Europe and the Pacific were no longer a closely integrated military machine, but rather had disintegrated to little more than large groups of individual replacements."[45] The peak American military strength in mid-1945 was 12 million service men and women. In mid-1946 the size of the Army, including the Army Air Forces, was fixed by Public Law 473 at 1,550,000 for July 1946, declining to 1,070,000 for July 1947. By mid-1947 personnel of all services totaled approximately a million and a half—a figure which would not significantly increase until the Korean War.[46]

The release of World War II draftees had of course been anticipated by Army planners. During World War II senior officials including Secretary of War Henry Stimson and Chief of Staff General George C. Marshall hoped to maintain postwar capabilities through reliance on a system of universal military training. UMT would avoid an "un-American" large professional army by requiring every male citizen to undergo a period of essentially military training which would allow him to serve effectively when called upon in a national emergency. President Truman was himself wholeheartedly convinced of the desirability of UMT, but despite strong support from many private organizations and individuals, several administration efforts to enact UMT failed to overcome congressional and public resistance.[47]

Lacking UMT, the maintenance of an adequate number of soldiers for occupation duties in Europe and the Far East depended upon the Selective Service System. The importance of the draft was dramatically demonstrated when Selective Service was allowed to lapse between March 1947 and June 1948. During this period the Army was unable to fill some 130,000 of its 669,000 slots and faced a worldwide personnel crisis.[48]

As noted earlier, President Roosevelt had believed that U.S. forces would remain on occupation duty in Europe for only one or two years after the end of hostilities. These duties were in fact extensive given the collapse of the German government and the initial Allied unwillingness to trust officials who had previously held positions under the Nazis. A force of some 30,000 troops, designated the Constabulary, provided police for the American zone, and U.S. soldiers were involved in various noncombat functions such as caring for POWs and refugees, administration of surplus property and supporting civilian officials of the military government.[49] Although it soon became clear that the Germans would not attempt violent resistance to the occupation and that significant numbers of officials of the former regime could be usefully employed in civil administration, U.S. troops continued to serve in essentially civilian functions into 1947 and beyond. In March 1948 the Army chief of staff, General Omar Bradley, explained to a congressional committee that the duties of U.S. forces in Germany remained

primarily those of occupation troops and in general they are pretty well scattered except for one regiment, and some artillery of the First Division, kept in general reserve, and one regiment of the constabulary which is kept as a reserve. The others in addition to these two units are primarily service troops and occupation troops guarding supplies, military government, and so forth.[50]

Increasing pressure for rapid demobilization and other uncertainties in the fall of 1945 necessitated some estimate of the extent of future requirements for occupation forces in Europe. Secretary of War Robert P. Patterson requested guidance from the State Department.[51] Byrnes responded that he could not predict how long U.S. troops would be needed, but added that "it is anticipated that occupation forces will be required in Germany on July 1, 1946, January 1, 1947 and July 1, 1947."[52] The State Department was coming to view U.S. forces as necessary for the restoration of German civil administration but also as providing tangible evidence of an American determination to play a role in the political future of Europe.[53] In April 1946 at the Paris Council of Foreign Ministers meeting Byrnes tabled a draft peace treaty with Germany which implied an American military presence for at least twenty-five years.[54] The following September, in his famous speech at Stuttgart on Germany's future, the secretary of state asserted that "security forces will probably have to remain in Germany for a long period. I want no misunderstanding. We will not shirk our duty. We are not withdrawing. We are staying here. As long as there is an occupation army in Germany, American armed forces will be part of that occupation army."[55]

Roosevelt's belief that domestic opinion would force the withdrawal of U.S. troops had been overtaken by a fear of Soviet aggression and an increasing American sense of responsibility for affairs in Europe. On the other hand, at a time of scarce military manpower it was difficult to justify large numbers of soldiers tied down in nonmilitary duties. The number of troops in Europe, known as the Occupation Troop Basis (OTB), had been initially set at 370,000, but was lowered to less than 300,000 in December 1945.[56] Although Selective Service was extended until March 1947, by the beginning of that year the U.S. troop strength had declined to 202,000.[57] Authorized levels were pegged at 117,000 for 1 July 1947, a figure based, as before, on police and not combat requirements.[58] It soon became clear that in view of Army-wide personnel shortages, even this number could not be maintained. By mid-1948 the U.S. Army in Europe consisted of some 9,700 officers and 81,000 enlisted personnel.[59]

The prospect of constantly declining numbers of U.S. troops in Europe had been a prime motivation for Byrnes to attempt to reach four-power agreement on the size of occupation forces. The issue was raised at the Council of Foreign Ministers meeting in New York in December 1946 when he proposed that the United States

and Britain maintain troop levels of 140,000 each, France 70,000
and the Soviets 200,000.[60] Soviet Foreign Minister Molotov evinced
no interest in the proposal, commenting only that it was "a new
question and a complicated one."[61] The United States raised the
issue again the following April at the Moscow CFM. In response
Molotov proposed that the total combined U.S. and British force
levels should equal that of the Soviet Union, implying that the
United States and Britain were linked in opposition to the Soviet
Union—a principle that neither of the two Western powers wanted
to acknowledge at that time. The question was referred to the
Allied Control Council, consisting of the four military commanders in Germany, for resolution. They discussed the issue in June
1947 but were unable to reach agreement in view of a Soviet insistence on the need for an extra 100,000 troops to maintain control of
Berlin (which would thus give them a total of 200,000 with the U.S.
and Britain each having 100,000). U.S. negotiators might have
accepted something close to the Soviet proposal since it essentially
coincided with U.S. manpower planning, but, to their annoyance,
the British representatives refused to accept anything other than
parity among the three powers. The British had a special interest in
having access to Germany for certain types of large-scale troop
exercises that could not be carried out at home, and had no desire
to reach an inequitable agreement which could perforce provide an
excuse for further American troop withdrawals.[62]

Although there was concern later in 1947 that the Soviets might
make a propaganda ploy by proposing a complete withdrawal of all
occupation forces from Germany,[63] the question of limiting forces
did not formally arise at the CFM which met in London in December 1947 and, in any event, broke down over other issues relating
to the future of Germany.

By 1947 the presence of U.S. troops in Germany was widely perceived as representative of American interest and commitment to
the future of Europe. The conviction held in the State Department
of the political and diplomatic utility of these forces was not, however, matched by a capability to resist any Soviet invasion of
Western Europe. Although, as noted above, these forces were in
large measure employed in civilian functions, beginning in the latter
part of 1947 combat training and organization into combat forma-
tions were undertaken in response to deteriorating East-West

relations, even as troop levels continued to decline. As has been noted, General LeMay, soon after his appointment as commander of the U.S. Air Forces in Europe in October 1947, energetically went to work to improve the training and readiness of the Air Force elements under his command.[64] General Lucius D. Clay, the commander of U.S. Forces in Europe, and his deputy, Lt. General Clarence R. Huebner, also began in the summer of 1947 an extensive program of more realistic combat training for U.S. troops, who by then could be freed from many of the occupation duties that were being turned over to German nationals.[65] In addition, the Army began the first steps in the gradual transformation of the Constabulary into a normal combat force.[66]

Even when American planning for the eventuality of war with the Soviet Union was underway, no major combat role was envisioned for these occupation forces. The emphasis was on a strategic bombing campaign launched from bases outside the European continent and eventually a repeat of the large-scale Normandy invasion of 1944. In the event of war, the plans continued to call for occupation forces to be evacuated as rapidly as possible to Britain or, at the most optimistic, to a bridgehead in the Low Countries. There was considered to be no possibility of holding the line in central Europe, much less of taking any offensive actions. The principal goal was to avoid losing the entire occupation force in the initial days of conflict.[67]

Planning for this unappealing eventuality began in early 1946— about the time American policy was becoming more hostile to the Soviet Union across the board—and was halted a year later at British insistence. The effort witnessed, however, the first postwar collaborative effort by American and British military officials to arrive at a common defense strategy vis-à-vis the Soviet Union; it was the direct antecedent, moreover, of the planning undertaken later in 1947 and 1948 when an effort was first being made to create viable, nonnuclear capabilities to resist Soviet aggression. As such, it warrants greater interest than its meager results in 1947 would suggest.

In the tense atmosphere of February 1946, General Lincoln, the Army planner, initiated contingency planning in order that any hostilities with the Soviets should not result in the loss of the entire U.S. Army of occupation.[68] Lincoln was interested in providing contingency guidance to General Joseph T. McNarney, the commanding general, U.S. Forces European Theater. Although the plans were built around the need for rapid withdrawal to the west, a central issue was the possibility of retaining a bridgehead on the Continent. McNarney's chief of staff, Major General Harold R. Bull, argued that holding any bridgehead would be an impossible mission once the OTB was reduced below 300,000.[69] Nonetheless General Eisenhower, who had relieved Marshall as chief of staff, insisted on the desirability of such an objective, arguing that, "If at all possible, we must hold a bridgehead, the size to be determined by the capabilities of ourselves and our allies at the time the conflict arises."[70] Eisenhower strongly held this opinion and reiterated it repeatedly even though the prevailing view on the Joint Staff was that "available estimates of Soviet and Allied capabilities indicate the complete inability of maintaining a bridgehead in Northwestern Europe in case the Soviets should bring against such an area that force which they are capable of quickly bringing up."[71]

The planning did not just involve the Army ground forces. As part of the effort AAF General Spaatz traveled to London in late June 1946 to arrange with his RAF counterparts for American use of British airfields. Similarly Vice Admiral Forrest P. Sherman, the deputy chief of naval operations for operations, was brought into this planning process at an early stage, as was Admiral H. Kent Hewitt, the commander of U.S. Naval Forces in Europe, who had command of the few U.S. Navy ships which were permanently stationed in European waters.[72]

It was soon apparent to all concerned that the British also had to be involved in the planning process. Truman administration spokesmen at the time were still backpedaling from an unfavorable public reaction to Churchill's suggestion at Fulton that a de facto military alliance be established between the United States and the British Commonwealth; thus any defense planning with the British was sensitive.[73] Nevertheless coordination was imperative; Lincoln's deputy, Lt. General J. E. Hull, acknowledged in February 1946 that "the direction of withdrawal and so forth would have to be tied in definitely with the British."[74] The chief of naval operations, Admiral Nimitz, considered that "naval support for any evacuation of occupation forces from North Europe and provision of the necessary lift therefore will be of necessity largely a

British responsibility and that such U.S. Naval units and shipping as are available in North European waters should be assigned to British control for this purpose."[75] Truman himself was briefed on plans for Anglo-American cooperation in the event of an evacuation. The president was told that McNarney was planning an emergency "to *join the British* in a lodgment in the Antwerp area . . . for at least the first couple of months the major Allied power in Europe immediately available is British . . . our detailed course of action must of necessity be resolved with the British."[76]

Liaison with the British was carried out between senior officers in Germany as well as between Army Staff officers and British representatives present in Washington as part of the British Joint Staff Mission/CCS apparatus.[77] Two "highly secret" meetings and several informal conversations were held. As a result of increased tension caused by the Yugoslav attacks on U.S. aircraft, Brigadier C. R. Price, secretary of the BJSM, returned to London in August 1946 to coordinate conversations between U.S. and British commanders in Europe and to discuss with the British Chiefs of Staff points on which Anglo-American agreement was required.[78]

Planning for hostilities in central Europe was a central topic when Eisenhower met "informally" with the British Chiefs of Staff in his October 1946 visit to London. There he agreed with the British on the need for combined planning and everyone at the meeting concurred that a bridgehead could be held, probably in Holland, at least long enough for an orderly evacuation.[79]

This entire effort was, however, brought to a sudden halt in January 1947 after the outlines of the plans had been presented to the British COS and to Prime Minister Attlee. They considered that the skeletal planning which had been made could, if necessary, be elaborated for implementation within six weeks. The danger of leaks, however, was grave and such could "provoke the very thing we want to avoid."[80] For this reason Attlee gave orders that no further work should be done by British planners on the project and U.S. records suggest that no further work was done by Washington planners.

The interruption of the planning process was no doubt a disappointment to energetic American and British staff officers who had been working closely together throughout the summer and fall of 1946. There were, nonetheless, a number of valid reasons which explain Attlee's special concern about leaks. Although in early 1947 there was no immediate fear of war with Moscow, revelations of detailed Anglo-American war planning, whatever its nature, could jeopardize the success of the CFM meeting scheduled for April. In addition, negotiations were underway with the French which would lead to the signing of the Dunkirk Treaty in early March 1947; any untimely discussion about plans for evacuating British and American troops from Europe would have seriously undercut French confidence in British support. The British Joint Planning Staff, in a comment suggesting that the Americans had no monopoly on pusillanimity in dealings with the French on this problem, noted that the draft wording of the Dunkirk Treaty "suggests that the Treaty might commit us to sending forces to the Continent if such an attack were to take place. We are informed, however, by the legal advisors of the Foreign Office that this expression is the standard wording for treaties of mutual assistance and leaves us free to decide what assistance we would be prepared to give."[81] Almost a year later the JPS warned the COS of the "extreme danger" of embarking on talks with the Americans regarding evacuating forces from the Continent "just at the moment when we are doing everything possible to bolster up the determination of the Western European Powers to oppose and eradicate Communist influence in their countries."[82] Some contingency planning apparently did go on, however, among naval commanders.[83]

The British remained deeply interested in close cooperation with Washington on European defense questions, but their ultimate goal was not to make plans to evacuate the Continent, but to ensure an American defense commitment which in their view would deter Soviet aggression. The planning process had in 1946 brought defense officials in Washington to realize that American military operations in Germany would have to be closely coordinated with those of their British counterparts. This particular set of discussions did not lead further. When, however, political and diplomatic relations between Washington and London on one hand and Moscow on the other reached crisis proportions in the spring and summer of 1948, there was a compelling need to renew combined planning for an emergency and ultimately establish a Western defense policy which would offer more than a chance to evacuate American and British troops. Defense planners had then to go back to work, but this time with a reasoned awareness of mutual dependence and with experience in postwar combined planning as well as World War II precedents.

THE NAVY

The U.S. Navy at the end of World War II inevitably had to look forward to a period of comparative austerity. Budgets would be drastically cut, sailors and officers released from active duty, ships built at enormous expense would be decommissioned, scrapped or mothballed. The Navy was likely to be a victim of its previous victories. The Pacific Ocean was at last an American lake. The Italian, German and Japanese fleets were in the hands of the Allies; even those who were most suspicious of Stalin's aims acknowledged that the Soviet Navy was incapable of sustained operations outside of coastal waters. U.S. naval activities in Europe were limited to winding up the war effort and making occasional port visits to show the flag and promote good will among friendly nations. The U.S. Navy's presence in the Mediterranean had been reduced by the beginning of 1946 to one light cruiser and two destroyers.

The postwar Navy in fact was facing a fight for its institutional life. The absence of maritime enemies, the drive for service unification and the assumption that nuclear weapons made conventional warfare irrelevant created an atmosphere in which budget cutters could not overlook the massive expenses involved in maintaining a 300-ship peacetime navy. Navy leaders saw a drift in the Truman administration and among the public which they "uniformly interpreted as threats to the very existence of their service as a key component of the U.S. defense establishment."[84] They had necessarily to justify the Navy's role in the postwar world or face relegation to a support service for the emergent Air Force.

As has been noted, the official assumption for postwar planning, accepted by the Navy and throughout the government, was that the Eastern Atlantic, the Mediterranean and the Indian Ocean remained the strategic responsibility of Great Britain. The United States would concentrate on the Western Atlantic and the Pacific.

This assumption was soon to be vitiated, on one hand by the absence of any likely threat to U.S. power in the Pacific and on the other by the great difficulties facing the British in maintaining their position throughout the world, particularly in the Mediterranean. National security interests and the requirements of institutional survival came together in the minds of senior naval officials. The decline of British postwar power, evolving American national interests and new technologies as well as the bureaucratic dynamics of a naval service flush with the greatest victories in its history led to altered naval missions, the replacement of battleships by aircraft carriers as the principal capital ships, and relocated geostrategic priorities. The success of the postwar Navy in adapting to changed conditions can be attributed in largest measure to the secrtary of the navy, James V. Forrestal, who would become the nation's first secretary of defense.[85] His influence on the shape of U.S. national security policy was enormous in the years between the end of the war and his untimely death in 1949.

As secretary of the navy from 1944 to 1947 Forrestal grasped the need to move beyond the self-imposed limitations of prewar and wartime naval planning. He had long been suspicious of Soviet policy and interested in the future of the Mediterranean and the Middle East.[86] Forrestal saw Moscow as posing not only a military threat—he was usually skeptical of dangers of imminent Soviet attacks—but also as a dynamic, expansionist, ideological enemy threatening the independence of neighboring states—Iran, Greece, Turkey—as well as Western interests. A good portion of this concern was based on the need for access to Middle Eastern energy resources. In early February 1946 Forrestal initiated with senior Navy officials

a discussion of the possibility that Russian military strategy might not in fact include the widely assumed initial transpolar bombing attack. Rather, they reasoned, the strategy might be to initiate no major war but rather a slow steady form of piecemeal military aggression, supported by political agitation and economic measures, around the periphery of the Soviet homeland especially in Southern Europe, the Middle East, and China.[87]

Forrestal believed that this strategy could be effectively countered with demonstrations of American strength and determination.

Early in 1946 when the State Department suggested the ceremonial return by warship of the ashes of the Turkish ambassador to Washington, who had died at his post, Forrestal seized the opportunity to initiate what would become a profound redirection of American naval policy.

The Navy assigned the task of transporting the ambassador's remains to the USS *Missouri*, the battleship named for the President's home state and on whose decks the Japanese had recently surrendered. Although there had been consideration of sending a number of ships as escorts for the *Missouri*, this was rejected in order to avoid too provocative a demonstration and because of the limited number of ships available at the time.[88] Nevertheless the trip was in fact a naval demonstration of American support to Turkey, which had been under continued Soviet pressure, and to Greece, threatened by an active leftist insurgency. The battleship made its intended point; it was joyfully received in both beleaguered countries, and the visits reinforced the hardening line of American diplomacy then being expounded by Secretary of State Byrnes.

Forrestal and the Navy planners began to perceive a Mediterranean presence not only as a way to reflect American opposition to Soviet pressure in the region but also as a means to guarantee the Navy a major role in postwar defense policy. Congressional hearings in the fall of 1945 had alerted them to the legislators' suspicions of the need for a large and expensive postwar fleet without apparent missions or potential enemies. The "carrier admirals" who had accounted for a series of brilliant victories in the war against Japan were also prepared to reorient naval strategy from ship-against-ship concepts (which now appeared to be irrelevant) to ship-against-shore attacks on land targets. These officers had come to wield great influence in the postwar Navy under the leadership of the former Pacific naval commander, Chester W. Nimitz, who had been appointed chief of naval operations in December 1945.[89] The Mediterranean offered scope for the Navy to serve as an instrument of national policy in peacetime and was an area where ships and support functions could be prepositioned for emergency use in a conflict with the only conceivable opponent. The combination of these factors made Mediterranean missions a matter of high priority both for Forrestal and the Navy staff.

Despite some earlier hesitations in the State Department, in June the navy secretary obtained Byrnes's agreement on the usefulness of more Mediterranean cruises "so that we may establish the custom of the American Flag being flown in those waters."[90]

The navy secretary's concepts of the Soviet danger were increasingly shared in the State Department by officials such as John Hickerson and H. Freeman Matthews of the Office of European Affairs, Loy Henderson of the Office of Near Eastern and African Affairs, Lincoln MacVeagh and Edwin G. Wilson, the ambassadors to Greece and Turkey respectively, and by Secretary Byrnes himself, who was spending long weeks in frustrating negotiations with the Russians. Support for a more assertive American role in European affairs also came from Vice Admiral Richard Conolly, the commander of U.S. Naval Forces in Europe, a member of the official U.S. delegation at the Paris Peace Conference, who considered it his mission

all the way through, to convince the nations of Europe that we would not revert to our policy of isolationism, as we had after World War I, but would continue to maintain a potent interest, an interest that we would back up with force, if necessary—by the show of force, the presence of force—in that area.[91]

The British quickly endorsed the American move into the Mediterranean. After World War II British power was slowly beginning to recede from the Middle East as a result of demobilization, economic pressures and Britain's increasingly untenable position in Egypt and Palestine. Although there was skepticism within the governing Labour party including, most notably, Prime Minister Clement Attlee, regarding the continued military and political significance of the Mediterranean, the Foreign Office and the Chiefs of Staff strongly supported the U.S. Navy's Mediterranean deployments, seeing them as a source of potential support for British interests in the region. Churchill, on his initial postwar visit to the United States, had expectably endorsed the decision to send the *Missouri* to Turkey although he had argued in favor of a larger contingent.[92] Just as warmly, Bevin also welcomed the prospect of U.S. naval deployments to the Mediterranean.[93] Nevile Butler of the Foreign Office indicated that it was "the general Foreign Office view . . . that we need American support in resisting Russian attacks upon our position and interests in Asia and the Middle East. This support will need to be stronger and steadier than anything we got out of the Americans between the wars—or recently."[94] The Joint Planning Staff in June 1946 reiterated its understanding that "an essential feature of our general policy is to associate the Americans as closely as possible in the defence of our interests throughout the world, and particularly in the defence of the Middle East."[95] The next month Forrestal, visiting London as part of an around-the-world trip, met with A. V. Alexander, the first lord of the admiralty, and Sir John Cunningham, the first sea lord. Both urged greater cooperation between the U.S. and Royal Navies and endorsed a large American naval presence in the Mediterranean.[96] It was clear in 1946 that Britain's previous Middle Eastern role could no longer be maintained unaided. Bevin sought to bring about a fusion of British and American policy which would, if necessary, provide a cover for the retreat of British power while retaining a means of defending Western interests. Although less convinced of the continuing importance of a large Mediterranean role, Attlee and other skeptics did not in the end obstruct Bevin's efforts.[97]

The U.S. Navy was prepared to assume Britain's Middle Eastern mantle. Immediately upon his return to Washington in July 1946 Forrestal forwarded a letter to the State Department, drafted by Vice Admiral Forrest P. Sherman, Nimitz' deputy for operations, asserting that "our national policies will require the maintenance of considerable naval strength not only in the Western Pacific but also in the Eastern Atlantic and the Mediterranean for some years to come."[98] The next day Forrestal submitted to the president (in response to a request by Clark Clifford for background for the latter's famous memorandum of September 1946 on U.S.-Soviet relations) a Navy position paper arguing that "in the event of Soviet aggression precipitating hostilities, it is considered that the Near or Middle East would be the initial 'focus of infection,' that consequent British involvement would be impossible of localization, and that the United States would sooner or later be drawn in." The paper included a strategic justification for the Navy's Mediterranean presence which would inter alia require the continued existence of a sizable navy. "The Mediterranean is the seaway deep into the land mass of Eurasia and Africa, through which naval and amphibious power can most effectively advance and support our Army air and ground forces for whatever operations may be required in the Middle East and Mediterranean area.''[99]

The intensification of Soviet pressure on Turkey in August 1946 combined with the Yugoslav shootdown of an American transport plane the same month led the administration once again to use naval forces to demonstrate its concern with events in the Mediterranean. The Adriatic contingent was strengthened, and ships previously scheduled for Mediterranean port visits were dramatically augmented by the newly commissioned aircraft carrier, the USS *Franklin D. Roosevelt*. The visit to the Eastern Mediterranean was one of the steps authorized at the White House meeting of 15 August 1946 which approved much stronger American support for Turkey in its ongoing disputes with Moscow.[100] In addition, the *Roosevelt's* deployment inaugurated a new policy, publicly announced by Forrestal at the end of September, that the United States would henceforth maintain a naval force, including carriers from time to time, in the Mediterranean.[101] This was the public charter for the Mediterranean buildup which would lead eventually to the creation of the Sixth Fleet. The *Roosevelt* was succeeded by the carrier *Randolph* in November 1946 and the *Leyte* arrived in March 1947.

The increased Mediterranean naval presence required day-to-day cooperation with the British. The U.S. Navy lacked shore facilities in the Mediterranean except for bases in Italy which would have to be given up in 1947 after the signing of the Italian peace treaty. Expanded operations in the Mediterranean required facilities for fuel, fresh food, water and other supplies as well as sites for occasional repair work and rest and relaxation for the crews. The Royal Navy, on the other hand, had large and well established facilities at Gibraltar, Malta and in the Suez Canal area. Thus, when Forrestal and Nimitz proposed an increased naval presence in the Mediterranean, they also recommended ''an informal arrangement by which the use by our ships of the British naval ports and facilities at Gibraltar and Malta would be authorized in exchange for corresponding use by British ships of our naval ports and facilities in the Western Pacific.''[102]

Although negotiations with Britain for bases in the Pacific foundered as a result of Australian demands for a regional defense agreement,[103] a relatively simple arrangement was agreed upon by the naval staffs of the two countries and approved by Bevin and Byrnes, who were together at the Paris Peace Conference.[104] The arrangement had advantages over a broader and more formal agreement since it did not require formal treaties or complicated exchanges of territory. As a result, the U.S. Navy soon made regular use of British bases at Gibraltar and Malta. The wartime spirit of cooperation was renewed among officers and sailors of the two fleets despite the usual difficulties inherent in scheduling use of port facilities and occasional altercations among sailors on liberty.[105]

As Forrestal had emphasized in his press release, the U.S. Navy intended to operate without its own shore facilities in the Mediterranean. Nonetheless the Navy sought to retain its access to Port Lyautey in French Morocco near the Atlantic approaches to Gibraltar. In November 1945 the JCS, when considering worldwide base requirements, had listed Port Lyautey as a secondary priority, but by June 1946 the Moroccan facility was one of six essential locations.[106] The base played a major role in support of Mediterranean operations by providing landing facilities for naval transport aircraft carrying personnel, mail and some supplies to ships deployed in the Mediterranean in addition to occasionally providing aircraft for training exercises.[107] Probably its most important role was in naval communications as it provided "the only adequate link between the continental United States and the Philippines and [was] indispensable for ships operating in the Mediterranean."[108]

Diplomatic negotiations to formalize the Port Lyautey arrangement were undertaken in Paris in June 1947 but proved inconclusive because of potential opposition in the French Chamber of Deputies.[109] An agreement was, however, worked out on a navy-to-navy basis and was subsequently approved at the diplomatic level. It provided for an American presence within a base under French control.[110]

The U.S. Navy did attempt to avoid complete dependence on Port Lyautey and the British bases. American ships rotated in and out of the Mediterranean on a periodic basis and were able to schedule major repairs and overhauls in United States ports. Much of the fuel oil and supplies was provided through American channels and by American supply ships. Access to British bases was nonetheless necessary, as senior naval officers readily acknowledged.[111] The two navies also operated together under a combined command in the northern Adriatic, a holdover from World War II. This naval presence underscored American and British opposition to Yugoslavia's efforts to absorb Trieste. (Elsewhere, however, the two navies operated under separate command.) Although the Americans did not intend to become involved in or identified with the unpopular roles played by the Royal Navy in Egypt or Palestine, at the same time the cooperation of the two navies underscored the common positions being taken by Byrnes and Bevin on most Eastern Mediterranean issues. The presence of a supreme allied commander in Italy provided a force structure which could be expanded in case of need. Forrest Sherman, for one, anticipated that the U.S. would eventually have the preponderance of forces in the Mediterranean and that the combined command there would eventually be transferred to an American commander.[112]

In 1947 U.S. naval operations in the Mediterranean increased as the U.S. officially accepted formerly British responsibilities for supporting Greece and Turkey. When the Greek insurgency grew more intense, an extensive series of visits to Greek ports was scheduled at the specific direction of the president in a demonstration of support for the beleaguered Athens government.[113] In the autumn of that year, senior American and British officials met together in the Pentagon Talks to formally approve a joint Mediterranean strategic policy.

The Mediterranean deployments were in large measure instances of naval diplomacy not immediately related to combat capabilities. They were designed to counter the threat of "slow and steady . . . piecemeal military aggression, supported by political agitation and economic measures, around the periphery of the Soviet homeland." Forrestal's intention, now shared by Byrnes, was to use the Navy to shore up the regional power balance in the Eastern Mediterranean region, which would fortuitously provide a continued role for the postwar Navy.[114] At the same time, however, the Joint Chiefs of Staff in early 1946 were giving consideration to potential wartime operations against the Soviet Union. The planners realized that attacks launched from the Eastern Mediterranean could be conducted on Soviet targets in regions which lay beyond the combat radii of aircraft based in other areas. In initial planning, the Joint

Staff envisioned a strategic attack (one by bombers carrying atomic weapons) from bases in such areas as Britain, the Suez Canal region, Karachi and Okinawa. This planning did not immediately result in an effort to acquire suitable air bases in the Middle East (such bases were only to be acquired after 1947) nor in the procurement of required numbers of aircraft.

Naval officers did not consider then or later that nuclear attacks on Soviet targets would be automatically decisive, but they saw such strikes as a prelude to conventional operations in which an offensive through the Mediterranean would be "preferable to one through Western Europe because it permits exploitation of our sea, air and amphibious strength in which we can be vastly superior."[115] This position was not abandoned even when the Navy began to acquire the capability to launch atomic attacks with carrier-based aircraft.[116]

The question of the sufficiency of nuclear attacks would become increasingly controversial in American defense circles in the late 1940s as budgetary pressures grew ever more intense. Air Force efforts to concentrate scarce resources on strategic bombers were countered by the Navy's emphasis on broader and more traditional concepts of warfare. The shift in American policy into the Eastern Mediterranean in both its diplomatic and naval aspects owed most of its impetus to geopolitical considerations such as desires to deter Soviet expansionism, to ensure access to regional resources and to position a naval capability in the region which could be expanded in the event of war. American naval policy in the Eastern Mediterranean was essentially in place before serious efforts were undertaken to find suitable bases for the Strategic Air Command. The shift in naval deployments to the Mediterranean would have occurred even in the absence of nuclear weaponry.[117]

Although central Europe was and is the crucial area of East-West rivalry, British and American postwar defense policies began to converge in the Eastern Mediterranean in 1946-1947. There the United States began its military commitment to the maintenance of the European balance of power. This first step had required neither congressional approval, greatly increased appropriations, nor the construction of large and controversial shore bases. The 1946-1947 deployments were carefully orchestrated to appear incremental and took place against the backdrop of steadily worsening East-West relations. Nevertheless, sustained Mediterranean deployments represented, literally and figuratively, a sea change in American defense policy that would in time involve the Army and Air Force as well.

NOTES

1. Robert J. Donovan, *Tumultuous Years: The Presidency of Harry S Truman, 1949-1953* (New York: W. W. Norton, 1982), p. 55.

2. Susan M. Hartmann, *Truman and the 80th Congress* (Columbia, Mo.: University of Missouri Press, 1971), p. 49.

3. See Samuel P. Huntington, *The Common Defense: Strategic Programs in National Politics* (New York: Columbia University Press, 1961), p. 41.

4. See Warner R. Schilling, "The Politics of National Defense: Fiscal 1950," in *Strategy, Politics, and Defense Budgets* by Schilling, Paul Y. Hammond and Glenn H. Snyder (New York: Columbia University Press, 1962), especially pp. 98-106.

5. See John Lewis Gaddis, *Strategies of Containment: A Critical Appraisal of Postwar American National Security Policy* (New York: Oxford University Press, 1982), pp. 93-95; Paul Nitze, "The Development of NSC 68," *International Security* 4 (Spring 1980): 171-73.

6. Schilling, "Politics of National Defense," p. 233.

7. On Air Force requirements for a seventy-group structure in the postwar period, see Smith, *Air Force Plans for Peace*, pp. 71-74; Robert Frank Futrell, *Ideas, Concepts, Doctrine: A History of Basic Thinking in the United States Air Force, 1907-1964* (Maxwell Air Force Base, Ala.: Air University, 1974), pp. 102-3; John T. Greenwood, "The Emergence of the Postwar Strategic Air Force, 1945-1953," in *Air Power and Warfare: The Proceedings of the Eighth Military History Symposium, United States Air Force Academy, 18-20 October 1978*, ed. Alfred F. Hurley and Robert C. Ehrhart (Washington: Office of Air Force History, Headquarters USAF and United States Air Force Academy, 1979), pp. 217-18; Wolk, *Planning and Organizing the Postwar Air Force*, pp. 62-64; Steven L. Rearden, *The Formative Years, 1947-1950*, vol. 1 of *History of the Office of the Secretary of Defense*, ed. Alfred Goldberg (Washington: Historical Office of the Secretary of Defense, 1984), pp. 313-16; United States, President's Air Policy Commission, *Survival in the Air Age: A Report by the President's Air Policy Commission* (Washington: Government Printing Office, 1948), p. 25.

8. Harry R. Borowski, *A Hollow Threat: Strategic Air Power and Containment Before Korea* (Westport, Conn.: Greenwood Press, 1982), p. 48.

9. See Converse, "United States Plans," pp. 163-64.

10. AAF input to the JCS planning process is discussed in ibid., pp. 136-46.

11. RG 218, CCS 360 (12-9-42), section 9.

12. Converse, "United States Plans," p. 170.

13. Joint Planning Staff, 217th Meeting, 1 September 1945, RG 218, CCS 360 (12-9-42), section 7.

14. See JCS to Byrnes, 7 November 1945, *FRUS* 1946, 1: 1112-17.

15. The Ryukyus were under U.S. occupation; Hawaii, the Marianas, Alaska, Puerto Rico and the Virgin Islands were U.S. territory; base rights in Newfoundland had already been granted and bases in the Philippines were to be part of the independence settlement. Diplomatic negotiations would, however, be required for bases or base access in the Galapagos Islands, Manaus Island, Iceland, Panama, Canton Island, Greenland, the Azores, the Cape Verde Islands and Ascension Island.

16. JPS 781, 8 January 1946, "Over-all Examination of Requirements for Transit Air Bases and Air Base Rights in Foreign Countries," RG 218, CCS 360 (12-9-42), section 12; JCS to SWNCC, 11 February 1946, *FRUS* 1946, 1: 1142-45.

17. See James L. Gormly, "Keeping the Door Open in Saudi Arabia: The United States and the Dhahran Airfield, 1945-46" *Diplomatic History* 4 (Spring 1980): 189-205.

18. Converse, "United States Plans," p. 173.

19. Memorandum for the Secretary of State, 1 May 1946, RG 353, Records of the State-War-Navy Coordinating Committee, File: 38/5; also filed in RG 59, 859A.20/5-146. These views were consistent with those of the JCS; see JCS 1641, "Soviet Interests in the Eastern Mediterranean," 13 March 1946, RG 218, CCS 092 USSR (3-2-45), section 6.

20. JCS to Byrnes, 7 November 1945, *FRUS* 1946, 1: 1113-14.

21. JCS 1518, 9 October 1945, RG 218, CCS 381 (5-13-45), section 2, quoted in James F. Schnabel, *The History of the Joint Chiefs of Staff: The Joint Chiefs of Staff and National Policy*, 1, *1945-1947* (Wilmington, Del.: Michael Glazier, 1979): 146.

22. Ibid., p. 148.

23. Converse, "United States Plans," pp. 195-97.

24. Minutes of Meeting of the Committee of Three, 20 February 1946, Reference File, Minutes of Meetings of Committee of Three, Legislative and Diplomatic Branch, NA.

25. SWNCC 38/35 published in *FRUS* 1946, 1: 1174-77. The listing of

Moroccan sites reflects the Navy's new interest in the Mediterranean.

26. SWNCC 38/46 was published in *FRUS* 1947, 1: 766-70.

27. Hoyer Millar to Secretary, COS, 10 August 1946, COS (46) 212 (O), CAB 80/102; see also my "Approach to Alliance: British and American Defense Strategies, 1945-1948," pp. 94-114; Donald E. Nuechterlein, *Iceland: Reluctant Ally* (Westport, Conn.: Greenwood Press, 1975, originally published 1961), pp. 37-72.

28. See below, p. 98.

29. NSC 2/1, "A Report to the President by the National Security Council on Base Rights in Greenland, Iceland and the Azores," 25 November 1947, RG 273. The potential role of these bases was publicly discussed; see, for instance, John C. Campbell, *The United States in World Affairs, 1945-1947* (New York: Harper and Brothers for the Council on Foreign Relations, 1947), pp. 40-46.

30. See Greenwood, "Emergence of the Postwar Strategic Air Force," pp. 225-26; Memorandum for General Spaatz from Bissell, 6 July 1946, Box: 250, File: Chief of Staff General Correspondence, July 1, 1946-July 31, 1946, Spaatz Papers, LC; Richard H. Willard, *Location of United States Military Units in United Kingdom, 16 July 1948-31 December 1967* (n.p.: United States Air Forces in Europe, Historical Division, Office of Information, Third Air Force, 1968), p. ii.

31. See Borowski, *Hollow Threat*, p. 102.

32. It is now well known that the bombers that actually deployed to bases in Britain in July 1948 were not among the few aircraft configured for carrying atomic bombs; see Kenneth W. Condit, *The History of the Joint Chiefs of Staff: The Joint Chiefs of Staff and National Policy*, 2, *1947-1949* (Wilmington, Del.: Michael Glazier, 1979): p. 179.

33. Converse, "United States Plans," p. 227.

34. See David Alan Rosenberg, "The U.S. Navy and the Problem of Oil in a Future War: The Outline of a Strategic Dilemma, 1945-1950," *Naval War College Review* 29 (Summer 1976): 58-59.

35. See Louis, *The British Empire in the Middle East*, pp. 241-44, 258-60.

36. Ibid., pp. 295-302; see also R. L. Swetzer, *Wheelus Field: The Story of the U.S. Air Force in Libya: The Early Days, 1944-1952* (n.p.: Historical Division, Office of Information, United States Air Forces in Europe, 1965).

37. *A Five Year Summary of USAFE History, 1945-1950* (Wiesbaden, Germany: Headquarters, United States Air Forces in Europe, Historical Division, 1952) [included in RG 319], pp. 62, 68, 76.

38. See Symington to Arnold, 17 September 1946, Box 256, File: Assistant Secretary of the Army for Air, Spaatz Papers, LC; Futrell, *Ideas,*

Concepts, Doctrine, pp. 109-10; James C. Selser, Jr., "The Bomber's Role in Diplomacy," *Air Force,* 39 (April 1956): 52-56.

39. Futrell, *Ideas, Concepts, Doctrine,* p. 109.

40. Borowski, *Hollow Threat,* pp. 74-75.

41. See Walton S. Moody, "United States Air Forces in Europe and the Beginning of the Cold War," *Aerospace Historian* 23 (Summer/June 1976): 72; Eisenhower, *Papers* 8: 1520 n. 5; 1563 n. 3; *Five Year Summary,* pp. 69-85.

42. *Five Year Summary,* pp. 81-83.

43. Curtis E. LeMay, with MacKinlay Kantor, *Mission with LeMay: My Story* (Garden City, N.Y.: Doubleday, 1965), p. 411.

44. Ibid., p. 413.

45. John C. Sparrow, *History of Personnel Demobilization in the United States Army* ([Washington]: U.S. Department of the Army, Office of the Chief of Military History, 1951), p. 360.

46. United States, Department of Commerce, *Historical Statistics of the United States, Colonial Times to 1970,* Part 2 (Washington: Government Printing Office, 1975), p. 1143.

47. See Frank D. Cunningham, "Harry S. Truman and Universal Military Training, 1945," *The Historian* 46 (May 1984): 397-415; Harry S. Truman, *Memoirs,* 2, *Years of Trial and Hope* (Garden City, N.Y.: Doubleday, 1956): 53-55; Richard F. Haynes, *The Awesome Power: Harry S. Truman as Commander in Chief* (Baton Rouge, La.: Louisiana State University Press, 1973), pp. 80-87.

48. See Clyde E. Jacobs and John F. Gallagher, *The Selective Service Act: A Case Study of the Governmental Process* (New York: Dodd, Mead, 1967), pp. 43-44.

49. See Brian Arthur Libby, "Policing Germany: The United States Constabulary, 1946-1952," (Ph.D. dissertation, Purdue University, 1977); Oliver J. Frederiksen, *The American Military Occupation of Germany, 1945-1953* (n.p.: Historical Division, Headquarters, United States Army, Europe, 1953), especially pp. 66-69; E. N. Harmon, *Combat Commander* (Englewood Cliffs, N.J.: Prentice Hall, 1970), especially pp. 279-94.

50. United States, Congress, Senate, Committee on Armed Services, *Universal Military Training, Hearings,* 80th Cong., 2d sess., p. 348. See also Lord Ismay, *NATO: The First Five Years, 1949-1954* (n.p., n.d. [Paris: 1954]), pp. 29-30.

51. Patterson to Byrnes, 1 November 1945, *FRUS* 1946, 1: 111-12.

52. Byrnes to Patterson, 29 November 1945, *FRUS* 1946, 1: 1129.

53. Ibid., 1132.

54. Proposal by the United States Delegation to the Council of Foreign Ministers, 30 April 1946, *FRUS* 1946, 2: 190-93.

55. "Restatement of U.S. Policy on Germany," 6 September 1946, *Department of State Bulletin*, 15 (15 September 1946): 499.

56. Eisenhower, *Papers*, 7: 603-604 nn. 6, 7.

57. Enclosure to Eisenhower to Hilldring, 26 February 1947, *FRUS* 1947, 1: 718.

58. Eisenhower to McNarney, 5 March 1947; *Eisenhower Papers*, 8: 1562.

59. United States, Army [U.S. Army Information School], *The Army Almanac: A Book of Facts Concerning the Army of the United States* (Washington: Government Printing Office, 1950), p. 633.

60. Proposal by the United States Delegation to the Council of Foreign Ministers, 6 December 1946, *FRUS* 1946, 2: 1466-67. Even earlier, in September 1945, Byrnes had suggested to a noncommittal Molotov that the potential withdrawal of American forces from Europe might lead to a "recrudescence of German aggression" and suggested four-power agreement on German demilitarization; Memorandum of conversation by Bohlen, 20 Septgember 1945, *FRUS* 1945, 2: 268.

61. United States Delegation Minutes, Council of Foreign Ministers, 11 December 1946, *FRUS* 1946, 2: 1528.

62. Lucius D. Clay, *Decision in Germany* (Garden City, N.Y.: Doubleday, 1950), pp. 154-55; Clay to War Department, 1 June 1947, *The Papers of General Lucius D. Clay: Germany, 1945-1949*, ed. Jean Edward Smith, 1 (Bloomington, Ind.: Indiana University Press, 1974): 368; Murphy to Marshall, 1 June 1947, *FRUS* 1947, 2: 871-72.

63. Smith to Marshall, 6 November 1947, *FRUS* 1947, 2: 896-98. See also Bullock, *Bevin*, p. 491.

64. See above, p. 82.

65. See *Occupation Forces in Europe Series: 1948, The Fourth Year of the Occupation, 1 July-31 December 1948*, 1 (Karlsruhe, Germany: Historical Division, European Command, 1949 [included in RG 319]), 44; Clay, *Decision in Germany*, p. 230.

66. See Libby, "Policing Germany," pp. 132-33; Frederiksen, *American Occupation*, pp. 172-74.

67. Contemporary estimates of Soviet forces available for combat can be found in such documents as Joint Intelligence Staff, "Russian Capabilities," J.I.S. 80/7, 23 October 1945, RG 218, CCS 092 USSR (3-27-45), section 2; Joint Intelligence Committee, "Estimate of Soviet Intentions and Capabilities, 1948-1955," 1 January 1948, RG 218, CCS 092 USSR (3-27-45), section 27. Matthew A. Evangelista, "Stalin's Postwar Army Reappraised," *International Security* 7 (Winter 1982/1983) argues that the JCS greatly overestimated Soviet forces. Evangelista's figures for Western forces before 1949 (p. 120 n. 34), however, include the troops of various

West European countries as if they were already part of a unified command, organized to resist a Soviet invasion.

68. Memorandum for the Record by T.D.R., 23 February 1946, RG 319, ABC 381 US-UK (23 February 1946).

69. See Bull to Hull, 15 April 1946, RG 319, ABC 381 US-UK (23 February 1946).

70. Eisenhower to McNarney, 17 April 1946; Eisenhower, *Papers*, 7: 1010.

71. Report of the Ad Hoc Committee, 15 November 1946, RG 319, ABC 381 US-UK (23 February 1946).

72. For Spaatz's arrangement with the British see above, p. 79. Transcript of conversation between Hull and Sherman, 29 April 1946, Norstad to Bull, 1 August 1946, both in RG 319, ABC 381 US-UK (23 February 1946).

73. War Department files are replete with injunctions to avoid leaks on these discussions; see Eisenhower, *Papers*, 7: 1157-58.

74. Transcript of conversation between Hull and Sherman, 29 April 1946, RG 319, ABC 381, US-UK (23 February 1946).

75. CNO to COMNAVEUR, 26 July 1946, RG 319, ABC 381 US-UK (23 February 1946).

76. Porter to Lincoln, 15 September 1946, RG 319, P & O 381 TS (Section III) (Case 66).

77. Lincoln to Hull, undated, RG 319, ABC 381 US-UK (23 February 1946); Eisenhower, *Papers*, 7: 1157-58; James V. Forrestal, *The Forrestal Diaries*, ed. Walter Millis (New York: Viking Press, 1951), p. 198; Leahy, diary entries for 5 and 16 September 1946, Leahy Papers, LC; Montgomery, *Memoirs*, pp. 391, 394-96.

78. Lincoln to Norstad, 29 August 1946, RG 319, P & O 381 TS (Section III) (Case 66).

79. RG 319, P & O 091 Great Britain (Oct.-Nov. 1946); see also Eisenhower, *Papers*, 8: 1344-45.

80. Mallaby to Lincoln, 15 January 1947, RG 319, ABC 381 US-UK (23 February 1946).

81. "Anglo-French Treaty of Alliance—Military Implications," J.P. (47) 14 (Final), COS (47) 23, DEFE 4/11.

82. Subjects for Discussion with the Americans, 6 January 1948, J.P. (48) 4 (Final), DEFE 4/10.

83. See, for instance, Memorandum for Admiral Conolly, 26 December 1947, OP-03/yg, Strategic Plans Division Records, NHC, enclosing an extract from a letter from General Hollis, chief of staff to the minister of defence, dated 18 December 1947.

84. Davis, *Postwar Defense Policy*, p. 180.

85. On Forrestal, see Robert G. Albion and Robert H. Connery, *Forrestal and the Navy* (New York: Columbia University Press, 1962); Arnold A. Rogow, *Victim of Duty: A Study of James Forrestal* (London: Hart-Davis, 1966); Joseph Zikmund, "James V. Forrestal," in *American Secretaries of the Navy*, ed. by Paolo E. Coletta, 2, *1913-1972* (Annapolis, Md.: Naval Institute Press, 1980): 729-44.

86. See Davis, *Postwar Defense Policy*, pp. 181-90.

87. Ibid., p. 223; see also Rosenberg, "The U.S. Navy and the Problem of Oil."

88. On the *Missouri* visit, see Dennis M. Pricolo, "Naval Presence and Cold War Foreign Policy: A Study of the Decision to Station the Sixth Fleet in the Mediterranean, 1945-1958," Trident Scholar Project Report No. 95 (Annapolis, Md.: U.S. Naval Academy, 1978); David J. Alvarez, *Bureaucracy and Cold War Diplomacy: The United States and Turkey, 1943-1946* (Thessaloniki: Institute for Balkan Studies, 1980), pp. 75-85; Stephen G. Xydis, *Greece and the Great Powers, 1944-1947: Prelude to the Truman Doctrine* (Thessaloniki: Institute for Balkan Studies, 1963), pp. 168-91.

89. See Davis, *Postwar Defense Policy*, pp. 149-150; 204-5.

90. Forrestal, *Diaries*, p. 171.

91. "The Reminiscences of Admiral Richard L. Conolly" (New York: Columbia University, Oral History Research Office, 1960), p. 294. Conolly's influence on Byrnes is noted by Melvyn P. Leffler, "The American Conception of National Security and the Beginnings of the Cold War, 1945-1948," *American Historical Review* 89 (April 1984): 370; Leffler, "Strategy, Diplomacy, and the Cold War: The United States, Turkey, and NATO, 1945-1952," *Journal of American History* 71 (March 1985): 814-15.

92. Forrestal, *Diaries*, pp. 144-45.

93. Minute by Piers Dixon, 4 March 1946, FO 371/51725.

94. Minute by Butler, 5 April 1946, FO 371/51630.

95. J.P. (46) 115 (Final), 21 June 1946, FO 371/51683.

96. Forrestal, *Diaries*, pp. 183-84.

97. Attlee, "The Future of the Italian Colonies," 22 February 1946, COS(46)54(o), CAB 80/100; Smith and Zametica, "Cold Warrior," 251.

98. Forrestal to Byrnes, 24 July 1946, RG 59, 811.20/7-2446; also found in RG 80, CNO Central File, 1946, Secret, file: L-24.

99. Forrestal to Truman, 25 July 1946, Clifford Papers, Box 15, Folder: Russia (folder 5), HSTL.

100. See below, pp. 127-28; also Acheson, *Present at the Creation*, p. 195.;

Alvarez, *Bureaucracy and Cold War Diplomacy*, p. 98; Jonathan Knight, "American Statecraft and the 1946 Black Sea Straits Controversy," *Political Science Quarterly* 90 (Fall 1975): 463-67.

101. The statement was reprinted in the *New York Times*, 1 October 1946, p. 14; see also Forrestal, *Diaries*, p. 211.

102. Forrestal to Byrnes, 24 July 1946, RG 59, 811.20/7-2446.

103. See Memorandum for Sherman from Hickerson, 26 July 1946, RG 80, CNO Top Secret Finish File, 1946, folder 2.

104. See Bullock, *Bevin*, p. 315; Byrnes to Hickerson, 26 September 1946, RG 59, 740.0019 Council/9-2646; Maclean to Hickerson, 19 September 1946, RG 59, 811.2341/9-1946; Memorandum of conversation by Hickerson, 9 December 1946, RG 59, 811.2341/12-946.

105. See Commander, U.S. Naval Forces, Mediterranean to Chief of Naval Operations, 7 January 1947, RG 80, CNO Top Secret File, 1947, Box 55, File L24-1.

106. *Cf.* Memorandum by the JCS, 7 November 1945, *FRUS* 1946, 1: 1112-17 and Memorandum by the JCS, 5 June 1946, *FRUS* 1946, 1: 1174-77.

107. See Commander, U.S. Naval Forces, Eastern Atlantic and Mediterranean to Director of Naval History, 9 May 1947, A12-1, ser 0108, Command History Files, NHC.

108. See Leon Borden Blair, *Western Window in the Arab World* (Austin, Tex.: University of Texas Press, 1970), pp. 126-27; Dennison to Nimitz, 14 October 1946, OP-35-oh, ser 000945P35, Double Zero Files, 1942-1947, Box 2, File 31, NHC.

109. See Caffery to Lovett, 7 October 1947, RG 59, 811.2351/10-747.

110. "The Port Lyautey Base Technical Agreement between the United States Navy and the French Navy," 15 September 1947 (filed in RG 59, 811.34551/9-1547).

111. The extent of American use of British Mediterranean facilities is discussed in Commander, U.S. Naval Forces, Eastern Atlantic and Mediterranean to Director of Naval History, 28 October 1947, ser 0203, A12-1, Command History Files, NHC. See also "The Reminiscences of Vice Admiral Bernard H. Bieri, U.S. Navy Retired" (Annapolis, Md.: U.S. Naval Institute, 1970), pp. 281-82, 298, 300, 305.

112. Minutes of the Joint Planning Staff, 252nd meeting, 18 June 1946, RG 218, CCS 334 JSP (3-6-46).

113. Marshall to Forrestal, 12 August 1947, RG 59, 811.3368/9-1047; see Edward John Sheehy, "The United States Navy in the Mediterranean, 1945-1947" (Ph.D. dissertation, George Washington University, 1983), pp. 246-52. Truman's interest in this effort is noted in his *Years of Trial and Hope*, p. 109.

114. See note 87 above; the now classic discussion of the use of navies to augment diplomacy is James Cable, *Gunboat Diplomacy, 1919-1979: Political Applications of Limited Naval Force*, 2nd ed. (London: Macmillan, 1981).

115. Sherman, Presentation to the President, 14 January 1947, RG 80, SECNAV/CNO Central Correspondence File, 1947, Top Secret, File: A16-3. This concept was also presented by Sherman to the Senate Armed Services Committee on 23 January 1947, same file. See also Navy Staff Study on Naval Base Sites in the Mediterranean Area (N.S.P.S. 9), 16 August 1947, Strategic Plans Division Records, NHC.

116. See David A. Rosenberg and Floyd D. Kennedy, Jr., "History of the Strategic Arms Competition, 1945-1972, Supporting Study: U.S. Aircraft Carriers in the Strategic Role, Part I—Naval Strategy in a Period of Change: Interservice Rivalry, Strategic Interaction, and the Development of a Nuclear Attack Capability, 1945-1951" (Falls Church, Va.: Lulejian and Associates, Inc., 1975), p. 77 [deposited at NHC]. Also, Pricolo, "Naval Presence and Cold War Foreign Policy," pp. 52-55.

117. Thus, not surprisingly, Air Force spokesmen were suspicious of Mediterranean commitments, seeing them as a convenient justification for larger naval forces at the expense of strategic bombers. See John T. Greenwood, "The Emergence of the Postwar Strategic Air Force, 1945-1953," p. 227. Melvyn Leffler is correct in emphasizing, with respect to U.S.-Turkish relations, the "important and often unexplained role of strategic imperatives in the shaping of foreign policy actions and alliance relationships" ("Strategy, Diplomacy and the Cold War," p. 808). This statement is valid, however, only if "strategic imperatives" are comprehensively defined to include not merely the search for bases for strategic bombers, but the whole range of American geopolitical interests.

CHAPTER 5

THE EVOLUTION
OF AMERICAN
FOREIGN POLICY

Harry S. Truman became president on 12 April 1945 upon the death of Franklin Roosevelt. Under Truman the United States assumed commitments to maintain the European—and the Asian—balance of power. Forty years later, American national security policy remains based on policies formulated and formalized in Truman's presidency. All subsequent administrations have worked within the context of the alliance framework which he and his officials created. Never again would the United States return to Fortress America; for good or ill, Washington became the Capital of the Free World, possessing permanent defense commitments across the Atlantic and around the world.

The administration which thus revolutionized American history was based on one created by Franklin Roosevelt. A native patrician of exceptional personal charm and political acumen, he pursued a style of government that was informal, disorganized and personalized. Truman, a plain-speaking, simpler man from the Missouri heartland, was far more straightforward in his approach to governing; he relied more heavily on his cabinet officers and less on personal intuition. But he too had the indispensable feel for the drift of public opinion that allowed him to survive in an atmosphere of uncertainty, change and political animosities that had their origins in the effects of the depression, World War II and long years of Democratic incumbency. Truman had above all the insight, courage and determination to recast American policy, to lead the American people to a new role in international affairs and to persuade them to provide, eventually, the resources to support it. This transformation was not achieved without missteps. Four secretaries of state and as many of defense wrestled with unprecedented difficulties and paid heavily for their efforts, variously leaving office alienated from the president, broken in mind or body or vilified by political opponents and the press. The armed services would be shamed by an interservice rivalry of unprecedented and unsurpassed bitterness. The administration became mired in a bloody but "unwinnable" war in Asia, alas not to be the last, and an atmosphere of vindictiveness and suspicion had poisoned political life as the Truman administration left office.

Truman cannot avoid responsibility for these disasters, but forty years later it is the solid accomplishments of his administration which appear to have had the most lasting consequences. The subsequent survival and vitality of Western Europe owe much to the policies he laid down. The defense policies of his administration made it possible for the United States and its allies to coexist, however tenuously it may have appeared at times, with the other superpower. They have provided whatever basis there has been for a peace among the great powers which thus far has endured.

Truman inherited Roosevelt's office and some of his former chief's political problems. The Democratic party was an uneasy coalition of urban ethnic groups, labor unions, liberal intellectuals and Southern conservatives. All had differing agendas in international affairs. Leaders of various ethnic groups—Italians, Greeks, Poles and the Jewish community—lobbied hard on issues of concern to their constituents. Unions feared unfair foreign competition. Liberals looked to former Vice President, and subsequently Commerce Secretary, Henry A. Wallace to guard the principles of idealistic internationalism that had been so frequently articulated by the late president.

Often neglected in subsequent accounts of this period has been the role of isolationist Republicans whose views on the dangers of the overcommitment of American resources or military power have long since become the proprietary interest of the most liberal wing of the Democratic party. Nonetheless it was midwestern Republicans, led by the able and conservative Senator Robert Taft of Ohio, who provided the most formidable opposition to the Truman administration. While firmly anticommunist, such Republicans opposed many of the heavy expenditures abroad and the expansion of the role of the federal government at home which was inherent in the Truman administration's foreign policies.[1] The possibility of a coalition between these men and one or more of the component groups within the Democratic party—and there were often grounds for common interest—could have wrecked the administration's policies abroad. Republican influence did in fact play a major role in the process by which defense budgets were reduced in the years 1946-1950 while defense commitments were constantly being expanded. The support—not unvarying—that the administration did receive from the Republican party came largely from its internationalists, principally the able Senator Arthur H. Vandenberg, chairman of the Senate Foreign Relations Committee in 1947 and 1948, a prewar isolationist who had come to believe in the necessity of much greater American involvement in postwar international life. Other internationalist Republicans, principally from the party's eastern wing, served to provide a basis for a working coalition on foreign policy in both the Senate and the House of Representatives.

In the first year of the Truman administration, American foreign policy (as distinct from defense policy) was radically redefined. The hope for a period of cooperation among the Big Three proved impossible of fulfillment. Senior officials in the White House and the State Department had recognized all along that the Soviets would seek to ensure that neighboring countries were friendly and sensitive to Moscow's interests, but public opinion had not been prepared for American recognition of a Soviet sphere of influence. The harsh and brutal methods of control which the Soviets employed intensified public outrage. The combination of sympathy for Poles and other Eastern Europeans and a naive belief that international covenants could easily and effectively regulate Moscow's relations with her neighbors contributed to a widespread perception that American diplomats had been duped again. Even (or perhaps especially) isolationists regarded events in 1945 and early 1946 as evidence of Soviet duplicity and signs that a conciliatory policy towards Moscow was simply a futile effort at appeasement. The need to articulate a tougher foreign policy vis-à-vis the Soviet

Union became by early 1946 a political necessity required by an outraged public and impatient congressional leaders, especially Vandenberg and Senator Tom Connally of Texas, then chairman of the Senate Foreign Relations Committee.[2] The efforts of Secretary of State Byrnes, who had been endeavoring since the previous summer to work out differences among Washington, London and Moscow through quiet diplomacy, were pulled up short by a president who intended to be perceived as a strong, determined leader unwilling to allow other countries to circumvent solemn agreements.[3]

BYRNES MEETS CHURCHILL

The decisive turning point in American policy towards the Soviet Union occurred in mid-February 1946. The shift was reflected in Secretary of State Byrnes' Overseas Press Club speech on 28 February 1946 in which he stated that despite "the mere legal veto" the United States "will stand with other great states in defense of the [U.N.] Charter,"[4] implicitly warning Moscow that Washington would not let the possibility of cooperative action be precluded by the Soviets' ability to stalemate the United Nations through the repeated use of the veto. At the same time Byrnes significantly hardened the American position on a number of issues relating to the implementation of the Potsdam accords on Eastern Europe and attempted to employ American economic leverage to induce Soviet agreement. Historian Fraser Harbutt argues that from February 1946 on,

both the American and Soviet governments began to recognize, and encourage their publics to recognize, the other as the principal adversary; to practice openly a unilateral rather than a cooperative diplomacy; and to consolidate their spheres of influence and prospective alliances in a rapidly bifurcating international system.[5]

Harbutt overstates and simplifies what was still a fluid and ambiguous international situation, and in fact the process of accommodation in Eastern Europe continued until peace treaties were finally signed and ratified in 1947, but he is correct in describing the changed tenor of American policy beginning in early 1946. FDR's confidence that American and Soviet interests were reconcilable no longer characterized American foreign policy.

This change in American policy was influenced by British leaders, in and out of office. Foreign Secretary Ernest Bevin's forceful opposition to Soviet efforts to intimidate Turkey and Iran at the January 1946 meeting of the United Nations had seized the imagination of the American people. *Time* invidiously compared the American delegation headed by Byrnes, "a habitual compromiser," with that headed by Bevin, who "rose above their level, tossed aside the numbing, ambiguous grandiloquence of traditional diplomacy which made international dialogue sound remote and ideal. He spoke as no statesman had ever spoken before in international councils. . . . He spoke up to the Russians as a great many plain people in pubs and corner drugstores had often wanted to speak."[6] The *Dallas Times Herald* suggested that Truman "swap Jimmy Byrnes to the British for Ernie Bevin and toss in any number of old destroyers it takes to clinch the deal."[7]

An even greater impact was made a few weeks later in Fulton, Missouri by former Prime Minister Winston Churchill, who wore the laurels of having warned of the Nazi threat long before it became obvious to others. In his famous Iron Curtain speech,[8] Churchill condemned in memorable phrases the police governments installed by Soviet power in Eastern Europe. His attack on Russia made a deep impression on the American public and Truman's presence on the speakers' platform clearly indicated official support for the somber message. In the same speech Churchill ventured onto more controversial ground, calling for closer Anglo-American defense cooperation. He urged the "continuance of the intimate relationship between our military advisors leading to common study of potential dangers, the similarity of weapons . . . continuance of present facilities for mutual security by the joint use of all Naval and Air Force bases in the possession of either country all over the world." This part of the speech was not well received by the American public, and both the president and Byrnes dissociated themselves from the concept of an Anglo-American military alliance. Truman and Byrnes had been aware in advance of the content of the speech.[9] Byrnes had even traveled to Florida, where Churchill was vacationing in mid-January, to confer on current issues and subsequently had held lengthy discussions with the former prime minister in Washington.[10] American opinion had not previously been exposed to an authoritative exposition of the Soviet danger. The "iron curtain" became a commonplace of the political vocabulary and the American public and policymakers alike internalized much of the former prime minister's analysis of Russian policy.

British spokesmen were not of course alone in describing the evils of Soviet policy. This was also the time when Washington was in receipt of a lengthy dispatch from the U.S. chargé in Moscow, George F. Kennan. The Long Telegram, which circulated widely among senior officials, analyzed the internal sources of Soviet hostility towards the West and argued for a doctrine of "containment."[11] He described a "political force committed fanatically to the belief that with US [the United States] there can be no permanent *modus vivendi*, that it is desirable and necessary that the internal harmony of our society be disrupted, our traditional way of life be destroyed, the international authority of our state be broken, if Soviet power is to be secure." Kennan argued that Russia is "impervious to logic of reason, and it is highly sensitive to logic of force. For this reason it can easily withdraw—and usually does—when strong resistance is encountered at any point."[12] Although Kennan and Churchill had different emphases, their audience found their messages mutually reinforcing.

After March 1946 American policy did begin to have a clearly anti-Soviet coloration. The familiar perception of a bipolar world, an epic contest between capitalist America and communist Russia, took hold of the popular imagination. As British observers noted, the Soviets replaced the Japanese as the principal national foe. Further, "The ordinary American, pre-1939, never considered it his country's job to control Germany, but did feel this as regards Japan, and Soviet Russia is now to the ordinary American in some ways a bigger and badder Japan."[13] Hereafter the rivalry with Moscow often appeared to be a zero-sum game in which every Soviet advance or success represented an equivalent American loss and vice versa.

The point was later driven home by the dramatic firing of Commerce Secretary Wallace in September 1946. Wallace, a spokesman for the liberal wing of the Democratic party, had long been critical of Byrnes' "get-tough" policies and closer U.S. cooperation with what he considered a still-imperialist Britain. His public expression of these views in a speech to a left-wing audience in New York City provoked a crisis when Byrnes, then at the Paris Peace Conference, threatened resignation unless Wallace was repudiated. Truman realized after much hesitation that he had no choice but to ask for the former vice president's resignation. Wallace left office and became a spokesman for improved relations with the Soviet Union. Despite his third-party campaign for the presidency in 1948, he still spoke for a significant section of the Democratic party.[14]

Although articulation of American policy changed in early 1946, it would be a mistake to assume that the substance of day-to-day U.S. policy had immediately altered. Obscured by the hard line that Byrnes was taking in public, diplomats continued to work out agreements over the peace treaties with Italy, Hungary, Bulgaria and Rumania. The administration's admittedly limited goal was to encourage a degree of moderation in Soviet relations with its neighbors.[15] Despite public expressions of animosity, the negotiating process continued and Eastern European issues (other than the persistent difficulties over Trieste) were resolved without leading to a major East-West crisis after 1946—a major and little recognized accomplishment of Secretary Byrnes.[16]

Yet the new diplomatic line of anti-Sovietism became part of American policy. The background of competition with Moscow, so often ideological and global in its expression, was a major factor in inducing American officials to perceive that the United States had truly vital interests in the Middle East and, most importantly, Western Europe. Common opposition to Soviet ideology naturally inclined American officials to work much more closely with their British colleagues. In dealing with postwar problems, American and British diplomats, with similar convictions about legitimate international behavior, were able to reconcile their differences and agree on a common position. They usually voted together (and often with other Western representatives) at the United Nations and other international gatherings.

The lengthy processes of conference diplomacy which occupied statesmen in 1946—the two Paris meetings of the Council of Foreign Ministers (25 April-16 May and 15 June-12 July), the long Paris Peace Conference (29 July-15 October), which included many more countries, and the New York Council of Foreign Ministers (4 November-12 December)—led naturally to a close working relationship between American and British diplomats trying to negotiate with difficult, abrasive and enigmatic Soviet diplomats headed by Foreign Minister Molotov. The range of issues discussed—the Eastern European treaties, the Italian-Yugoslav border, the Italian treaty—were those that tended to bring the United States and Britain together, a tendency carefully nurtured by Bevin and his associates to draw the United States into closer and long-lasting involvement with European affairs.

A fact of crucial importance bringing American and British diplomacy into alignment was that in regard to economic conditions in Germany and Austria, American and British interests were coming to coincide. The Potsdam agreements had envisioned Germany being treated as a single economic unit. The Soviets, however, had unilaterally transferred key agricultural regions in the east to Poland, and had refused to allow shipments of foodstuffs from their zone to the largely nonagricultural regions which had been assigned to the Western allies, areas that in addition were flooded with refugees from the East. The cost of providing even a subsistence diet for the Western zones soon became a drain on American and especially British financial resources. As a result the two countries were both unwilling to continue previously agreed-upon reparations to the Soviet Union. By mid-1946 efforts were underway to combine the British and American zones in order to make them economically self-sustaining. While this was a move which clearly had the potential to lead to a divided Germany, it was seen at the time as the only expedient to shore up the Western occupation zones.[17] Cooperation in Bizonia set the stage for cooperation on larger European economic issues in 1947 under the auspices of the Marshall Plan.

During 1946 American opinion of Britain was rapidly shifting. The almost universal lack of sympathy with which Americans in 1944 observed British policies in Italy and Greece had dissipated. The Labour government did not share the imperial pretensions of Churchill, and some degree of independence for India and Egypt seemed likely. As concerns over the Soviet Union mounted, there was a corresponding tendency to see the British as valuable collaborators and as bastions of democracy in a threatened world. Fear of involvement in an Anglo-Soviet conflict disappeared as it became desirable to have allies. This shift did not occur uniformly; there was strong resistance to a military alliance with the British, and important segments of American opinion continued to resent vestiges of colonialism. The American Jewish community was especially critical of British efforts to prevent large numbers of displaced persons from entering Palestine.[18] The negotiation of a $3.75 billion loan to Britain dragged on for months, bringing out isolationist sentiment and recollections of British inability or unwillingness to repay the World War I loans. The loan was eventually approved in mid-July 1946, but only on the basis of the value of British partnership in a world menaced by a rising threat of communism.[19]

There emerged by the end of the year a clear "parallelism" of British and American policy which the *New York Times* described as resulting "from the inevitable reaction of two democratic nations to developments since the war."[20] In February 1947 Charles Bohlen, the counselor of the State Department, noted:

No one knows better than Mr. Bevin that in the diplomatic field there has been no preconcerted Anglo-American bloc in negotiations with the Soviet Union. The fact that the U.S. and Great Britain have come to adopt in these negotiations similar positions on the points at issue is merely an entirely natural result of our common civilization, and, therefore, common and it may be added innocent objectives in world affairs.[21]

The State Department officials who were most directly concerned with questions of defense policy were H. Freeman Matthews, the director of the Office of European Affairs, and his deputy and successor, John D. Hickerson. Both men had had extensive experience in Anglo-American relations, Matthews having been counselor at the London embassy before returning to Washington in 1943. Hickerson, who spent most of his career dealing with West European affairs in the State Department, had served previously as chief of the Division of British Commonwealth Affairs and a member of the Permanent Joint Board on Defense, U.S.-Canada which had brought him into security planning involving U.S., Canadian and British interests. Both men realized the weakened postwar position of Britain and argued that the United States should attempt to bolster British power. Matthews and Hickerson, who worked closely with Pentagon officials, saw to it that there was at least some congruence between American foreign and defense policies in the first postwar years.

FOREIGN POLICY AND DEFENSE
POLICY INTERSECT

The evolution of American foreign policy in 1946, based on public antipathy towards the Soviet Union and the increasing alignment of U.S. and British diplomacy in the long series of conferences, served as background for a simultaneous reassessment of American defense policy. Postwar plans had been based on the assumption that continued great-power cooperation would be possible and that American and Russian interests were focused in different regions of the world and thus would not come into direct conflict. Once this set of assumptions was overturned, a new defense policy would be necessary. If American opposition to Soviet ambitions were the established American policy, what military implications would be entailed? Defense planners, who shared their colleagues' concerns about Soviet policies, were of several minds. Airpower advocates argued for a greater strategic bombing capability. The Navy saw the need for American military power to be augmented in likely areas of confrontation, especially in the Eastern Mediterranean. Obviously the existence of bureaucratic self-interest on the part of the military services, which would soon be starved for funds and qualified personnel, cannot be discounted. Nevertheless, defense policy changed while appropriations did not rise for almost five years. Defense policy was revolutionized from within; it did not result from congressional appropriations or public pressure. This came about as a result of the changed perceptions of senior officers and administration officials regarding the nation's security interests.

American planners came to assume that British interests in the Mediterranean and in Europe were vital American concerns as well. This was accepted by senior officials in the spring of 1946; when it was acted upon in 1947 and thereafter, the regionalism previously inherent in American defense policy had been undermined and superseded. The planning process had, moreover, radical implications for the future size and structure of the American defense establishment that were only dimly perceived even by the planners themselves and certainly not by most administration officials or an economy-minded Congress.

Within the limited circle of officials concerned with national security planning, the official view in mid-1945 had centered on the need to avoid entanglement in British and Soviet disputes in Europe and the Middle East. At Potsdam the U.S. had finessed the issue of Soviet demands on Turkey for a hand in the control of the Turkish Straits by suggesting that there be unrestricted navigation on all international waterways, thereby avoiding the need to side with traditional British interests in the Eastern Mediterranean against equally traditional Russian aims to control the Straits. Although the concept of the United States as a mediator between Britain and the Soviet Union was reflected in official documents and undoubtedly to some extent in official thinking throughout most of 1945 from Potsdam on some American officials were beginning to recognize that U.S. interests were inextricably tied to those of the British.[22] The extent of the influence which British officials had on this shift in American official thinking cannot be precisely gauged. The opportunity for influence was provided by the CCS/BJSM infrastructure in Washington and in cooperative defense endeavors elsewhere. The British had a consistent policy and they advocated it relentlessly.

In the context of continuing Soviet pressure on Turkey, Secretary of State Byrnes asked the JCS in early March 1946 the effect, from the U.S. military point of view, of Soviet demands being granted. The JCS response reflects the shift in official thinking:

The defeat or disintegration of the British Empire would eliminate from Eurasia the last bulwark of resistance between the United States and Soviet expansion. After this the military potential of the United States together with the military potential of possible allies bound to her ideologically might be insufficient to match those of an expanded Soviet Union. Militarily, our present position as a world power is of necessity closely interwoven with that of Great Britain.

The JCS argued, as a result, that the United States should buttress the British Empire against an aggressive Soviet imperialism, a conclusion which would hardly have gained universal public support at the time. Similar views were coming to the fore in the State Department. On 1 April 1946, H. Freeman Matthews provided guidance to the military planners in the form of a "Political Estimate of Soviet Policy for Use in Connection with Military Studies":

If Soviet Russia is to be denied the hegemony of Europe, the United
Kingdom must continue in existence as the principal power in Western
Europe economically and militarily. The U.S. should, therefore, explore its
relationship with Great Britain and give all feasible political, economic,
and if necessary military support within the framework of the United
Nations, to the United Kingdom and the communications of the British
Commonwealth.[24]

These comments were related to the beginning of the process of
creating war plans in March 1946. These plans, identifying the
Soviet Union as the likely adversary, also assumed cooperation
with British forces and, inasmuch as they were based on a strategy
of air strikes, using nuclear weapons, on the Soviet homeland,
reflected the fact that Britain offered the best bases for air
operations. But the larger significance was a belief in "interwoven"
British and American interests in denying Moscow the hegemony of
Europe.[25]

This identification of American and British defense interests was
of course highly sensitive in light of the public furor over
Churchill's proposal for a virtual Anglo-American alliance at
Fulton and the persisting controversy over passage of the British
loan. Leakage could also have greatly complicated Byrnes' efforts
to continue negotiations to work out a settlement for German as
well as Eastern European issues.

Truman was well aware of the line of thinking by Pentagon and
State Department officials, but was probably not yet completely
persuaded.[26] A keen student of American history, he appreciated
the vast implications that such policies would eventually have for
American society in general. Truman mulled over the question of
the state of relations with the Soviet Union in the summer of 1946
and on 12 July launched what turned out to be a full-scale
reappraisal of American defense policy culminating in the September memorandum by his special counsel, Clark M. Clifford.[27]
Much of the staff work for the project was done by Clifford's
assistant, George M. Elsey, who requested inputs from the various
parts of the government. The final report incorporated large
sections which had been originally drafted by the State Department
and the Joint Staff. The Clifford memorandum gave a history of

recent Soviet-American relations and provided a gloomy assessment of the likely future course of a Soviet leadership "increasing their military power and the sphere of Soviet influence in preparation for the 'inevitable' conflict, . . . trying to weaken and subvert their potential opponents by every means at their disposal."[28] The final section, dealing with U.S. policy towards the Soviet Union, recommended maintaining American military strength, particularly the capability to wage atomic and biological warfare; the "mere fact of preparedness may be the only powerful deterrent to Soviet aggressive action and in this sense the only sure guaranty of peace."[29] The United States should, in addition, be prepared to support "all democratic countries which are in any way menaced or endangered by the U.S.S.R. Providing military support in case of attack is a last resort; a more effective barrier to communism is strong economic support."[30]

The report acknowledged the dangers of a Soviet conquest of Europe, but it gave little attention to cooperation with allies or potential allies including Great Britain; instead the focus was on "preparedness" and economic assistance. This emphasis was, however, Clifford's or more likely Elsey's, both of whom were very much attuned to the political difficulties posed by closer Anglo-American ties, especially within important ethnic constituencies of the Democratic party. Clifford had in fact left out discussion of U.S. cooperation with its allies, which was of major concern to officials dealing regularly with policy issues. The Navy's input, forwarded by Forrestal, had minced no words, recommending the "formulation of a coordinated naval policy with appropriate members of the British Commonwealth."[31] The JCS noted that "a basic element in our military policy is establishment and strengthening of relationships with naturally friendly people, particularly those that adhere firmly to our basic concepts of government and way of life."[32] War Department emphases did focus on the need for "long range air power, supplemented by atomic and long range weapons, and adequate ground forces," but specifically urged that "Soviet efforts to divide Britain and the United States be defeated."[33]

Discussion of the need for cooperation with other allies was not included in the final report, possibly because Clifford and Elsey considered close ties with the British to be politically out of the

question; perhaps because the heaviest emphasis on such cooperation derived from the Navy which was fighting the president's unification efforts; and most likely because Elsey in particular did not
accept this approach. A handwritten draft paragraph from Elsey's
papers with the notation "omit" suggests the latter:

Should the United States become involved in a war with the U.S.S.R., this
country would not be able to rely on allies to stave off the enemy during
mobilization. A future war would begin—and might well end—in a very
short time. The strength of the United States must be such that it need not
rely upon assumed or potential allies. The United States could be attacked
directly from the Soviet Union by long-range planes armed with atomic
bombs.[34]

This line of thought, influential in Air Force circles, would be a recurrent theme in the late 1940s, but it did not reflect the whole story.

Clifford sent the report on to the president, who read it carefully
and, because of its sensitivity, at once impounded all copies.[35] It
nonetheless served to advise the president that continuing bad relations with the Soviet Union were likely and that the country would
have to lend its efforts to resisting Soviet aggrandizement. It undoubtedly confirmed in the president's mind the rationale for an
anti-Soviet foreign policy. Remaining locked in the White House
safe, it did not, however, provide an operational plan for the
bureaucracy. Elsey and Clifford were not full-time national security advisers and they soon turned their attention to other matters
more directly related to domestic politics.

State Department and Pentagon officials meanwhile proceeded
with their own plans for appropriate American defenses, efforts
which eventually would channel the unfocused anti-Sovietism that
had come to pervade American politics in 1946 into defense policies
which could provide the basis of North American and West European security in the postwar decades. The process by which these
defense policies were created was a cooperative endeavor in which
much of the initiative would be taken by Britain and other nations
that would eventually constitute the Atlantic alliance. Initiatives
made in military planning channels, reinforced at the diplomatic
level, would create a military policy for this alliance.

THE MIDDLE EAST AND
EASTERN MEDITERRANEAN

The shared perception of interwoven Anglo-American strategic interests had highly visible impact in a geographical region—the Eastern Mediterranean and Middle East—where the United States and Britain had long had different and to some extent conflicting interests. On 10 November 1945 a group of senior State Department envoys had warned President Truman that governments in the Middle East "know from bitter experience and present trends that Britain and France will make every effort to consolidate their pre-war spheres of influence; they look especially to us to support them in their efforts to block any such development. If the United States fails them, they will turn to Russia and will be lost to our civilization; of that we feel certain. On the other hand, there need be no conflict between us and Russia in that area. On the contrary, Russian policy has thus far closely paralleled our own." Truman agreed that there was no reason for Soviet-American conflict in that area and said he would like these countries to turn towards both Russia and the United States.[36] Nevertheless in a matter of months the United States came to share British concerns in this important region.

Anglo-American cooperation in the Eastern Mediterranean and the Middle East developed gradually as the two countries faced crises in Iran, Greece, Turkey and Yugoslavia. In March 1946 the continued presence of Soviet troops in Iran resulted in a confrontation at the United Nations, with the United States and Britain being publicly aligned against the Soviets for the first time. Moscow had pledged to remove the troops at the end of the war, but there had been rumors that the Russians might try to annex the Iranian province of Azerbaijan and attempt to establish greater influence throughout the entire country. Early in 1946 reports of Soviet troop movements in the direction of Tehran were circulating. Bevin protested at the U.N. Security Council with U.S. backing. Soviet Foreign Minister Molotov walked out in protest, but the Soviet and Iranian governments eventually signed an agreement calling for the withdrawal of Soviet troops by early May and recognizing Azerbaijan as part of Iranian territory. Although the accord gave the

Soviets a majority interest in a joint Soviet-Iranian oil company, the Iranian parliament subsequently rejected this provision without forceful Soviet protest.[37]

The Iranian crisis demonstrated to Washington and to the American public Moscow's inclination to lean on its neighbors. It fueled concerns that the Soviets had Middle East ambitions and were seeking direct access to the Persian Gulf oil supplies traditionally controlled by American and British firms. The resolution of the crisis indicated that, in the face of a united front by the United States and Britain and the determination of a local country to defend its rights, Moscow would back down.

Turkey provided a second source of great-power dispute. The Soviets deeply resented Turkey's neutrality during World War II and various actions that Moscow interpreted as pro-German. Soviet determination to force Ankara to be more accommodating resulted in March 1945 in a denunciation of a 1925 treaty of friendship and an announcement of Moscow's determination to seek revision of the 1938 Montreux Convention governing transit of the Turkish Straits. Moscow also pressed the Turks for Soviet bases in the Straits at least in time of war and demanded the cession of the Kars-Ardaban district in eastern Turkey which had been under Russian control from 1878 until 1921.

Throughout 1945 Turkish security was considered a matter of greater concern to London than to Washington. There was little American interest in committing the United States to assist Turkey if she were attacked.[38] In early November Washington proposed an international conference to consider opening the Straits to warships of the Black Sea powers at all times and provide for stricter limitations on the passage of ships belonging to non-Black Sea powers. Even though the United States had not been a signatory of the Montreux Convention, the Turkish government was informed that Washington, "if invited, would be pleased to participate in such a conference."[39] The Turkish government, aware of the relative strengths of the great powers, indicated that in fact American participation would be the sine qua non for holding a conference.[40] The Soviets, however, declined to make an official response and stood by their earlier proposal.

From the end of 1945 through July 1946 the question of the

Straits remained in suspense. No one called for a conference to revise the convention. Moscow concentrated on intimidating the Turkish government by propaganda attacks and menacing troop movements, anticipating that Turkey could, in Molotov's arch formulation, be "elevated in its relations with the Soviet Union to the atmosphere of cordiality which prevailed between the Soviet Union and Poland."[41]

Through most of 1946 Turkish security was a question of more direct importance to London than to Washington. Up to this point American concerns for the Straits had reflected a general interest in international law governing waterways and a desire to accommodate reasonable Soviet security requirements. Truman had refused to join the British in a démarche to Moscow in support of Turkey in July 1945.[42] American officials, however, were gradually coming to see Soviet pressure on Turkey as reflecting a highly unwelcome determination to improve its position in the Middle East and Eastern Mediterranean vis-à-vis Britain and as part of a plan to dominate Turkey politically in a manner consistent with Soviet tactics in Eastern Europe.[43]

Soviet pressure against Turkey persisted into the summer of 1946, until on 7 August Moscow addressed a note to the Turkish government proposing a new agreement for the Straits that would have effectively limited the influence of Britain and other signatories of the Montreux Convention. The reaction in Washington was far different than it would have likely been a few months earlier. Although the Joint Chiefs of Staff discounted the military importance of control of the Straits, since the area could be effectively interdicted by airpower, they also had come to recognize that Soviet pressure on Turkey threatened Britain's role as a world power, a position now seen as one with which America's own position was linked.[44] On 15 August 1946 a memorandum, personally presented to the president by the secretaries of war and the Navy and Dean Acheson, as acting secretary of state, suggested the Soviet goal in the note to Turkey was to introduce troops into that country and to use them to gain control that in turn would result "in Greece and the whole Near and Middle East, including the Eastern Mediterranean, falling under Soviet control and in those areas being cut off from the Western world." They recommended that the United States should resist any "Soviet aggression against Turkey."[45]

This was a new departure in American policy. It was neither a question of upholding World War II agreements with the Soviet Union nor of protecting a traditional sphere of influence. By August 1946 leading American officials had concluded that the Eastern Mediterranean was vital, that lines had now to be drawn against Soviet expansion and that Turkey, neutral during World War II, was the place to draw them.[46] The president shared this assessment; he indicated that he was prepared to support Turkey "to the end." The Turkish government shortly received the not unwelcome news that the "government of the United States cannot agree to the proposal that Turkey and the Soviet Union organize joint means of defense of the Straits."[47]

Despite a willingness to support Turkey "to the end," American efforts centered on nonmilitary aid—economic assistance, Export-Import Bank credits, assistance to the Turkish merchant marine, and the like. The responsibility for providing military aid was considered to remain with London. Should the British be unable to carry through with military support, the State Department suggested in October 1946 that "the United States is prepared to consider the possibility of furnishing such supplies to Great Britain for delivery to the Turks. In a very exceptional case we might consider furnishing supplies direct." The ambassador in Ankara was instructed, nonetheless, to discourage the Turks from asking the United States for arms and military equipment and to advise them to direct such requests to London.[48]

Yet another Mediterranean crisis confronted Washington in the summer of 1946. On 9 August Yugoslav fighters shot down an unarmed American C-47 transport flying supplies from Austria to Italy and held the crewmembers captive. On 19 August another C-47 was shot down, this time with a loss of five crewmembers. The State Department issued a sharp ultimatum, demanding the release within forty-eight hours of the crewmen held since the 9 August incident. The Yugoslavs felt obliged to comply with the demand and released the crew, and the following month Belgrade also agreed to make sizable payments to the families of the crewmembers killed in the 19 August incident.[49] Nevertheless, relations with Yugoslavia continued to be tense as a result of persistent difficulties over the activities of American diplomatic personnel and, more importantly, Yugoslav ambitions to annex Trieste, a city in the northern Adriatic with a mixed Italian and Slavic population. The August 1946 crisis and its aftermath was especially significant in that its resolution required a more pointed American military response directed at cautioning a country regarded at the time as a willing satellite of the Soviet Union. Secretary of State Byrnes had recommended on 22 August that transport flights be resumed with fighter escorts. The Joint Chiefs of Staff proposed instead that resupply be conducted by armed bombers and such flights did commence on 27 September. In addition Truman ordered the augmentation of American troops along the line separating troops under combined Anglo-American command from Yugoslav forces at the disputed border with Italy. U.S. air forces in northern Italy were also reinforced.[50] Additional American and British naval forces deployed into the Adriatic. In a delayed reaction to this crisis a group of B-29 bombers also was sent to Europe in November 1946, an early use of airpower as a diplomatic tool.[51]

This series of military moves further reflected the shift in American opinion which had occurred since the autumn of 1945 when President Truman had been distinctly reluctant to contemplate any armed confrontation with the Yugoslavs.[52] Although, in a narrow sense, the problems over Trieste were part of the World War II legacy, the nature of the bellicose Yugoslav attacks contributed significantly to the hardening American attitudes towards the new Communist states in Europe and the willingness of American officials to employ military force in the Mediterranean area.

The situation in Greece proved to have the most decisive impact on relations among the great powers. Greece had always been an area of special British concern, particularly during World War II. Churchill had dispatched troops to Greece in 1940 despite the imminent threat of a cross-channel invasion of Britain itself. The Greek government in exile spent the years of occupation in Egypt under British sponsorship. Largely to ensure a pro-Western Greece, Churchill and Eden had proposed the "percentages deal" to Stalin in 1944. British forces had played an important role in forcing out the German army in the final months of 1944. On the other hand, the United States had by and large stood aloof from British involvement in Greece and there was a lingering suspicion of British imperial motives and of the monarchial government in Athens. Throughout 1945 Greek public opinion shifted to the right in large measure as a result of leftist excesses against alleged former collaborators with the Germans. In March 1946 an election monitored by American, British and French observers returned a strongly right-wing parliament with a conservative government; that September a plebiscite restored the king to his throne. To put an end to right-wing retaliation then in full sway, the Americans and British worked together to encourage the monarch and the government to promote reconciliation among Greeks.

During the latter half of 1945, however, Greek survival seemed to be under constant challenge. The Soviet press launched a sustained propaganda campaign against the "monarcho-fascist" government and its British supporters. Although in retrospect there was probably little Soviet involvement in the armed raids into Greece (the Yugoslavs and others were undoubtedly active), Washington saw similarities between the situation in Greece and conditions in other Eastern European countries. Ukrainian attacks on Greece in the United Nations were described by an American diplomat as part of a Soviet effort to " 'break' Greece and to try to bring about a situation in Greece comparable to the situations in Rumania and Bulgaria.''[53]

American officials, having been involved in monitoring the March 1946 Greek elections, felt some obligation to support the government which resulted from them.[54] More decisive, however, was growing concern about the strategic balance in the Eastern Mediterranean which had motivated the *Missouri* visit to Athens in April 1946. In October 1946 the State Department's Office of Near Eastern and African Affairs suggested that "many signs indicate that Greece is becoming a focal point in strained international relations and that its fate during the next few months may be a deciding factor in the future orientation of the Near and Middle East.''[55]

Confronted with the threatening situation facing Greece, American officials reviewed their options. They saw the continuing presence of British troops as essential. William L. Clayton, the acting secretary of state, had noted in early September that "US military and [State] Dep[artmen]t believe that their continued presence is [a] stabilizing factor and we hope that UK will not commence an early withdrawal following plebiscite [on retention of the monarchy] which we have understood is their intention.''[56] Contrary to Clayton's hopes, the British troops did commence withdrawing from Greece, but at a slow rate, beginning their departure from urban areas where the security situation was not as acute as in the northern countryside.[57]

Along with a series of conspicuous visits by American warships to Greek ports throughout the rest of 1946, Washington's own support to Greece was concentrated on diplomatic and economic measures. As was the case with regard to Turkey the question of the supply of arms to Greece demonstrated the limiting parameters of American policy. Acheson explained to Byrnes that discussion of the supply of military aid to Greece

did not mean that any such sales are now envisioned but was intended to provide for future eventuality in case situation develops in which Brit[ain] cannot provide minimum Greek requirements. It is Dep[artmen]t's feeling, as it is yours, that US assistance should be primarily economic.[58]

Byrnes and Bevin subsequently agreed in Paris on 15 October 1946 that the United States would provide economic aid and the British military assistance unless the British were unable to provide sufficient arms. In that case the United States would provide the arms to the United Kingdom who would in turn supply them to Greece. In early November the American ambassador in Athens was instructed to discourage the Greek government from asking the United States for arms and to refer them to London.[59] In a subsequent memorandum of 20 December 1946, Byrnes advised Truman of this arrangement.[60]

American officials were now convinced that the United States had a significant security interest in an independent Greece. Although hope remained that the British would continue to take the lead in military assistance, there was a psychological readiness to accept greater responsibilities even in the defense area if the British had to pull back. Bevin moved carefully and consulted regularly with Byrnes at the various conferences in 1946. Avoiding precipitous moves, he sought to induce the Americans to accept ever-increasing responsibility for the beleaguered countries of the Eastern Mediterranean. As Bruce Kuniholm has concluded:

With the help of Britain and [ironically] the Soviet Union, the Truman administration by the fall of 1946 had arrived at a clear conception of Greece,

Turkey, and Iran in their collective historical role of dividing East and West. . . . Their territorial integrity, moreover, was defined in terms of the strategic interests of the United States. As the viability of three governments continued to be threatened . . . the United States found itself increasingly committed to the continuation of earlier British policies.[61]

THE TRUMAN DOCTRINE, MARCH 1947

The need to accept even more British responsibilities was not long delayed. Throughout late 1946 the British cabinet had wrestled with its financial difficulties, and attention was often drawn to the outflow of funds required to maintain the traditional British position in the Eastern Mediterranean and the Middle East. Many in the Labour party and some, including the prime minister, in the cabinet believed the game was no longer worth the candle. Bevin and the Chiefs of Staff had put up a long struggle, but the dwindling of currency reserves was inexorable and the Treasury's demands for spending reductions had to be met. Bevin had done his best to see that a common Anglo-American position was in place. He was successful. Between the delivery of two British notes on the afternoon of Friday, 20 February 1947, indicating that His Majesty's Government could no longer bear the financial burden of supporting Greece and Turkey, and the proclamation of the ringing terms of the Truman Doctrine on 12 March, American foreign policy was formally redefined. The hitherto secret assessments of administration officials became the official public policy of the United States government, defined by President Truman and the new secretary of state, George Marshall, who took office in January 1947.

The British notes addressed the question of economic assistance, estimating that London could provide only some £40 million of the £60-70 million which Greece was estimated to require for meeting its civilian and military needs in 1947. London also proposed that the strategic and military position of Turkey should also be considered and steps taken to "bring the Turkish Armed Forces up to a reasonable state of preparedness which would involve a plan of economic development."[62] The burden would have to be borne now by Washington.

There was virtual unanimity within the Truman administration on the need for the United States to meet Greek and Turkish requirements. As Joseph M. Jones, a State Department official who subsequently wrote an authoritative account of the period, described the events,

Marshall's reaction was similar to that of all the others in the [State] Department who had heard the news. Without any exception known to the writer, everyone in the executive branch recognized what this meant, and saw that if Russian expansion was to be checked the United States must move into the defaulted position in the Middle East.[63]

The bureaucratic consensus which had formed throughout 1946 now coalesced into a plan for action. At a meeting on 24 February 1947, State, War and Navy representatives concurred that

it was vital to the security of the United States that Greece and Turkey be strengthened; that only the United States was in a position to do this; and that the President should therefore ask Congress for the necessary funds and authority.

The president, according to Jones, "required no convincing" and at once accepted the State-War-Navy recommendations.[64]

Approaching Congress would not be simple; the new Eightieth Congress, Republican in both houses, had been elected on a platform of spending reductions and lower taxes. On 14 February 1947 the Joint Congressional Committee on the Legislative Budget had recommended a cut of $6 billion in the President's $37.5 billion budget, and a cut of $1.75 billion was proposed in the operating budgets of the Army and Navy. In addition, $1 billion requested by the administration for preventing starvation, disease and unrest in Germany and Japan was to be cut in half.

Senator Arthur Vandenberg, a former isolationist now chairman of the Foreign Relations Committee, advised Truman that any request to Congress for aid to Greece and Turkey would have to be accompanied by a presidential message underlining the "grim facts of the larger situation."[65] By this Vandenberg meant that the aid request had to be justified by portraying it as a response to the Soviet aggressiveness that had already alienated the American public. One account has Vandenberg remarking to Truman, "Mr. President, if that's what you want, there's only one way to get it. That is to made a personal appearance before Congress and scare hell out of the country."[66]

The president's speech of 12 March 1947 embodied Vandenberg's suggestion. Delivered to a packed chamber of both houses, Truman described the dire needs of Greece, ravaged by war, "threatened by the terrorist activities of several thousand armed men, led by Communists, who defy the government's authority at a number of points, particularly along the northern boundaries." Recognizing the imperfection of the Greek government, he argued that it was still representative of 85 percent of the members of the parliament elected under international observation in 1946.

Turkey received less emphasis, but Truman suggested that Ankara needed assistance for the modernization "necessary for the maintenance of its national integrity . . . essential to the preservation of order in the Middle East." To accomplish the goal of supporting the two countries, the president asked for authority for aid in the amount of $400 million in addition to maximizing relief assistance to Greece from previous appropriations.

Moving beyond a straightforward request for funds, however, Truman placed the Greek and Turkish situations in a broad ideological context. The United States, the president urged, should

support free peoples who are resisting attempted subjugation by armed minorities or by outside pressures. I believe that we must assist free peoples to work out their own destinies through economic and financial aid which is essential to economic stability and orderly political processes.[67]

This enunciation of the Truman Doctrine caught the attention of contemporary listeners and has occasionally provided historians with an all-purpose explanation of the cold war. Yet, despite the intimation of globalism and the martial rhetoric, the administration's aims were focused on the Mediterranean and its goals were to be achieved through economic assistance. This could be easily misunderstood since the Truman Doctrine, not strategic interests, supplied the public justification for offering aid and served to provide an ideological basis for American foreign policy. For political reasons, the administration had to play down the extent to which the United States was consciously moving to fill ailing Britannia's shoes. A closed meeting of Democratic senators had approved the concept of aid to Greece only with the express reservation that it not be employed to further British policies in the region.[68] Senator Allen Ellender of Louisiana was quoted by the *New York Times* as saying "I am for giving aid to the people of Greece, but as to money for maintaining British soldiers in Greece, I would say 'Nix!' "[69]

Nonetheless the administration's tactics were effective. Aid to Greece and Turkey was approved by both House and Senate in lopsided votes. The president signed the authorization bill on 22 May 1947.

The passing and receiving of the torch of Mediterranean defense from Britain to the United States did not go off without difficulties and misunderstandings. In Britain the Treasury exerted unrelenting pressure to end expenditures on British forces in Greece. American officials sought to ensure a smooth turnover, noting with concern that British forces in Greece were scheduled to be reduced to one brigade and that the brigade itself would be withdrawn during the coming summer.[70] (This brigade was in addition to a training mission of some 1,400 men which was to remain.) Officials in Washington also realized that it would be impossible to launch the aid program to Greece by the date scheduled for the end of British assistance, 31 March 1947, and relayed to London their hope that British aid could be extended.

Despite the strong reservations of Hugh Dalton, the chancellor of the Exchequer, who had in any event little sympathy for the regime in Athens, the British agreed to provide £2 million a month until American aid became effective but for no more than three months. However, on 8 March 1947 the British ambassador, Lord Inverchapel, advised Acheson that these military advances would be made in the form of loans to Greece which would have to be repaid as soon as possible either by the United States or by the Greek government out of funds made available to it by Washington. Acheson's umbrage at this effrontery was soothed only when Inverchapel assured him that he himself had already sent a strong protest to London.[71] On reconsideration, the British agreed to provide at least £1 million in aid with reimbursement from Greek funds held in London under a 1944 arrangement, but they made no commitment for further aid.

This was not the end of the difficulties. Bevin also advised Marshall on 22 March 1947 that there were additional problems in funding the training mission and he did not want to have to approach the Commons again; he proposed instead that the cost of the mission be defrayed by the Greeks, presumably out of American loans.[72] Acheson cabled Marshall (then in Moscow) that "this British proposal to be repaid in dollars from our loan would produce storm of protest here [in Washington] and undoubtedly an amendment specifically prohibiting it." (The bill, as enacted, did in fact include such a stipulation.[73]) The United States in response noted that the British troops then in Greece would still have to be paid wherever they were stationed and the costs were after all "too trifling to warrant serious embarrassment to us which such picayune haggling would cause."[74] The British finally agreed to pay the sterling costs of the mission in Greece, and in the end their troops remained in Greece until 1950 in cooperation with the American training mission.

An American aid mission arrived in Athens on 22 May 1947, but the guerrilla war actually intensified. The administration considered involving U.S. troops in the fighting, but contented itself with an extensive series of naval visits to various Greek ports.[75] It was to be several years before Greece's endemic economic and social problems were partially ameliorated and Turkey's military put on a more efficient basis. The problem, however, was by then one that Washington considered its own; the British had come to be the junior partners.

THE TALKS AT THE PENTAGON, OCTOBER 1947

Continuing concern over the unsettled situation in the Middle East and the Eastern Mediterranean led in the autumn of 1947 to the holding of the so-called Pentagon Talks between senior American and British officials. These discussions reflected the still uncertain state of American policy and while they did not produce any concrete results, they did represent a further step in the merging of British and American defense and foreign policies.

They prepared the way for conversations on more important questions relating to the defense of central Europe.

The Pentagon Talks originated in the concern of American officials about the prospect of further British troop withdrawals from the Mediterranean region and the end of the Italian occupation which required the departure of U.S. and British troops and the closing of bases there. British troops in Greece could not soon be replaced by American forces inasmuch as Congress had been promised by the administration during the negotiations for economic support to Athens that no U.S. troops would be sent to Greece.[76] In response to American protests (and Field Marshal Montgomery's warnings), Bevin made a "purely personal suggestion" that the United States and Britain

jointly review the whole position in the Middle East including Cyrenaica [part of today's Libya], Egypt, Palestine, Iraq and Persia, for the purpose of arriving at a "gentlemen's understanding" in regard to a common policy and joint responsibility throughout the area, with the British acting as the front and [the Americans] supplying the moral support.[77]

A compromise on the British troop withdrawals had been arranged whereby some eight hundred men would be quietly withdrawn from Greece with the rest remaining until at least 15 December 1947, and the talks were scheduled to begin in mid-October 1947.

American preparatory papers reflect awareness of Britain's economic difficulties and her inability to maintain her traditional position in the Middle East. American officials had no desire to move in quickly with military forces to fill the void: "Given our heavy commitments elsewhere and Britain's already established position in the area, it is our strong feeling that the British should continue to maintain primary responsibility for military security in that area."[78] Nonetheless American officials did consider that the decision taken by Washington in August 1946 to "resist overt Soviet aggresison against Turkey should apply with equal force to the Eastern Mediterranean, including specifically Italy, Greece, and Iran, as well as Turkey."[79] An important American goal was finding ways to improve British relations with local states, particularly since it was apparent that the British would be faced with continuing demands for the evacuation of Egypt and that alternate locations for bases would be useful.

The talks began on 16 October 1947 in the Pentagon, where it was possible to ensure tight security. The high-level British delegation included Lord Inverchapel, Sir John Balfour, British minister in the United States, Michael Wright, the assistant under secretary of state in the Foreign Office, Lt.-Gen. Sir Leslie Hollis, chief of staff to the minister of defence and various other Foreign Office and Ministry of Defence officials. The American side was represented by Robert Lovett, the acting secretary of state, Loy Henderson, the director of the Office of Near Eastern and African Affairs, John Hickerson, George Kennan and other State Department officials as well as Vice Admiral Sherman from the Navy, Lt. Gen. Lauris Norstad from the Army and Major General A.M. Gruenther, the director of the Joint Staff.[80]

Lord Inverchapel opened by emphasizing the importance of the Middle East area in a future war when it would,

as proved to be the case in both the last wars, be a strategic theatre second only in importance, or perhaps equal in importance, to the United Kingdom. The reasons which [the British Chiefs of Staff] adduce are not merely that the Middle East is a vital theatre of communication for the Commonwealth, or that it contains vital supplies of oil, although both these reasons are valid. But they adduce the still more important argument that in meeting future aggression conditions of modern warfare will not permit of merely passive or even active defence, but require counter offence. The Middle East is perhaps the one area from which offensive action could be taken, both to relieve the pressure of attack on the United Kingdom and from which to strike at the aggressor where he is vulnerable.[81]

Inverchapel argued in addition that it was necessary to have bases within reach of the Middle East, for example in Aden or Africa, and that advance bases within the Middle East were necessary in peacetime. Noting that Britain had treaty rights in various parts of the region (Transjordan, the Persian Gulf, the Sudan), Inverchapel stated, however, that major strategic facilities would be lacking since it appeared improbable that bases could be maintained either in Egypt or Palestine. He argued that "the whole question whether we can retain adequate strategic facilities in peace time therefore turns upon Cyrenaica."[82]

An American paper prepared by State Department officials accepted the proposition that the "security of the Eastern Mediterranean and of the Middle East is vital to the security of the United States" and that thus the United States should "be prepared to make full use of its political, economic and, if necessary, military power in such manner as may be found most effective."[83] The American paper did not, however, indicate specific plans other than making the Soviets aware of the firm American commitment to the region.

The talks, which concluded on 7 November, resulted in a series of agreed statements reflecting a close harmony of views and promising close consultation in the future. Diplomatic support would be forthcoming in Cairo on behalf of the British military facilities in Egypt which contributed to overall Middle Eastern security. Agreement was made on the desirability of assuring British facilities in northern Africa, and American negotiators promised to recommend United States support for the granting of a British trusteeship over Cyrenaica (which was ultimately unrealizable). Other issues were dealt with in platitudinous terms or, as in the intractable case of Palestine, carefully finessed. The talks served as an opportunity for frank discussions of respective concerns about the area and underlined the desirability from the participants' points of view of closely aligning the two countries' policies—particularly on political and economic matters. They did not commit the United States to any new obligations in its defense policy nor did the Truman administration provide the across-the-board backing for British policy in the Mediterranean area that London had desired. In essence, there was to be no Anglo-American policy for the region.

Although a brief summary of the conversations was approved by the newly established National Security Council on 21 November 1947 and President Truman indicated his concurrence a few days later, no new American initiatives flowed from the conclusions of the talks. Lovett noted in a cable to Marshall that

we have taken great pains to make it abundantly clear to all concerned that no agreement is involved. Conversations represented merely exchange of views. Documents emanating from conversations were proposed statements of respective policies subject to confirmation. It is understood that these statements even after approval could not be considered as agreements; that no obligations were taken; and the policies outlined were subject to change to meet new conditions.[84]

On 4 December 1947 Bevin and Marshall discussed the Pentagon
Talks again and agreed that

> there was no agreement nor even an understanding between the two Gov-
> ernments on the questions which had been discussed at Washington; it had
> merely happened that each of the Governments had been presented by their
> officials with recommendations which substantially coincided.[85]

It is apparent that after the conclusion of the talks there had been
some American backpedaling from their implications. In part this
may have resulted from political considerations—United States cooperation with the British on "colonial" questions was inevitably a
sensitive matter, and especially in regard to Palestine. More inter-
esting, however, was the reaction of the JCS to whom the paper
was referred by Forrestal, now secretary of national defense. On
reflection, the JCS considered that the security of the Eastern Mediterranean was of "critical" rather than "vital" importance to the
United States and explained that "any additional deployments of
U.S. armed forces to this area will, in view of our present extended
position, automatically raise the question of the advisability of
partial mobilization."[86]

The JCS, at this point greatly concerned about declining troop
levels, did not seek new commitments without concomitant personnel augmentation. The Air Force in particular saw any new Middle
East strategy as justifying large naval programs and complicating
its efforts to construct an effective strategic bombing capability.

The results of the Pentagon Talks reflect at the least a settled
American view that there were valid United States interests in
resisting Soviet expansion in Europe and the Middle East. As
Charles Bohlen, the counselor of the State Department, had written
the previous August, "The United States is confronted with a con-
dition in the world which is at direct variance with the assumptions
upon which, during and directly after the war, major United States
policies were predicated."[87] Carefully calculated appreciations of
national interest by State Department officials with considerable
input from the Pentagon had, in the two and a half years since the
end of hostilities, merged with public outrage over Soviet domination of Eastern European countries and Moscow's unrelenting
antipathy towards the United States and the British Common-

wealth. There was an American willingness to accept the fact that, in Bohlen's words, "there are, in short, two worlds instead of one." The United States, he added, should become involved in the "drawing together and consolidation of the non-Soviet world."[88] Even Admiral Leahy, who had strong reservations about American involvement in Greek and Turkish affairs, now felt that "the only possibility of establishing a durable peace in Europe is by the establishment of a balance of military power between Western and Eastern Europe."[89]

NOTES

1. For background on this important political group, whose role is often neglected, see Ronald Radosh, *Prophets on the Right: Profiles of Conservative Critics of American Globalism* (New York: Simon and Schuster, 1975); and Justus D. Doenecke, *Not to the Swift: The Old Isolationists in the Cold War Era* (Lewisburg, Pa.: Bucknell University Press, 1979).

2. See John Lewis Gaddis, *The United States and the Origins of the Cold War, 1941-1947* (New York: Columbia University Press, 1972), pp. 294-96.

3. In a conversation between Truman and Byrnes on 5 January 1946, Truman reportedly emphasized the need to stop "babying the Soviets" and take a much firmer line. The two men later gave radically different accounts of the tone of the meeting, but there seems little doubt that at that time Truman was concerned that continued efforts to pursue a conciliatory policy towards the Soviet Union would play into the hands of Republican critics of his administration. See the careful treatment of this incident by Robert L. Messer, *The End of an Alliance: James F. Byrnes, Roosevelt, Truman and the Origins of the Cold War* (Chapel Hill, N.C.: University of North Carolina Press, 1982), pp. 156-66.

4. Address by the Secretary of State, 28 February 1946, *Department of State Bulletin* 14 (10 March 1946): 355-58.

5. Fraser Harbutt, "American Challenge, Soviet Response: The Beginning of the Cold War, February-May, 1946," *Political Science Quarterly* 96 (Winter 1981-1982): 624; see also Gaddis, *United States and the Origins of the Cold War*, pp. 282-315.

6. "UNO: Great Commoner," *Time*, 18 February 1946, pp. 25-26.

7. Quoted in Anderson, *United States, Great Britain, and the Cold War*, p. 109.

8. Churchill's title for the address was "The Sinews of Peace." It is reprinted in *Churchill: Complete Speeches*, 7: 7285-93.

9. See Hathaway, *Ambiguous Partnership*, pp. 240-42; Anderson, *United States, Great Britain, and the Cold War*, pp. 114-16.

10. Henry B. Ryan, "A New Look at Churchill's 'Iron Curtain' Speech," *Historical Journal* 22 (December 1979): 903-5.

11. For the impact of this message, see George F. Kennan, *Memoirs, 1925-1950* (Boston: Little, Brown, 1967), pp. 293-97; Forrestal, *Diaries*, pp. 135-40; John Lewis Gaddis, *Strategies of Containment*, pp. 19-21.

12. Kennan to Byrnes, 22 February 1946, *FRUS* 1946, 6: 706, 707.

13. Butler to Sargent, 25 September 1946, FO 371/51731; the same point is made in Embassy Washington to Foreign Office, Weekly Political Summary, 22 June 1946, FO 371/51608.

14. This incident has been discussed by Robert J. Donovan, *Conflict and Crisis: The Presidency of Harry S Truman, 1945-1948* (New York: W. W. Norton, 1977), pp. 222-28; and J. Samuel Walker, *Henry A. Wallace and American Foreign Policy* (Westport, Conn.: Greenwood Press, 1976), pp. 149-58.

15. See Mark, "American Policy toward Eastern Europe," pp. 333-34.

16. See Patricia Dawson Ward, *The Threat of Peace: James F. Byrnes and the Council of Foreign Ministers, 1945-1946* (Kent, Ohio: Kent State University Press, 1979); John Gimbel, *The Origins of the Marshall Plan* (Stanford, Calif.: Stanford University Press, 1976), pp. 97-111.

17. Clay, *Decision in Germany*, p. 78; Bullock, *Bevin*, pp. 309-10. As Bullock writes, "Neither [the Americans nor the British] had much doubt that the logical conclusion was the establishment of a West German government, but both were careful to avoid any move which could be taken to commit them to this" (p. 309).

18. Anglo-American differences over Palestine presented a major exception to the generally increasing cooperation between the two countries. The British attempted to avoid permanently antagonizing Arab opinion by refusing to allow large numbers of displaced persons from Europe to emigrate to the Palestine mandate. American officials were sympathetic to this concern, but the Truman administration supported such emigration and the creation of an independent state of Israel. Bevin and Attlee swallowed their resentment of Washington's policies in order to get on with more important areas of Anglo-American cooperation. See Bullock, *Bevin*, pp. 164-83, 254-58, 292-306, 559-65; also Richard Leonard Jasse, "Zion Abandoned: Great Britain's Withdrawal from the Palestine Mandate, 1945-1948" (Ph.D. dissertation, Catholic University, 1980).

19. On the British loan see Hathaway, *Ambiguous Partnership*, pp. 186-201, 230-48; Gardner, *Sterling-Dollar Diplomacy*, pp. 188-254; Richard P. Hedlund, "Congress and the British Loan, 1945-1946: A Congressional Study" (Ph.D. dissertation, University of Kentucky, 1976).

20. *New York Times*, 24 October 1946, quoted by Bullock, *Bevin*, p. 314.

21. "Recent Developments in Anglo-Soviet Relations," 15 February 1947, Bohlen Papers, Legislative and Diplomatic Branch, NA.

22. See, for instance, Memorandum for the Secretary, JCS, 17 December 1945, RG 218, CCS 092 United States (12-21-45), which forwarded a State Department document suggesting that "within the limits of the principles of our foreign policy, we must act as mediator and conciliator between Britain and Russia."

23. JCS 1641/3, 13 March 1946, RG 218, CCS 092 USSR (3-27-45), section 6. See also Walter S. Poole, "From Conciliation to Containment: The Joint Chiefs of Staff and the Coming of the Cold War, 1945-1946," *Military Affairs* 42 (February 1978): 14.

24. Memorandum by Matthews, 1 April 1946, *FRUS* 1946, 1: 1170.

25. Poole, "Conciliation to Containment": 14.

26. Ibid., p. 16 n. 17.

27. The Clifford memorandum was published in Arthur Krock, *Memoirs: Sixty Years on the Firing Line* (New York: Funk and Wagnalls, 1968), pp. 419-82.

28. Krock, *Sixty Years*, p. 476.

29. Ibid., p. 478.

30. Ibid., p. 479.

31. Forrestal to Truman, 25 July 1946, Clifford Papers, Box 15, File: Russia, HSTL.

32. Leahy to Truman, 26 July 1946, Clifford Papers, Box 14, File: Russia, HSTL.

33. Patterson to Truman, 27 July 1946, Clifford Papers, Box 15, File: Russia, HSTL.

34. George Elsey Papers, Box 63, File: Foreign Relations-Russia (1946-Report "American Relations with the Soviet Union"), Folder: 9, HSTL.

35. See Margaret Truman, *Harry S. Truman* (New York: William Morrow, 1973), p. 347. Daniel Yergin, believing that the Clifford memorandum had major significance in defining U.S. policy, suggests that it indicated that "the Americans were convinced that they faced a cunning, sure-footed enemy, engaged in a never-ending drive for world hegemony" (*Shattered Peace*, p. 245). More likely, Clifford and Elsey were attempting to describe U.S. policy in a way which would not run against the grain of traditional American distaste for the old world entanglements which defense and foreign policy officials in Washington then were coming to advocate. In any event, as Elsey would later recall, "There was no group of White House staff members who were regarded as foreign policy experts or

who were *expected* to be foreign policy experts." (George M. Elsey, Oral History Interview [Independence, Mo.: HSTL, 1974], pp. 354-55).

36. Henderson to Byrnes, 13 November 1945, *FRUS* 1945, 8: 14, 16.

37. See Bruce Robellet Kuniholm, *The Origins of the Cold War in the Near East: Great Power Conflict and Diplomacy in Iran, Turkey, and Greece* (Princeton, N.J.: Princeton University Press, 1980), pp. 304-50, 383-98.

38. See Jonathan Knight, "America's International Guarantees for the Straits: Prelude to the Truman Doctrine," *Middle Eastern Studies* 13 (May 1977): 248-49.

39. Byrnes to Wilson, 30 October 1945, *FRUS* 1945, 8: 1265-66.

40. Wilson to Byrnes, 5 November 1945, *FRUS* 1945, 8: 1269-70.

41. Quoted in Harry N. Howard, *Turkey, the Straits and U.S. Policy* (Baltimore, Md.: Johns Hopkins University Press, 1974), p. 240.

42. See above p. 63.

43. Wilson to Byrnes, 23 March 1946, *FRUS* 1946, 7: 821-22.

44. JCS to Patterson and Forrestal, 23 August 1946, *FRUS* 1946, 7: 857-58.

45. Acheson to Byrnes, 15 August 1946, *FRUS* 1946, 7: 840-42.

46. See Knight, "American Statecraft and the 1946 Black Sea Straits Controversy": 474.

47. Acheson to Byrnes, 15 August 1946, *FRUS* 1946, 7: 840; Acheson to Wilson, 16 August 1946, *FRUS* 1946, 7: 843.

48. Acheson to Wilson, 8 November 1946, *FRUS* 1946, 7: 916-17; see also Memorandum on Turkey prepared in the Division of Near Eastern Affairs, 21 October 1946, *FRUS* 1946, 7: 894-97.

49. See *Department of State Bulletin* 15 (1 September 1945): 415-19; *FRUS* 1946, 6: 955-56. Relations with Belgrade had been tense since the final weeks of World War II when Yugoslav troops, which had occupied parts of Austria, were obliged to withdraw as a result of a joint demarche by Churchill and a somewhat reluctant Truman; see Herbert Feis, *Churchill, Roosevelt, Stalin: The War They Waged and the Peace They Sought* (Princeton, N.J.: Princeton University Press, 1957), pp. 626-32; Feis, *Between War and Peace*, pp. 39-51, 280-86.

50. Byrnes to Acheson, 22 August 1946, *FRUS* 1946, 6: 927; Acheson to Byrnes, 22 August 1946, *FRUS* 1946, 6: 927-28.

51. See Selser, "The Bomber's Role in Diplomacy."

52. See Hathaway, *Ambiguous Partnership*, p. 141. For a discusison of the Trieste question, see Bogdan C. Novak, *Trieste, 1941-1954: The Ethnic, Political and Ideological Struggle* (Chicago: University of Chicago Press, 1970); and Robert G. Rabel, "Between East and West: Trieste, the United States and the Cold War, 1943-1954," (Ph.D. dissertation, Duke University, 1984).

53. Memorandum of Conversation by Hiss, 9 September 1946, *FRUS 1946*, 7: 208. Subsequent investigation has indicated that the unrest in northern Greece was probably not a result of direct Soviet instigation. Stalin apparently adhered to his "percentages deal" in regard to Greece and Tito's support for the Greek insurgency may have contributed to the fissures then beginning to emerge between Moscow and Belgrade. Albanian support for Greek rebels was evident and was probably not unrelated to Athens' efforts to claim Northern Epirus. See Lawrence S. Wittner, *American Intervention in Greece, 1943-1949* (New York: Columbia University Press, 1982), pp. 57-60; William H. McNeill, "The View from Greece," in *Witnesses to the Origins of the Cold War*, ed. Thomas T. Hammond (Seattle, Wash.: University of Washington Press, 1982), p. 127; Kuniholm, *Origins of the Cold War in the Near East*, pp. 402-4; D. G. Kousoulas, "The Truman Doctrine and the Stalin-Tito Rift: A Reappraisal," *South Atlantic Quarterly* 72 (Summer 1973): 427-39; on Greek-Albanian relations, see especially Jacobs to Byrnes, 21 September 1946, *FRUS 1946*, 7: 222.

54. McNeill, "The View from Greece," p. 120.

55. Memorandum Prepared in the Office of Near Eastern and African Affairs, 21 October 1946, *FRUS 1946*, 7: 242.

56. Clayton to Johnson, 5 September 1946, *FRUS 1946*, 7: 199.

57. MacVeagh to Byrnes, 11 September 1946, *FRUS 1946*, 7: 209.

58. Acheson to Byrnes, 11 October 1946, *FRUS 1946*, 7: 236 n.2.

59. Acheson to MacVeagh, 8 November 1946, *FRUS 1946*, 7: 263; see also Memorandum by British Embassy in Greece to American Embassy in Greece, 5 November 1946, describing a conversation between Byrnes and the British minister of defence, A. V. Alexander, on 15 October 1946, *FRUS 1946*, 7: 913-15.

60. Byrnes to Truman, RG 59, 868.00/12-2046. In fact, the State Department did authorize the transfer to the Greek government of eight C-47 transport aircraft which the British were unable to supply, but RAF pilots were asked to ferry the planes from Cairo to Athens; see Acheson to MacVeagh, 13 December 1946, *FRUS 1946*, 7: 278-9.

61. Kuniholm, *Origins of the Cold War in the Near East*, p. 382.

62. The two British notes are printed in *FRUS 1947*, 5: 32-37. The extent to which the British were waiting for a timely moment to present the notes has been much discussed; see Anderson, *United States, Great Britain and the Cold War*, pp. 171-75; Hugh Dalton, *High Tide and After: Memoirs, 1945-1960* (London: Frederick Muller, 1962), pp. 206-9; Peter G. Boyle, "The British Foreign Office and American Foreign Policy, 1947-1948," *Journal of American Studies* 16 (December 1982): 373-789; Bullock, *Bevin*, pp. 338-40, 368-71; a version emphasizing British exasperation with Greek politicians is found in Louis, *British Empire in the Middle East*, pp. 93-102.

63. Joseph M. Jones, *The Fifteen Weeks (February 21-June 5, 1947)* (New York: Harcourt, Brace and World: A Harbinger Book, 1964, originally published 1955), p. 130. Jones was special assistant to the assistant secretary of state for public affairs.

64. Ibid., pp. 135, 138.

65. Ibid., p. 142. Acheson in his memoirs recalled telling the assembled legislators, "In the past eighteen months . . . Soviet pressure on the Straits, on Iran, and on northern Greece had brought the Balkans to the point where a highly possible Soviet breakthrough might open three continents to Soviet penetration. Like apples in a barrel infected by one rotten one, the corruption of Greece would infect Iran and all to the east. It would also carry infection to Africa through Asia Minor and Egypt, and to Europe through Italy and France, already threatened by the strongest domestic Communist parties in Western Europe. The Soviet Union was playing one of the greatest gambles in history at minimal cost. It did not need to win all the possibilities. Even one or two offered immense gains. We and we alone were in a position to break up the play. These were the stakes that British withdrawal from the eastern Mediterranean offered to an eager and ruthless opponent." *Present at the Creation: My Years at the State Department* (New York: W. W. Norton, 1969), p. 219.

66. Eric F. Goldman, *The Crucial Decade—and After: America: 1945-1960* (New York: Vantage Books, A Division of Random House, 1960), p. 59.

67. The speech is printed in United States, *Public Papers of the Presidents: Harry S. Truman, 1947* (Washington: Government Printing Office, 1963), pp. 176-80.

68. Acheson, *Present at the Creation*, pp. 221-22.

69. Quoted by C. P. Trussell, "Greek Aid Favored on Reserved Basis," *New York Times*, 7 March 1947. The significance of the administration's shift was not lost on British observers. A Foreign Office commentator considered Truman's address the "most heartening development in many months." Gallman to Marshall, 13 March 1947, RG 59, 868.00/3-1347. Harold Macmillan, then a Tory backbencher, asked the House of Commons, "Has there ever been a more dramatic reversal of policy than that of the United States towards Greece in two short years? Has there ever been a more complete endorsement of British policy?" Great Britain, Parliament, *Parliamentary Debates* (House of Commons), 5th series, 437 (1947): 1945. Subsequent references to *Parliamentary Debates* will be abbreviated according to the following model: 437 H.C. Deb. 5s. 1945 (16 May 1947). See also Macmillan's *Tides of Fortune, 1945-1955* (London: Macmillan, 1969), p. 114.

70. Department of State to the British Embassy, 1 March 1947, *FRUS 1947*, 5: 72. The British had agreed with the Soviets to withdraw their

troops from Greece ninety days after the entry into force of the Bulgarian peace treaty.

71. Memorandum of Conversation by Acheson, 8 March 1947, *FRUS* 1947, 7: 105.

72. Memorandum of Conversation by Marshall, 22 March 1947, *FRUS* 1947, 5: 128-29; Marshall to Acheson, 11 April 1947, *FRUS* 1947, 5: 141-42.

73. Public Law 75, 22 May 1947, Section 3(e).

74. Acheson to Marshall, 12 April 1947, *FRUS*, 1947, 78: 144.

75. See Sheehy, "The United States Navy in the Mediterranean," p. 274.

76. See COS (47) 116th Meeting, 5 September 1947, DEFE 4/6; United States, Congress, Senate, Committee on Foreign Relations, *Report on S. 938, Assistance to Greece and Turkey*, Senate Report 90, 80th Cong., 1st sess., 1947, p. 15.

77. Douglas to Marshall, 1 September 1947, *FRUS* 1947, 5: 323; COS (47) 128th Meeting, 15 October 1947, DEFE 4/6.

78. Memorandum prepared in the Department of State, undated, *FRUS* 1947, 5: 514.

79. Memorandum of conversation by Hare, 9 October 1947, *FRUS* 1947, 5: 561.

80. Papers relating to the Pentagon Talks of 1947 are printed in *FRUS* 1947, 5: 485-626.

81. Draft Notes for Remarks by the United Kingdom at the Opening of the United States-United Kingdom Talks on the Middle East, 16 October 1947, *FRUS* 1947, 5: 566-67.

82. Ibid.

83. Memorandum prepared in the Department of State, "The American Paper," undated, *FRUS* 1947, 5: 575-76.

84. Lovett to Marshall, 25 November 1947, *FRUS* 1947, 5: 1289 n. 5; Note of Discussion between the Secretary of State and Mr. Marshall, 24 November 1947, FO 371/61114.

85. Jones to Henderson, 8 December 1947, *FRUS* 1947, 5: 625. General Hollis felt, after all the effort put into the talks, "a little crestfallen" at the meager results; Leslie C. Hollis, *One Marine's Tale* (London: Andre Deutsch, 1956), p. 157.

86. JCS to Secretary of Defense, 19 November 1947, RG 218, CCS 381 EMMEA (11-19-47), section 1, quoted in Condit, *History of the Joint Chiefs of Staff*, p. 28; see also Leahy, diary entry for 19 November 1947, Leahy Papers, LC.

87. Memorandum by Bohlen, 30 August 1947, *FRUS* 1947, 1: 763.

88. Ibid., 763, 764.

89. Leahy, diary entry for 31 December 1947, Leahy Papers, LC.

CHAPTER 6

FROM LONDON TO
BRUSSELS TO NATO

At the meeting of the Council of Foreign Ministers in London in November-December 1947 it became apparent that a final impasse between East and West had been reached. The Western powers found Soviet proposals for German unification unacceptable and they were not prepared to forego their plans to introduce economic reform measures in Germany which they considered vital for the resuscitation of the European economy as a whole. Compromise seemed impossible. The United States, Britain and France concluded that they would have to attempt a resolution of the German question themselves; otherwise a collapsing German economy would bring down all of Western Europe, including the United Kingdom. All recognized that economic policies would have to be changed to encourage the gradual raising of levels of production and promote German economic self-sufficiency.

Marshall adjourned the council without arranging for a future meeting. The French now agreed to join their zone to Bizonia in the spring of 1948. The collapse of the council not only set the stage for new economic policies, but also led Bevin to consider that the time had arrived to tackle as well the defense questions that he considered closely related. As noted earlier, various proposals had been made during and immediately after the war for closer British relations with the Western European countries. After the signing of the Anglo-French Treaty of Dunkirk of March 1947, Belgium and the Netherlands had expressed interest in entering into an alliance with the British and the French. This possibility was weighed by the Foreign Office and the Chiefs of Staff during 1947. Bevin, despite enthusiasm for the project, realized that overtly rapid movement towards the creation of a broad alliance would appear to split Europe into blocs and make relations with the Soviet Union over Germany even more difficult. Once, however, the foreign ministers had definitely failed to reach a decision on the all-important German question, Bevin saw closer relations with the Western European states as the only way to stabilize western Germany's political and economic situation and to bring the west German economy into a working relationship with those of its neighbors. Bevin's ideas were not immediately crystallized, but he set to work at once to provide a security linkage among the United States, Britain and the West Europeans, a goal he doggedly pursued for the rest of his tenure at the Foreign Office.

BEVIN'S INITIATIVE

The Council of Foreign Ministers had been adjourned on 15 December; two days later Bevin spoke with Bidault and then met informally with Marshall. The British foreign secretary suggested that in view of the failure of the council it was time to decide on the next step:

His own idea was that we must devise some western democratic system comprising the Americans, ourselves, France, Italy etc. and of course the Dominions. This would not be a formal alliance, but an understanding backed by power, money and resolute action. It would be a sort of spiritual federation of the west.[1]

He noted the need for discussions of the future of western Germany being held among the British, French and Americans with the aim of creating "an eventually united Germany." Beyond this, however, Bevin emphasized the problem of security, recalling that there had been some idea of a three-Power treaty on the lines of the original Byrnes Treaty. He himself thought it might be better to have some treaty or understanding which also brought in Benelux and Italy. The communist inroads would be stopped. The issues must be defined and clear.[2]

Marshall agreed with the need for continued American cooperation with Britain and other West European states and referred to the "material regeneration" which would result from the European Recovery Program, as the Marshall Plan was officially known. Further, the American secretary of state "felt that what was already being done on the material plane should now be given greater dignity. But it was not necessarily [necessary?] to write everything down in detail."[3]

Although further discussions in London appear to have been related to technical questions regarding the German problem, it was in this rather oblique and offhand manner that the first direct steps were taken towards an Atlantic alliance. Marshall's concept of providing greater "dignity" to current European plans of cooperation was a tacit and perhaps unconscious association of American foreign policy with the British foreign secretary's larger design which was shortly to become publicly known.[4]

The day following the conversation with Marshall, Bevin had vented his exasperation with Moscow's policies to the House of Commons:

We have no aim and no desire to divide the world. But the termination of the Conference and the manner of its ending, I have no doubt, will cause many people furiously to think. We cannot go on as we have been going on. We have hoped against hope that four-Power collaboration would work. Most of the world Powers can find a basis of agreement; they cannot all be wrong.[5]

Early in January 1948, Bevin set forth more fully developed ideas to the cabinet. Echoing Churchill's address at Fulton almost two years earlier, the Labour foreign secretary pointed out:

It must be recognised that the Soviet Government has formed a solid political and economic block behind a line running from the Baltic along the Oder, through Trieste to the Black Sea. There is no prospect in the immediate future that we shall be able to re-establish and maintain normal relations with European countries behind that line. . . .

In the situation in which we have been placed by Russian policy halfmeasures are useless. If we are to preserve peace and our own safety at the same time, we can only do so by the mobilisation of such a moral and material force as will create confidence and energy on the one side and inspire respect and caution on the other. The alternative is to acquiesce in continued Russian infiltration and helplessly to witness the piecemeal collapse of one Western bastion after another.

Bevin advocated that Great Britain must in response

organise and consolidate the ethical and spiritual forces inherent in this Western civilisation of which we are the chief protagonists. This in my view can only be done by creating some form of union in Western Europe, whether of a formal or informal character, backed by the Americans and the Dominions.

Bevin envisioned a Western democratic system, but not necessarily a formal alliance, comprising, in addition to the United Kingdom, Scandinavia, the Low Countries, France, Portugal, Italy and Greece. Eventually the system would include Spain and Germany "without whom no Western system can be complete."[6]

The following day Bevin set out another memorandum providing his analysis of the drift of Soviet foreign policy, arguing that Moscow "is actively hostile to British interests everywhere." Underlining a key British concern, he pointed to

the deflection of the food resources of Eastern Germany, Poland, and Hungary to the East [that] largely deprives Western Europe of important sources of non-dollar supplies, and worsens the balance of payments position of Western Germany and Western Europe, with incalculable effects upon our own economic position.

The Russian threat was portrayed largely in economic terms; Bevin suggested that Moscow believed that the fruits of war could be obtained without having to engage in hostilities. The Soviets, he suggested,

probably realise that for the present at any rate their long-term chances in a war against the West are not good and that the best result they could hope for would be mutual destruction. Technically they are still backward compared with the Americans and ourselves, and their war losses were heavier.

Nevertheless, Moscow and its policies presented a clear danger to Britain:

It is evident that if the Russian political plans for Southern and Western Europe were to succeed, they would be in a position . . . to put us in a hopeless position strategically. Their submarine fleet, in which they are incorporating all the latest German inventions, would be operating from forward bases and would be a serious menace to our sea communciations. They would be in a position to dominate the Mediterranean and the difficulty of defending our interests in Africa and the Middle East would be immeasurably increased, quite apart from any direct threat to the Middle East.

Without the oil reserves of South Persia and the Middle East neither the British Government nor even America can exert their full strength. Furthermore, the threat to the security of these islands would be very great. Finally, the Russians have developed and improved the V1s and V2s, to say nothing of other secrct German weapons and of inventions of their own.

It is thus evident that the success of Russian expansionist plans would threaten, if not destroy, the three main elements of Commonwealth defence, the security of the United Kingdom, the control of sea communications, and the defence of the Middle East.[7]

A third memorandum from Bevin to his colleagues, dealing with British publicity policy, was designed to demonstrate to his Labour colleagues the distinctive approach of a socialist government to a Communist challenge. He noted that "Soviet propaganda has, since the end of the war, carried on in every sphere a vicious attack against the British Commonwealth and against Western democracy." In response:

It is for us, as Europeans and as a Social Democratic Government, and not the Americans, to give the lead in spiritual, moral and political spheres to all the democratic elements in Western Europe which are anti-Communist and, at the same time, genuinely progressive and reformist, believing in freedom, planning and social justice—what one might call the "Third Force." . . .

In general we should emphasise the weakness of Communism rather than its strength. Contemporary American propaganda, which stresses the strength and aggressiveness of Communism tends to scare and unbalance the anti-Communists, while heartening the fellow-travelers and encouraging the Communists to bluff more extravagantly. Our propaganda, by dwelling on Russia's poverty and backwardness, could be expected to relax rather than to raise the international tension.[8]

The British cabinet considered these memoranda at a meeting on 8 January 1948 and approved them with the suggestion that:

It would be necessary to work out more precisely the purposes for which a closer union of Western Europe was to be advocated. Co-operation might be for the purpose of defence or in economic or cultural fields; but, unless some positive point of focus were devised, it would be difficult to make any satisfactory progress. It might be advisable, in the first instance, to try to work out the basic principles in consultation with the French Government.

The cabinet noted further that:

It would give much-needed encouragement to the Social Democratic leaders in Germany if in any proposals for closer union in Western Europe it was made clear that there would in due course be a place for Germany in the union.[9]

NEGOTIATION COMMENCES

The State Department was given advance notice of this decision. On 13 January 1948 Lord Inverchapel, the British ambassador in Washington, sent Marshall an outline of Bevin's views generally along the lines of his cabinet memoranda:

It is clear that from secure entrenchments behind their lines the Russians are exerting a consistently increasing pressure which threatens the whole fabric of the West. In some Western countries the danger is still latent, but in others the conflicting forces are already at grips with one another. The Soviet Government has based its policy on the expectation that Western Europe will sink into economic chaos and they can be relied upon to place every possible obstacle in the path of American aid and of Western European recovery.

The proposals Bevin had made to Marshall in the previous month were reiterated:

We should seek to form with the backing of the Americas and the Dominions a Western Democratic system comprising Scandinavia, the Low Countries, France, Italy, Greece and possibly Portugal. As soon as circumstances permit we should, of course, wish also to include Spain and Germany without whom no Western system can be complete.[10]

The American response to Bevin's proposal was completely favorable at that point. Marshall wrote to Inverchapel:

The initiative which he [Bevin] is taking in this matter will be warmly applauded in the United States. I want him to know that his proposal has deeply interested and moved me and that I wish to see the United States do everything which it properly can in assisting the European nations in bringing a project along this line to fruition.[11]

Hickerson elaborated on Marshall's message in a conversation with Inverchapel on 21 January 1948. Dealing with the issue of United States involvement in a European defense structure, Hickerson suggested that there were two general alternatives:

He had envisaged the creation of a third force which was not merely the extension of US influence but a real European organization strong enough to say "no" both to the Soviet Union and to the United States, if our actions should seem so to require. We would be willing to take our chance in dealing with any such organization of freedom-loving nations confident that we could settle any differences with them.

On the other hand, should the

European nations decide that no regional defense organization could be completed without the United States and that this would give, as Lord Inverchapel had suggested, more assurance to the smaller nations, we felt that this country would be sympathetically disposed and would at least give it very careful consideration. If it were closely associated with the Charter of the United Nations, it might receive a favorable reception. The important aspect of this question was, however, that any such concept should be and should give the impression that it is based primarily on European intitiative.[12]

After Inverchapel had briefed the State Department, Bevin brought the conclusions of the cabinet meeting of 8 January 1948 to the House of Commons on 22 January. Bevin described

a policy on the part of the Soviet Union to use every means in their power to get Communist control in Eastern Europe, and, as it now appears, in the West as well. It therefore matters little how we temporise, and maybe appease, or try to make arrangements.

Bevin noted Soviet and Communist policies in Eastern Europe, Greece, Trieste, Germany and the "flood of abuse against ourselves and the world by M. Vyshinski [the Soviet representative at the United Nations] in New York." His primary point was that "the free nations of Western Europe must now draw closely together. . . . I believe the time ripe for a consolidation of Western Europe." Reaffirming that close relations with France, as reflected in the Dunkirk Treaty, represented "an important nucleus in Western Europe," Bevin indicated that talks were being proposed with Belgium, the Netherlands and Luxemburg and that "we shall have to consider the question of associating other historic members of European civilisation, including the new Italy, in this great conception." Bevin also took note of the potential contribution of the vast colonial holdings of the European states.[13]

Bevin's grand design for the free world as anticipated in his cabinet memoranda and in his speech to the House of Commons represents a major turning point in postwar history. In the historiography of the period it has been given little attention, while buckets of ink have been expended on explications of the Truman Doctrine and Churchill's speech at Fulton. Yet Bevin's policy, as first publicly set forth in January 1948, was perhaps much more significant; it led directly to fundamental changes in international relations while the Truman Doctrine and the Iron Curtain address impacted most directly on generalized public opinion in the United States. The creation of the Western European Union by the Treaty of Brussels of March 1948 was a direct result of Bevin's initiative; Brussels was NATO in embryo. Bevin clearly indicated that western Germany would be integrated into Western Europe along with Italy and even Spain. All this has come to pass. Bevin set forth the method of dealing with the Soviet Union—the creation of a strong and united West which could "inspire respect and caution" on the part of Moscow. This too has been characteristic of subsequent international relations.

Bevin clearly understood, as many at the time did not, the close relationship between military strength on the one hand and political stability and economic development on the other. He appreciated that all the economic assistance which Washington made available would not be useful without a sense of security on the part of the Western Europeans, and that this required a firm conviction that they would not be an easy prey to either military attack or political subversion. Bevin knew also that this conviction would depend not just on a few American superweapons but also upon cooperation among the states of Western Europe for their own defense. The persuasive logic of the shrewd analyst merged with the fierce determination of a lifelong trade union organizer to mold and shape the policies of Europe and North America for more than one generation.

The Brussels Treaty, the first step in Bevin's design, was negotiated in early March by British, French and Benelux diplomats. The Benelux countries clearly realized that they would always be vulnerable and isolated if they could not associate themselves with the larger European states. After lengthy discussion of the best form for a security guarantee, the Dunkirk formulation regarding defense against Germany was, in part as a result of advice given by Hickerson,[14] rejected as inappropriate since it was clear beyond quibble that the threat now came from the Soviet Union. The five countries signed the Treaty of Economic, Social and Cultural Collaboration and Collective Self-Defence at Brussels on 17 March 1948. Article IV of the treaty read:

If any of the High Contracting Parties should be the object of an armed attack in Europe, the other High Contracting Parties will, in accordance with the provisions of Article 51 of the Charter of the United Nations, afford the Party so attacked all the military and other aid and assistance in their power.[15]

Much of the impetus for the quick agreement on the Brussels Treaty derived from an immediate fear of further Communist takeovers. The treaty was signed in the shadow of the Communist coup in Czechoslovakia in late February 1948, continuing difficulties over Berlin, rumors of Soviet pressure on Norway and Finland, persisting insurgency in Greece and intense political agitation on the part of the Communist parties of France and Italy.

The historian John Baylis has written that Bevin "saw it more in terms of a convenient device to convince the Americans that West European states were prepared to stand on their own feet. That, he hoped, like his initiative after Marshall's Harvard speech, would encourage direct American participation."[16] President Truman's response was gratifying; he welcomed the Brussels Treaty on the day of its signature in a speech delivered in person to a joint session of Congress. Truman criticized the Soviets for having "persistently obstructed the work of the United Nations by constant abuse of the veto," and hailed the Brussels Treaty whose

significance goes far beyond the actual terms of the agreement itself. It is a notable step in the direction of unity in Europe for the protection and preservation of its civilization. This development deserves our full support. I am confident that the United States will, by appropriate means, extend to the free nations the support which the situation requires. I am sure that the determination of the free countries of Europe to protect themselves will be matched by an equal determination on our part to help them to protect themselves.[17]

Truman's forceful words to Congress on 17 March, in large measure responsive to the Communist coup in Prague, did not reflect the persisting ambivalence within the U.S. government (and perhaps within the president's own mind) regarding a formal defense relationship with the Europeans. The negotiating process, which has been described in a number of authoritative accounts,[18] demonstrates the extent to which Bevin and his colleagues kept constant pressure on the American administration, which was beset by inevitable opposition in Congress and differences within the State Department as well as a determination by the JCS and Forrestal that any assistance to the Europeans must not come at the expense of efforts to meet the United States' own pressing needs. Bevin succeeded in large measure because of a number of like-minded American officials and as a direct result of the public reaction to the Communist coup in Czechoslovakia, Soviet pressure on Norway and Finland, Communist agitation in France and Italy and the steadily increasing tension in Germany which culminated in the imposition of the Berlin blockade in June 1948.

Throughout the first half of 1948 Bevin again and again sought Washington's support for and involvement in an Atlantic security system that would provide the French and other West Europeans the necessary security for reconstructing their societies. This was a long-term proposition. As the crisis atmosphere in Europe intensified, Bevin and his colleagues also sought to involve American military representatives in planning for military actions in case of a sudden Soviet attack. The two approaches came together only later, after the signing of the North Atlantic Treaty and, in reality, the establishment of credible defenses in West Europe was assured only in the 1950s after Bevin's death.

The British were the ones who were doing the asking; they desperately desired American military support and eventual U.S. participation in a defensive alliance. The United States had the strength, both in material and morale, which the British and the Europeans lacked. If the U.S. government proceeded in these negotiations with a certain amount of reluctance, the reason was that the American people would have to foot the bill and plan for the possibility of yet another European war. The U.S. government and the American people came through, it seems in retrospect, without excessive or undue delay and have continued to play an important role alongside their allies in maintaining West European defenses. What is striking, contrary to much of the historiography dealing with this period, is the hesitancy shown by senior American officials faced with involvement in European defense arrangements.

On 27 January 1948 Inverchapel, following up Bevin's initiatives, told Under Secretary of State Robert Lovett that the foreign secretary desired to see the United States and Britain consider "the possibilities of concluding some defense agreement between them to provide against aggression which could reinforce the defense project Mr. Bevin had proposed for Western Europe."[19] Not as enthusiastic as Marshall had earlier been to a more generalized British proposal, Lovett appeared to be somewhat taken aback, remarking that "what Mr. Bevin was now suggesting would in fact mean consideration of a military alliance between the United States and Great Britain." He quickly added that any such approach would have to be considered by the National Security Council, the president and congressional leaders—which Inverchapel would be sure to appreciate as a daunting prospect.[20]

Inverchapel was not to be put off. In a follow-up letter he described Bevin's desire for American support. The foreign secretary, he wrote, considered that

> the treaties that are being proposed cannot be fully effective nor be relied upon when a crisis arises unless there is assurance of American support for the defence of Western Europe. The plain truth is that Western Europe cannot yet stand on its own feet without assurance of support.[21]

On 2 February 1948 Lovett formally replied to the British. He noted the complications involved in such discussions and suggested that any American involvement at the preliminary stage of negotiations would be premature. He suggested, however, that once the Europeans had decided upon appropriate defense measures the United States would consider what role it could play.[22]

Lovett was aware not only of the political problems that the British initiative would create, but also of opposition from within the State and Defense Departments. George Kennan, the director of the Policy Planning Staff, joined by Charles Bohlen, the counselor of the State Department, were skeptical of the advisability of creating a military alliance between the West European countries and the United States. Their opposition (not recalled by Bohlen in his memoirs, but discussed at considerable length in those of Kennan[23]) was based on the belief that a formal alliance and a permanent U.S. military presence in Europe were inconsistent with American tradition and unlikely to be continued in the long run. They saw, as Kennan wrote some months later, the appropriate eventual goal to be a withdrawal of both U.S. and Soviet troops from the "heart of Europe" and "the encouragement of the growth of a third force which can absorb and take over the territories between the two."[24] Yet Kennan and Bohlen were both well aware of the need for the United States to provide military support to the Western Europeans and both encouraged close cooperation in defense planning. Neither pushed his opposition forcefully and, in the end, it may have served as a useful corrective to the enthusiasm of Hickerson and others who tended to be in advance of what the American political process could bear.

Skepticism from the Pentagon was based on concern that funds badly needed for American requirements not be directed into a bottomless pit of European rearmament. For instance, in mid-April 1948 the JCS urged that supplying machine tools to the European countries for their rearmament be considered "only when their exploitation does not interfere with our own needs and that due consideration should be given to the possibility that the Soviets may easily capture armament plants in certain locations."[25] Later in the month they reiterated the point in a letter to Forrestal affirming their belief that assistance to the Europeans was desirable, but that

it is also clear that its extent must be limited by the necessity for avoiding either undue reduction of resources essential to our national security or undue interference with our own military requirements. We must also avoid the harmful influence on our global strategy that might result from decision [sic] regarding assistance of this sort dictated by foreign demand rather than appropriateness to strategic plans."[26]

The following month they expressed opposition to "any agreement that might unduly influence or jeopardize our optimum over-all global strategy in favor of either direct military assistance or distribution of equipment." The overall strategy was of course based on strategic bombing attacks, not on ground fighting in Europe.[27]

More significant still was the situation in Congress where the administration was making a major push for Marshall Plan funding in an election year. As Lovett advised Inverchapel on 7 February,

If it became known in Congress that in addition to the economic commitments involved in the European Recovery Program the United States is asked to assume new and extensive military and political commitments it might well adversely affect the prospects for the approval by Congress of the European Recovery Program.[28]

Bevin was no doubt disappointed by evidence of American hesitancy, but he quickly returned to the charge, deploring the possibility of a vicious circle in which the Americans could not discuss involvement in European defense measures until they were agreed

upon by the Europeans, while the latter could not really make
progress unless they could be assured of the security that only the
United States could offer.[29]

Meanwhile the State Department began to face up to the demands Bevin was making of the United States. On 8 March 1948
Hickerson addressed Bevin's importunings in a memorandum to
Marshall. Personally convinced of the need for the United States to
join with the Europeans, Hickerson argued that

no security arrangement for Europe can be effective unless the free European governments and peoples are prepared to pool their resources and to
resist by every means at their disposal, including armed force, any threat to
the independence of any member whether from within or without. A substantial start is being made in the present Anglo-French-Benelux
negotiations. On the other hand, the willingness of this Government to participate in or support such an arrangement is essential to its success and will
enormously increase European confidence that it is possible to prevent
extension of the area of dictatorship and worthwhile to fight if necessary to
prevent it.[30]

Hickerson went on to suggest that the president take up with the
National Security Council and congressional leaders the question
of the "magnitude and nature of the military commitment this government is in a position to assume with respect to Europe," ways to
deter "fifth-column aggression on the Czech model," and the
"possibility of U.S. participation in a North Atlantic-Mediterran-
ean regional defense arrangement. . . ." He recommended that a
security program be separate from, "although parallel and related
to, ERP [the European Recovery Program] to avoid driving the
Scandinavians, Swiss and possibly others out of ERP."[31]

On 11 March 1948, the day after Jan Masaryk, the Czech foreign
minister, jumped or was pushed to his death, Inverchapel once
again sought United States support for Western European defense
arrangements. Noting Soviet efforts to intimidate Norway, the
ambassador indicated that "Mr. Bevin considers that only a bold
move can avert the danger." The British and American governments, he argued,

should study without any delay the establishment of such an Atlantic security system, so that if the threat to Norway should develop, we could at once

inspire the necessary confidence to consolidate the West against Soviet infiltration and at the same time inspire the Soviet Government with enough respect for the West to remove temptation from them and so ensure a long period of peace. The alternative is to repeat our experience with Hitler and to witness helplessly the slow deterioration of our position, until we are forced in much less favourable circumstances to resort to war in order to defend our lives and liberty.[32]

Alarmed by the coup in Prague and concerned about Soviet pressures on Norway and Finland, the administration was finally ready to move. Shortly thereafter Marshall, having spoken with Truman, advised Inverchapel on 12 March 1948 that "we are prepared to proceed at once in the joint discussions on the establishment of an Atlantic security system." He suggested the prompt arrival of British representatives in Washington.[33] A message from Marshall to the French Foreign Minister on the same day further indicated a readiness to discuss the next steps with British and French representatives.[34]

TRIPARTITE TALKS

In his 17 March message to the joint session of Congress, Truman hinted at American cooperation with the Western defense effort. Now with the signing of the Brussels Treaty, reinforced by Bevin's persistent approaches to the State Department as well as the air of crisis hanging over Europe, the administration moved to enter discussions aimed at providing American backing for European security arrangements. The United States had in effect accepted Bevin's premise that the security of Western Europe from Soviet attack had become a vital American interest. This was an event with major implications for American defense policy. The program to aid Greece and Turkey had not involved American ground combat forces, but no one could assume that the same would be true about this commitment to the West Europeans.

The first step in the planning process which Washington had initiated was the holding of six United States-United Kingdom-Canada "Security Conversations" at the Pentagon from 22 March to 1 April 1948. Involving both diplomatic and military officials, these talks addressed the question of American assistance to the Brussels powers and the creation of an eventual Atlantic pact.

Inverchapel and Gladwyn Jebb, who had come over from the Foreign Office, pressed for an American commitment to provide military aid in the event of any aggression in Europe. Ambassador Douglas, who had also returned from London, parried with the suggestion that "US full support should be *assumed*, for the purpose of the current conversations, since such support was more than implied in the president's 17 March message to Congress and since no commitments could be developed in any case without support of the Congress."[35] This position, undoubtedly dictated by concern over the possibility of an election-year leak, was "somewhat reluctantly" accepted by the British representatives.

Much of the attention at these conversations was focused on the question of the relationship between the Brussels powers and the United States, Italy and other countries. U.S. representatives were concerned that any Atlantic alliance include Norway, Denmark and Iceland to ensure U.S. access to North Atlantic bases.[36] The American delegation, aware of inevitable congressional opposition towards an automatic requirement for the United States to go to war, argued in favor of language regarding signatories' obligations to react to external attacks with appropriate measures rather than the more specific obligations which had been assumed by the signatories of the Brussels Treaty.

At the sixth meeting of the group on 1 April, Hickerson introduced a summary paper concluding that a formal defense alliance should be attempted covering Western Europe, North America and islands in the North Atlantic. Washington, Hickerson proposed, would first approach the five signatories of the Brussels Treaty to secure their approval for extending the treaty to include Norway, Sweden, Denmark, Iceland, Italy, Canada, Eire and Portugal along with the United States. The United States, it was envisioned, would declare its intention, pending the conclusion of this pact, "to consider an armed attack in the North Atlantic Area against a signatory of the Five-Power [Brussels] Treaty as an armed attack against the United States to be dealt with by the United States in accordance with the United Nations Charter."[37] In addition there would be an Anglo-American declaration, harking back to the Pentagon Talks of the previous autumn, that the two countries would not countenance any attack on the political independence or territorial integrity of Greece, Turkey, or Iran, and that in the event of such an attack and pending the possible negotiations of some general Middle Eastern security system, they would feel bound fully to support these states under Article 51 of the Charter of the United Nations.[38]

The final draft of the summary adopted Hickerson's suggestions. It outlined various provisions of the proposed collective defense agreement which would establish its relationship to the United Nations Charter. It reflected the commitment by each signatory to resist attack by taking immediate measures until coordinated measures had been agreed upon—this led to efforts to coordinate American and British plans in the event of a sudden Soviet attack. It also delineated the area covered, the duration of the agreement, and the like. It was noted that Germany (or the three Western Zones) and Spain should be invited to join "when circumstances permit," although this objective *"should not be publicly disclosed."*[39]

The paper did imply a commitment by the United States, but Hickerson warned that it represented "only a concept of what is desired at the working level, and that British expectations should be based on nothing more than this."[40] On reflection American officials were still doubtful. In particular, it was feared that military conversations with the Brussels powers could create undesirable pressure for changes in American strategy unless they were limited to the coordination of production and supply.[41]

On 9 April 1948 Bevin affirmed British backing for the calling of a conference as proposed, and indicated to the State Department that he and Attlee considered that more than a presidential declaration of potential support would be necessary: "Again, any such declaration not having the backing of the Senate would make people here very doubtful as to whether they had incurred any reciprocal obligation." He pointedly recalled:

One of my great anxieties in this business is whether, if trouble did come, we should be left waiting as in 1940 in a state of uncertainty. In view of our experience then it would be very difficult to be able to stand up to it again unless there was a definite worked out arrangement for the Western area, together with other assistance, on the basis of collective security to resist the aggressor.[42]

Lovett was offended; he considered Bevin's comment "highly unfortunate," and asked Douglas so to inform the foreign secretary.[43] Bevin was not very apologetic; the ambassador reported that the foreign secretary gave only

assurances that although the UK would fight with determination, she was relatively so much weaker now than in 1940, that she could not hope for a successful stand against the Soviet hordes for a protracted period while we were considering whether we would participate actively.[44]

A PERIOD OF DOUBTS

Although the Tripartite Security Conversations seemed to point directly towards United States involvement in a collective security arrangement, uncertainty prevailed in the Truman administration and Lovett was pessimistic.[45] Senator Arthur Vandenberg, the chairman of the Senate Foreign Relations Committee, told Lovett in a conversation on 11 April 1948 that "an attempt to get a two-thirds vote in the Congress on a pact involving the type of military guarantees envisaged by the proposals was doubtful and dangerous at this time." The Michigan Republican indicated that the Senate would be especially opposed to allowing accidents occurring abroad to obligate the United States to go to war. Lovett pressed the Senator, nonetheless, for a congressional resolution in favor of "the determination of this country to take such steps as might be necessary to bring about the international peace for which the UN was presumably designed." Vandenberg agreed to consider the point further.[46]

While discussions with the congressional leadership were proceeding, the first draft of an NSC paper, NSC 9, *The Position of the United States With Respect to Support for Western Union and Other Related Free Countries*, was circulated by the State Department. The report, which was a compromise between the Hickerson draft of 1 April and a study by the Policy Planning Staff, concluded that the United States should not at that point join the Brussels pact but should declare its intention to regard an attack on any of the signatories as an attack on the United States. However,

Fear of Soviet-Communist aggression is sufficiently strong that many of
the free nations of Europe are willing to cooperate in close association, provided they are assured of military support by the United States.

This assurance should be given on a basis of reciprocal military under-
takings which would predicate resolute action on their part, and which
should take the form on our part of a firm commitment to extend military
and other support (in the President's words to Congress on March 17 "the
support which the situation requires") but leave maximum freedom of
method compatible with effective assurance of reciprocal support from
them.[47]

NSC 9 concluded also that key European nations should be
invited to draw up a "collective defense agreement" for the North
Atlantic area. Further it recommended that "military conversations should be initiated in the immediate future with parties to the
Five-Power Treaty, with a view initially to strengthening the collective security through coordinating military production and supply."[48]
There was no mention of the United States entering an alliance,
but, given Bevin's attitude that only such an effort would provide
European security, the momentum of negotiations would make it
increasingly difficult to avoid this step.

On 17 April 1948 the United States was officially advised by
Bevin and Bidault that the Brussels powers had agreed upon the establishment of a consultative council and the early initiation of
military talks. The two leaders also urged that conversations be initiated by the United States to "organise the effective defence of
Western Europe which at present cannot stand alone."[49] These
talks were to be conducted at a higher level than that of the Tripartite Security Conversations (of which the French and Benelux
governments had not been informed) and would include all Brussels powers. The State Department replied on 22 April that it was
necessary that any American assurances have "maximum country-
wide support and backing of the Congress" but that preparations
were underway and that a definite date would shortly be set.[50]

A week later, on 29 April, George Kennan of the Policy Planning
Staff, just returned from the Far East and a stay in the hospital,
expressed concern that the United States was being insufficiently
forthcoming in assuring the Europeans. He argued that exploratory
staff talks with the Europeans should be undertaken "with a view
to seeing what can be done about coordination of military measures
in the event of war with Russia." Kennan felt that what was needed

was "not so much a public political and military alliance (since the very presence of our troops between Western Europe and the Russians is an adequate guarantee that we will be at war if they are attacked)." Nonetheless he proposed that the American military establishment be encouraged to indicate to the Europeans that the United States was "willing to explore with them all serious suggestions as to how a Russian advance could be at least delayed and impeded in the early stages and possibly eventually halted at some point or another."[51]

Kennan prepared a revision of NSC 9 which was generally along the lines of the original, but which also addressed the possibility of an American political commitment "to bolster public confidence in western Europe," although nothing would be undertaken without the "fullest bipartisan clearance" and nothing would be undertaken which would require congressional action before the end of 1948 (that is, until after the elections were over).[52]

When Marshall returned to Washington from a conference in South America, he and Lovett met with Vandenberg and John Foster Dulles, a New York attorney who was increasingly accepted as a principal Republican foreign policy spokesman. All agreed that the United States should not be in the position of inviting other countries to present Washington with requests for arms or military guarantees. The approach favored was for the State Department to request a senate resolution on United States support for European defense efforts; then, with Senate passage of such a resolution secured, it would be arranged for the signatories of the Brussels Treaty to ask the United States to consult with them on matters of international peace and security; then the president would announce "in effect, that this country was prepared to accept an invitation to consider association on the basis of self-help and mutual aid among the European participants with such regional arrangements as affect its national security."[53] The two Republicans also argued that the paragraphs dealing with Greece, Turkey and Iran were still unacceptable since the American position regarding the first two had already been made known and, in the case of Iran, "they felt that there was not much we could do and that an undertaking along the lines contemplated would be an empty gesture on which we might be called and thereafter disclose our inabilty to make good."[54]

While this draft was under consideration, Bevin again made a plea for "definite acceptance of obligations on the part of the United States." In a message to the State Department on 14 May 1948, he suggested that

the mere fact that the United States was prepared to enter into some kind of regional defensive system would, by itself, encourage the democratic forces all over the world and be far the best deterrent to any Soviet miscalculation, which probably constitutes the only serious danger of war in the near future.

Bevin reiterated the clear need for "some positive and spectacular move by the Administration" and affirmed his view that it was

of the highest importance that the United States should, in the near future, open negotiations for the conclusion of a North Atlantic Pact. Otherwise he fears that a golden opportunity will be missed for rallying the democratic nations of the world, and thus calling a halt to an aggressive attitude we have all had to face.[55]

At this point it became evident that Bevin was beginning to push too hard. When queried on 19 May by a British embassy official (the egregious Donald Maclean) about the wisdom of presenting another message from the foreign secretary urging the negotiation of a treaty, Theodore Achilles, a State Department official who was working closely with Hickerson, discouraged its presentation since "it might merely produce a reply indicating United States unwillingness to conclude such a treaty."[56] That such views were appreciated by the Foreign Office is reflected in a comment one British diplomat made to Kennan:

No one in England is deceiving himself that there would be any chance of getting ratification on a security pact before the next Congress. What they hope is that by consenting to conduct discussions along these lines we will keep the ball rolling and keep up the hopes of peoples in Europe.[57]

Responding to Bevin's entreaties, Marshall noted that the resolution approved by the Senate Foreign Relations Committee on 19 May 1948 "reflects the development of public opinion in . . . these matters and the seriousness and good will with which they are being studied in Washington." Marshall cautioned, however, against "hasty or ill-prepared action [that] could easily promote disunity rather than unity both in the United States and among European countries." Since there was no chance that Congress could consider such matters before its impending adjournment, he suggested instead that the rest of the year could be well used for diplomatic examination of the issues.[58]

In a 1 June message, apparently not delivered until a 14 June meeting between Marshall and Sir Oliver Franks, the new British ambassador, Bevin praised the American secretary of state's desire for "a firm and determined course" in the face of "a determined opponent of everything that democracy represents." At the same time he warned of the success of a recent Soviet peace offensive in Europe and the possibility of a neutral Scandinavian bloc. He repeated his view that talks should be held between the United States and the Brussels powers as soon as possible, irrespective of congressional deliberations.[59] On the 14th, with the situation in Germany more ominous, Marshall advised Franks that while he preferred to wait to see how the House of Representatives acted on a resolution similar to the Vandenberg Resolution, he was prepared to proceed on the basis of the Senate's action alone.[60]

THE BERLIN CRISIS FORCES DECISION

The situation in Germany and Berlin ultimately had the most decisive impact on American willingness to pursue serious discussions with the Europeans. On 18 June the three Western powers began to introduce a common currency into their zones to stabilize the German economy. The move was quickly denounced by the Soviets who saw it as a move to divide Germany. On 24 June all land and water traffic between the Western zones and Berlin was halted indefinitely. The United States, along with Britain and France, was faced with a major Soviet challenge to its specific rights as an occupying power as well as its general position in Europe. There was serious talk of war.

The Vandenberg Resolution had passed the Senate on 11 June. It put the Senate on record as favoring "progressive development of regional and other collective arrangements for individual and collective self-defense in accordance with the purposes, principles, and provisions of the [U.N.] Charter;" it further accepted the principle of "association of the United States, by constitutional process, with such regional and other collective arrangements as are based on continuous and effective self-help and mutual aid, and as affect its national security."[61]

On 23 June 1948 the embassies of Britain, France, Canada, Belgium, the Netherlands and Luxemburg were notified that the United States was ready to begin top secret exploratory talks pursuant to the Vandenberg Resolution. The talks would begin on 29 June and would be conducted by regular diplomatic representatives without military officials or special envoys. The proposed agenda included the situation in Europe as it affected security, including estimates of Soviet intentions; security measures taken and to be taken in Europe by Brussels signatories; and the nature of the American association with European security arrangements.[62]

On 1 July 1948 the National Security Council adopted the final version of NSC 9 (NSC 9/3). It was basically unchanged from previous versions. United States military representatives should, it concluded, attend London five-power military talks on a "non-membership basis with a view to participating in conversations on military plans," rather than, as stated in an earlier version (NSC 9/2), participate in the London talks "with a view to: (a) concerting military plans . . . and (b) drawing up a coordinated military supply plan."[63] This weakening of the wording, it should be noted, derived from a recommendation by the JCS.[64]

Truman approved NSC 9/3 on 2 July 1948 and directed that its conclusions be implemented under the coordination of the secretary of state. Four days later the first meeting of the Washington Exploratory Talks on Security were opened by Lovett, who welcomed the ambassadors by recalling Bevin's approach to Washington earlier in the year and concurring in the foreign secretary's belief that the political, economic and spiritual forces of Western Europe must be integrated into "some form of union, formal or informal, backed by the United States."[65] JCS representatives shortly departed for London to attend the five-power military conversations beginning in mid-July.

The Washington Exploratory Talks extended through the summer of 1948. The conferees recommended in September that "those nations having a primary interest in the security of the North

Atlantic area should collaborate in the development of a regional or collective defence arrangement for that area"[66] and forwarded draft provisions which might be suitable for inclusion in a North Atlantic security pact.[67] For all intents and purposes this put NATO on track; the Canadians and the Brussels pact countries shortly indicated their concurrence in negotiating a treaty. There was discussion of the territorial extent of the alliance, with the U.S. insisting on the inclusion of Denmark, Iceland and Portugal to facilitate secure access to base facilities. Various texts were considered to find a way to meet the Europeans' need to have a reliable guarantee of U.S. support without doing violence to the prerogative of the U.S. Congress to declare war. By December of 1948 an outline of a draft treaty had been prepared and the American elections were safely past. After further revisions of the December draft, the North Atlantic Treaty was signed, in Washington, on 4 April 1949. Through it the United States became formally committed to the defense of Western Europe. The long-standing goal of British policy was thus achieved.

NOTES

1. Memorandum of conversation by Bevin, 17 December 1947, FO 371/64250; also printed in *FRUS* 1947, 2: 815-22.

2. Ibid.

3. Ibid.

4. In response to a suggestion by Marshall, the British, French and American officers attached to their respective United Nations missions met near New York to discuss the problem of the military defense of Europe. They agreed on the need for a common policy and a global strategy, but these talks were not carried to a higher level. See Lawrence S. Kaplan, "Toward the Brussels Pact," *Prologue* 12 (Summer 1980): 74.

Other conversations were held in Paris by Major General Harold R. Bull, who was serving as Eisenhower's personal representative. The French chief of staff, General Georges M. J. Revers, had suggested to the American military attaché in Paris in October 1947 that the United States, France and Britain work out strategic plans to make maximum use of French forces in the event of war. This proposal had duly circulated through the Army Staff and the State Department but did not generate much enthusiasm in view of the difficulty of explaining to the French that initial plans involved a hasty evacuation of the Continent. Bull, however, during a stop in Paris in

January 1948 was warned by French cabinet officers of a widespread "fear psychosis" in Western Europe stemming from the belief that Western Europe would be abandoned in the event of a war with the Soviet Union. The French again urged "coordinated general defense plans for Europe in terms of the immediate future," and sought American participation and arms supplies. See Memorandum for the Chief of Staff from Wedemeyer, 31 December 1947, RG 319, P & O 091 France (Section 1) (Cases 1-9); Caffery to Lovett, 30 January 1948, *FRUS* 1948, 3: 620-21.

5. 445 H. C. Deb. 5s. 1882 (18 December 1947).

6. "The First Aim of British Policy," 4 January 1948, C.P. (48) 6, CAB 129/23.

7. "Review of Soviet Policy," 5 January 1948, C.P. (48) 7, CAB 129/23.

8. "Future Foreign Publicity Policy," 4 January 1948, C.P. (48) 8, CAB 129/23.

9. C.M. 2 (48), CAB 128/12.

10. Inverchapel to Marshall, 13 January 1948, *FRUS* 1948, 3: 5.

11. Marshall to Inverchapel, 20 January 1948, *FRUS* 1948, 3: 9.

12. Memorandum of conversation by Hickerson, 21 January 1948, *FRUS* 1948, 3: 11.

13. 446 H.C. Deb. 5s. 384: 395-97 (22 January 1948).

14. Hickerson called the attention of the British to the Rio pact (the Inter-American Treaty of Reciprocal Assistance, signed at Rio de Janeiro, 2 September 1947) and its formulation, "automatic action against aggression from without or within." See Memorandum of conversation by Hickerson, 21 January 1948, *FRUS* 1948, 3: 11.

15. Treaty of Economic, Social and Cultural Collaboration and Collective Self-Defence between the United Kingdom, Belgium, France, Luxembourg and the Netherlands, 17 March 1948; reprinted in Great Britain, *British and Foreign State Papers* 150, Part 1 (London: Her Majesty's Stationery Office, 1956): 672-77.

16. John Baylis, "Britain, the Brussels Pact and the Continental Commitment," *International Affairs* 60 (Autumn 1984): 627.

17. "Special Message to the Congress on the Threat to the Freedom of Europe, 17 March 1948," United States, *Public Papers of the Presidents, Harry S. Truman, 1948* (Washington: Government Printing Office, 1964), pp. 183, 184.

18. See especially Lawrence S. Kaplan, *The United States and NATO: The Formative Years* (Lexington, Ky.: The University Press of Kentucky, 1984); Alan K. Henrikson, "The Creation of the North Atlantic Alliance," in *American Defense Policy*, ed. John F. Reichart and Steven R. Sturm, 5th ed. (Baltimore, Md.: The Johns Hopkins University Press, 1982); Sir Nicholas Henderson, *The Birth of NATO* (Boulder, Colo.: Westview

Press, 1983); Escott Reid, *Time of Fear and Hope: The Making of the North Atlantic Treaty, 1947-1949* (Toronto: McClelland and Stewart, 1977); Theodore C. Achilles, "U.S. Role in Negotiations that Led to Atlantic Alliance," *NATO Review* 27 (August 1979): 11-14; (October 1979): 16-19.

19. Memorandum of conversation by Lovett, 27 January 1948, *FRUS* 1948, 3: 13.

20. Ibid.

21. Inverchapel to Lovett, 27 January 1948, *FRUS* 1948, 3: 14.

22. Lovett to Inverchapel, 2 February 1948, *FRUS* 1948, 3: 17-18.

23. See Charles E. Bohlen, *Witness to History, 1929-1969* (New York: W. W. Norton, 1973), pp. 267-68; Kennan, *Memoirs, 1925-1950*, pp. 397-414.

24. Memorandum by Kennan, 24 November 1948, *FRUS* 1948, 3: 287.

25. Reported in Forrestal to NSC, 17 April 1948, *FRUS* 1948, 1 (pt. 2): 563.

26. Forrestal to NSC, 28 April 1948, RG 330, CD 6-2-49, quoted in Rearden, *Formative Years*, pp. 462-63.

27. Summarized in Forrestal for Executive Secretary, NSC [20 May 1948], CD 6-2-49, quoted in Rearden, *Formative Years*, p. 463.

28. Memorandum of conversation by Hickerson, 7 February 1948, *FRUS* 1948, 3: 22.

29. Inverchapel to Lovett, 6 February 1948, *FRUS* 1948, 3: 19-20.

30. Hickerson to Marshall, 8 March 1948, *FRUS* 1948, 3: 41.

31. Ibid., 41-42.

32. British Embassy to Department of State [11 March 1948], *FRUS* 1948, 3: 48.

33. Marshall to Inverchapel, 12 March 1948, *FRUS* 1948, 3: 48.

34. Marshall to Caffery, 12 March 1948, *FRUS* 1948, 3: 50.

35. Minutes of the First Meeting of the United States-United Kingdom-Canada Security Conversations, 22 March 1948, *FRUS* 1948, 3: 60.

36. Minutes of the Third Meeting of the United States-United Kingdom-Canada Security Conversations, 24 March 1948, *FRUS* 1948, 3: 66; Minutes of the Sixth Meeting of the United States-United Kingdom-Canada Security Conversations, 1 April 1948, *FRUS* 1948, 3: 73-74. See Henrikson, "Creation of the North Atlantic Alliance," p. 303.

37. Final Draft, enclosure to the Minutes of the Sixth Meeting of the United States-United Kingdom-Canada Security Conversations, 1 April 1948, *FRUS*, 1948, 3: 73.

38. Ibid., 74.

39. Ibid., 75.

40. Minutes of the Sixth Meeting of the United States-United Kingdom-Canada Security Conversations, *FRUS* 1948, 3: 72.

41. Lovett to Douglas, 6 April 1948, *FRUS* 1948, 3: 78.

42. Bevin to [Marshall], [9 April 1948], *FRUS* 1948, 3: 79-80.

43. *FRUS* 1948, 3: 89 n. 5.

44. Douglas to Lovett, 16 April 1948, *FRUS* 1948, 3: 89.

45. See Henderson, *Birth of NATO*, p. 21. Bevin calculated that the chances that the United States would adhere to a treaty were about even; see Cees Wiebes and Bert Zeeman, "The Pentagon Negotiations March 1948: The Launching of the North Atlantic Treaty," *International Affairs* 59 (Summer 1983): 362.

46. Memorandum of conversation by Lovett, 11 April 1948, *FRUS* 1948, 3: 82-83.

47. Report by the Executive Secretary of the NSC, 13 April 1948, *FRUS* 1948, 3: 85-86.

48. Ibid., 88. The Policy Planning Staff Report of 23 March 1948 is printed in *FRUS* 1948, 3: 61-64.

49. Bevin and Bidault to Marshall, 17 April 1948, *FRUS* 1948, 3: 91.

50. Marshall to Bidault, 21 April 1948, *FRUS* 1948, 3: 99. Bevin may have informally advised the French foreign minister, Robert Schuman, about the Tripartite Conversations; see Bullock, *Bevin*, p. 536.

51. Kennan to Marshall and Lovett, 29 April 1948, *FRUS* 1948, 3: 108-9. This emphasis on military measures was consistent with a talk Kennan gave at a June 1948 meeting of the Permanent Joint Board on Defense, U.S.-Canada in which he argued that "we should not conclude that, since Russia does not plan war, adequate defense preparations are unnecessary. If Russia does not plan such a war it is because of the military strength of her potential opposition." Furthermore, "In solution of our national defense problems we must: a. Have *real* military strength—the Russians will not be fooled by false strength. We must be strong. b. We must not only be strong but we must appear strong. c. We must be prepared. This is the really difficult problem." Memorandum for the Record by Maddocks, 8 June 1948, enclosure to Journal of Discusssions and Decisions at the meeting of the Board, Trenton, Ontario, 3-4 June 1948, RG 59, PJBD Records, box 15.

52. Kennan to Lovett, 7 May 1948, *FRUS* 1948, 3: 116-17.

53. Memorandum of conversation by Lovett, 27 April 1948, *FRUS* 1948, 3: 107.

54. Ibid., 108.

55. British Embassy to Department of State [20 May 1948], *FRUS* 1948, 3: 122-23.

56. Achilles to Hickerson, 19 May 1948, *FRUS* 1948, 3: 128.

57. Kennan to Lovett and Marshall, 24 May 1948, *FRUS* 1948, 3: 128-29.

58. Comments by Marshall, enclosure to Lovett to Balfour, 28 May 1948, *FRUS* 1948, 3: 133.

59. Bevin to British Embassy, Washington, 1 June 1948, enclosure to memorandum of conversation by Marshall, 14 June 1948, *FRUS* 1948, 3: 138-39.

60. Memorandum of conversation by Marshall, 14 June 1948, *FRUS* 1948, 3: 137.

61. The Vandenberg Resolution (Senate Resolution 239 of 11 June 1948) was reprinted in *FRUS* 1948, 3: 135-36. The important role played by the Michigan senator is described by Daryl J. Hudson, "Vandenberg Reconsidered: Senate Resolution 239 and American Foreign Policy," *Diplomatic History* 1 (Winter 1977): 46-63.

62. See Marshall to Caffery, 23 June 1948, *FRUS* 1948, 3: 139.

63. Report by the NSC, 28 June 1948, *FRUS* 1948, 3: 140-41.

64. Condit, *History of the Joint Chiefs of Staff*, p. 366.

65. Minutes of the First Meeting of the Washington Exploratory Talks on Security, 6 July 1948, *FRUS* 1948, 3: 149.

66. Memorandum by the Participants in the Washington Security Talks, 9 September 1948, *FRUS* 1948, 3: 238.

67. Ibid., 245-48.

CHAPTER 7

A STRATEGY FOR
AN ALLIANCE

The North Atlantic Treaty Organization became in the years following its establishment in 1949 not merely an expression of pious intent, but a key determinant of North American and Western European defense policy and programs. Governments on both sides of the Atlantic recognized that if the alliance were to provide a credible deterrent to Soviet aggression it would have to possess strong military forces in an effective combat organization. Only in this way could Western Europe retain the confidence in American support necessary to sustain the reconstruction of economic, political and social life and the United States avoid the dangers that would be entailed if all Eurasia came under the domination of a single, inherently hostile superpower.

In 1948-1949, or even thereafter, the idea that a Soviet attack could be held at the Rhine was not one which could gain ready assent from defense planners either in Washington or London. The focus of defense planning in the United States had been on the establishment of a capability to launch a strategic bombing campaign. The Pincher series of plans initiated in 1946 led to the first official American war plan for use in a conflict with the Soviet Union under the codename Broiler. It was considered by the JCS in late 1947 and based on the premise of a Soviet attack on the United States in FY 1949. It centered on atomic bombs delivered by air-

craft flying from bases in Britain, Egypt, northwestern India and
Japan or the Ryukyus. It assumed that the British would be
involved in the conflict and that both British and American occupation forces would be withdrawn from the Continent.[1] Prior to early
1948, British planners, however much they might have wanted to
see the United States committed to maintaining the European
balance of power, did not accept the necessity for a new continental
commitment. They too placed their confidence in an American
nuclear deterrent while undertaking preparations for a British
atomic capability.

American and British forces in Germany were a military anomaly.
These troops had miniscule combat capabilities and the war plans
of both countries, to the extent that any existed, envisioned their
hasty evacuation from the Continent in the event of a Soviet push
westward. In the course of the momentous year 1948, however, the
occupation forces began to acquire a role symbolic of Anglo-
American determination not to be pushed out of Germany that at
least provided the basis for an eventual capability to maintain a
"stopline" at the Rhine or even further east. The acquisition of
true ground combat capabilities would not occur until several years
later, and an element of linkage with strategic nuclear forces was,
as it has always remained, an essential element of NATO strategy.
Nonetheless 1948 was the watershed year when British and American planners cooperatively worked out the strategic concept for the
defense of Western Europe that has ever since been an essential
element of Washington's defense planning as well as the central
security concern of British and other European countries. In
addition, it made American adherence to a military alliance with
West European countries imperative.

The acceptance of a strategic concept requiring a capability to
hold the Soviets in Germany was achieved despite opposition from
strongly entrenched interests. Pouring money into vulnerable
ground combat forces ran counter to the prevalent strategic
thought of the day, as well as to deeply ingrained traditions of both
the British and the Americans. It jeopardized efforts to create a
credible strategic attack capability for the U.S. Air Force and
represented also a major challenge to those who wanted to reduce
government expenditures or redirect them from military spending.
The new strategic concept was, however, accepted because only

thus could central strategic and diplomatic interests, as they came to be understood by senior British and American officials, be maintained. The ramifications of this strategy, established during the international crises of 1948, constituted a revolution in American defense policy and achieved a European balance of power which has persisted for over three and a half decades.

With the collapse of the London Council of Foreign Ministers meeting in December 1947 and the launching of Bevin's efforts to achieve a Western security arrangement, there was a clear requirement for the British Chiefs of Staff to review their own defense plans. A paper by the Joint Staff Planners in late January 1948 analyzed three options: an air strategy—deterring the Soviet Union by the capability to launch a large scale strategic air offensive; a continental strategy—holding the line in central Europe with large scale ground forces; and a semi-continental strategy—holding on to a redoubt beyond the Pyrenees.[2] The Staff Planners implicitly argued for the air strategy option while dismissing the continental strategy as being beyond British capabilities. This view, supported by sound assumptions and analysis, nonetheless ran into vehement opposition from the chief of the Imperial General Staff, Field Marshal Montgomery, who in a paper of his own drafting argued to the contrary, that only by creating a credible force able to resist any Russian attack on Western Europe could Soviet intimidation or blackmail be avoided:

We must agree that, if attacked, the nations of the Western Union will hold the attack as far to the east as possible. We must make it very clear that Britain will play her full part in this strategy and will support the battle with the fullest possible weight of our land, air and naval power.

Unless this basic point in our strategy is agreed, and is accepted wholeheartedly by Britain, the Western Union can have no hope of survival, and Britain would then be in the greatest danger.[3]

This assertion produced a strong division among the COS and had to be taken to the prime minister. In a 6 February 1948 meeting with the COS, Defence Minister A. V. Alexander and Bevin, Attlee listened to the arguments pro and con. The Navy and Air Force remained opposed and the prime minister was himself skeptical, recalling that "previous experience had shown how Continental com-

mitments, initially small, were apt to grow into very large ones."
Montgomery, however, gained support from Bevin, who cast the
question in terms of overall West European cooperation extending
now into the military sphere as it was doing in the economic arena.
The COS, Bevin suggested, should study how "the forces of the
United Kingdom, France, the Benelux countries and possibly Italy
should be organised and rationalized so as to form one effective
whole." Once this was done, Bevin indicated, he "would then
make America face the fact that they had got to be in any future war
from the beginning." By placing the need for a continental strategy
in the context of the Attlee government's overall policy of allying
Britain (and, it was devoutly hoped, the United States) with the
Western Union countries, Bevin persuasively urged its eventual
adoption over the objections of the Navy and the Air Force and the
qualms of the prime minister.[4] The government shortly accepted
Montgomery's position.[5] The focus of British defense policy was
now shifted to cooperation with the West Europeans. Montgomery
regarded the success of his initiative with customary modesty:
"This was a great triumph."[6] The triumph in truth belonged as
much to the foreign secretary.

While the policy of contintental commitment was being considered
in London, concern over the danger of war in the aftermath of the
Czech coup in late February 1948 gripped military commanders in
Germany and in Washington as well. Fearing the possibility of a
sudden Soviet attack in Germany, British planners traveled to the
United States in April 1948, shortly after the Tripartite Security
Conversations had been held 22 March-1 April at the diplomatic
level, to coordinate war plans. This combined planning was of a
scale and realism which had not been seen since the end of the war.
Agreement was reached on "unilateral but accordant" plans for
use in an emergency situation (one with no time to enlarge existing
forces). The American emergency plan, Halfmoon, later called
Fleetwood, was coordinated with the British plan Doublequick, or
Speedway, and envisioned strategic air attacks from bases in Britain,
Okinawa and Egypt.[7] The navies of the two countries would defend
lines of communication through the Eastern Mediterranean and, to
an undefined extent, participate in strategic air operations.[8] As this
emergency plan was not based on force levels beyond those then
existing, no serious effort was considered possible for slowing the

projected Soviet push westward; the goal remained to extract as
mány troops and dependents as possible to French and Italian sea-
ports for evacuation. Although Halfmoon was thus consistent with
previous U.S. and British planning, the British had now to make
some attempt to bring it into alignment with commitments to their
Brussels pact allies. For the moment, the COS accepted that British
forces should "stay and fight," but "there should be no reinforcement other than the necessary administrative backing."[9]

The strategic concept of fighting as far to the east in Germany as
possible was adopted by the defense ministers and chiefs of staff of
the Brussels powers. The results were communicated on 14 May
1948 to the American ambassador in London, Lewis Douglas:

In the event of an attack by Russia, however soon it may come, the five
powers [of the Western Union] are determined to fight as far east in
Germany as possible. If Russia overruns the countries of western Europe,
irreparable harm will be done before they are liberated, owing to the
Russian policy of deportation and pillage. Their preparations are therefore
aimed at holding the Russians on the best position in Germany covering the
territory of the five powers in such a way that sufficient time for the American military power to intervene decisively can be assured. The five powers
are now assessing their resources and fully recognise that an attack in the
near future would find them militarily weak. They also recognise that their
plans must be very closely linked to the American strategic concept and the
deployment of such forces as they are prepared to provide for the defence
of western Europe from the outset.[10]

The need for West European defense planning to be tied into
American plans was increasingly recognized. U.S. planning remained focused on long-range bomber attacks, but some American
officials had also been having second thoughts about a strategy
almost wholly dependent on strategic bombing as a deterrent in the
light of recent talks with the British on emergency plans. A study
forwarded in March 1948 by the Army to the State Department
argued:

We can proceed no longer on the "strategic concept" basis that Europe
must first be conquered and occupied by the Soviets, and ourselves first
denuded of active Allies, before there can be any prospect of adopting a
strategy of victory for our arms.[11]

Another Army study maintained:

The assumption, in our current plans, that the Armed Forces of ourselves
and our Allies now on occupation duties in former enemy countries would
be evacuated from Western Europe immediately, is an unsound and untenable hypothesis. The material effect of such an ill-considered action would
be that equipment would be diverted from its proper task of reinforcing the
Channel coast to the cowardly one of opening the way for the enemy to
over-run Western Europe at will and establish himself on the Channel
coast.[12]

The prevalent trends in strategic planning had also been under
attack from another quarter. In many ways the Navy had had the
most to lose from the emphasis on strategic bombing campaigns in
which carrier air strikes would have at best been ancillary to the
bombers' principal role. There was in fact a genuine fear among
senior naval officers that tight defense budgets combined with
expansionist doctrines of air power would result in sharp cutbacks
in naval roles and missions and thus drastically lower funding for
the Navy. Thus naval officers had been seeking, out of bureaucratic self-interest as well as genuine conviction, to overturn the
planning assumptions of Broiler and Halfmoon/Fleetwood. The
chief of naval operations, Admiral Louis E. Denfeld, argued in
April 1948 in favor of an effort to hold the Soviets in central
Europe in coordination with the Western Union powers.[13] This
strategy had the distinct advantage from the Navy's perspective of
requiring more extensive capabilities for ocean transport and sea
control.

An April 1948 report by the Joint Strategic Plans Committee discussed the problem in the context of U.S. relations with the
Western Union:

Combined staff conversations, however, cannot be undertaken on the basis
of a "strategic concept" which abandons Western Europe and the Mediterranean nations without a struggle and hands over to the USSR their
resources, manpower, and industrial capacity for exploitation against us.
To do so would nullify Western Union's present strong psychological
position and destroy its determination to strive for development of a
common defense which would hold reasonable prospects of future military

security. No attempt should be made to conceal present weakness and difficulties in the development of emergency war plans with our friends. But we must be prepared to assure them that our forces in Europe will fight with them, against any odds, in defense of their liberties as well as our own, and will move forward towards preparation of a common defense that will provide maximum assurances of future security.[14]

Such arguments quickly ran into the hard reality of limited budgets as well as the strong belief in a strategy based on air bombardment within the administration and the Congress. There were neither the funds nor the inclination, especially in the Air Force, to revamp the American "strategic concept." As the JCS stated in regard to NSC 9, "We should not be committed to any agreement that might unduly influence or even jeopardize optimum over-all global strategy in favor of either direct military assistance or distribution of equipment."[15]

United States representatives were present on a "non-membership" basis at the Western Union Chiefs of Staff talks in London in July 1948. The JCS instructions to General Lyman L. Lemnitzer, who headed the American delegation (but was relieved by Major General A. Franklin Kibler the next month), emphasized the ambiguous American position vis-à-vis the Western Union:

The current Western Union strategic concept is to fight "as far east in Germany as possible." . . . In this connection, the Western Union powers should be brought to realize in due course that American forces for the defense of Europe would initially consist significantly only of those already in Europe. However, those U.S. Forces employed in long-range warfare would contribute substantially to the defense of Western Europe, even though deployed in other areas.[16]

The intensification of the Berlin crisis in late June 1948 made it necessary to undertake further plans for the contingency that what appeared to be a very real threat of a Soviet attack might materialize. As a result of a widely perceived danger of imminent war, the commanders in Germany with direct responsibility for the safety of their troops had to adjust their evacuation plans. Clay and his British counterpart, General Sir Brian Robertson, received authorization to begin detailed staff planning in June 1948.[17]

Although the JCS were not prepared to commit additional forces to Europe, they accepted the need for the occupation forces to stay and fight in Germany, which was consistent with Truman's determination that the United States was going to stay in Berlin. The willingness to approve American participation in planning to hold on in central Europe had far-reaching implications that neither the JCS nor certainly the Truman administration were prepared to address in the election summer of 1948. Despite the efforts to improve the training and combat readiness of American occupation troops in Germany, the occupation forces still constituted no significant military capability in and of themselves. They had, however, as early as Secretary Byrnes's Stuttgart speech in 1946, taken on enormous significance as a reflection of American commitment to Europe quite unrelated to their military capabilities. In the aftermath of the 1948 Czech crisis, despite the continuing reduction in force levels, Truman had affirmed in his 17 March 1948 speech to Congress the "vital importance" of keeping "our occupation forces in Germany until the peace is secure in Europe."[18] The importance was underscored (and exaggerated) a few months later by State Department Counselor Charles Bohlen in commenting to European diplomats, "The maintenance of U.S. forces in Western Germany should be sufficient assurance of our concern with the immediate aspects of military security of Western European countries."[19]

In longer term considerations, the JCS assumed that ultimately the West Europeans could supply sufficient manpower to field adequate defense forces if they were properly trained, equipped and organized. The initiative for proper organization was being launched by the Europeans themselves through the Western Union. It was anticipated that the United States would provide military assistance as it was doing for the Greeks and Turks, although a new program could hardly be introduced in the midst of the election campaign of 1948.[20]

JCS planners believed in mid-1948 and even into 1949 that, with West European armies rebuilt and properly organized, the American military contribution would chiefly lie in linking European defense with U.S. strategic bombing capabilities. This would continue to remain the focus of all American strategic planning; it was in any event the only approach that had a realistic chance of being funded. The presence of American ground forces in Germany would ensure the Europeans of the necessary linkage with the strategic arsenal and provide a needed strengthening of capabilities in Europe in the period during which West European armies were being rebuilt. The United States, it became apparent, could also provide leadership for Western defense that was not mired in traditional national jealousies.[21]

The British, however, were caught between contradictory planning efforts—whereas their emergency war plans, coordinated with the U.S., envisioned a quick pullout from the Continent, their commitments to the Brussels pact required that they stay and fight as far east in Germany as possible. In July representatives of the COS traveled to Washington to discuss their new strategic concept with the American planners. They presented a summary on 9 July 1948, known as RDC 5/10 (which was declassified in 1986) which described the intention to hold the enemy in Europe. The JCS recognized that this concept had to be accepted as the basis for discussion but emphasized that American support would not be in terms of ground forces.[22]

While American defense officials began working out the implications of support for the Brussels powers' strategic concept, complications arose which would ultimately undermine the foundations of American defense policy. The question of command in a potential war had to be faced. American, British and French troops were present in Germany; if war broke out, who would be in charge? The British and French, as members of the Western Union, had by September 1948 agreed to a single commander in chief, and Montgomery was duly appointed to the new post. The advantages of a single commander for all Western forces were obvious; the JCS had recommended, and on 23 August the president approved, the concept of American forces coming under the wartime command of the supreme commander of the Western Union forces. Truman noted, however, that "we must be very careful not to allow a foreign commander to use up our men before he goes into action *in toto*."[23]

Yet the United States was not part of the Western Union and there were obvious difficulties in placing American troops under a command structure on which there was no official American representation. Various approaches to this impasse went back and forth between the Pentagon and Clay's headquarters in Germany. Clay, always blunt, forcefully pointed out the unedifying implications of the situation. When war came, the U.S. commander would be required to turn over command of his troops to the Western Union commander, who would be in charge of the retreat to the coast. Hinting at resigning, Clay indicated that when such plans became known, the U.S. commander's "position and influence will be very much less than at present." He was candidly advised that Washington did "not want an American commander too closely associated with the overall initial debacle which on an overall basis may not be too successful. Secretaries Marshall, Forrestal and Royall all feel very strongly on this point."[24] This nonsolution to the command problem was only a stopgap pending the conclusion of negotiations for an Atlantic alliance and the holding of the American elections.[25] As much as any other factor, the need to avoid having to turn over U.S. forces to a foreign commander dictated American participation in the Atlantic alliance as a full member.

During these negotiations over command in the event of war in Europe, the role of the Combined Chiefs of Staff resurfaced. The JCS suggested that the CCS could coordinate the efforts of the Western Union commander with other aspects of a worldwide struggle with the Russians. Such an arrangement would give the United States a role in the command of the Western forces in Germany; its great disadvantage was the exclusion of the French from an ultimate command authority consisting only of English-speaking powers. Although Marshall assured the French ambassador in August 1948 that the CCS had been allowed to lapse,[26] in actuality the JCS were then giving serious thought to its potential role in the event of hostilities.[27] In view of the leading role envisioned for French ground forces by both British and American planners, it would hardly have been possible to retain the supreme direction of the war in Anglo-American hands. A new approach was clearly necessary. A full NATO command structure had to be worked out.[28]

Despite the prevailing belief in Washington in late 1948 that the defense of Europe would remain essentially a problem only for the Europeans, American officials had in fact undermined the basis on which their forces had previously been planned. This was not immediately apparent since budgetary stringencies continued (and would not be lifted for another two years). However, once it was accepted that U.S. forces would fight alongside British and other European troops in central Europe, questions of weapons, equipment, supply and reinforcement of an adequate force structure had to be faced. Such questions could only exacerbate the Truman administration's efforts to keep a tight lid on Pentagon spending. The administration's FY 1950 defense budget request, which was submitted in January 1949, totaled $14.4 billion and Congress appropriated $13.9 billion. After excruciating deliberations throughout 1949, caused by even stricter presidentially imposed budget guidelines, the administration requested $13.1 billion for FY 1951.[29] Significant increases came only with the outbreak of war in Korea. The FY 1952 budget, submitted in April 1951, totaled $55.5 billion and was subsequently overfunded by Congress.[30]

With the 1948 elections over and Truman surprisingly reelected, Washington was now able to move forward. The discussions that had been conducted in the summer of 1948 had produced a clear consensus that the United States should become a full member of an Atlantic alliance. Other considerations reinforced this conclusion. The Vandenberg Resolution had indicated that the U.S. should associate itself to a security arrangement "by constitutional process," i.e., by treaty, not by a presidential declaration. Availability of base facilities in Greenland, Iceland and the Azores would be far easier to obtain if there were a collective security arrangement including all involved parties rather than the existing situation in which the U.S. had to ask Denmark, Iceland and Portugal to provide bases for assistance in defending North America. For the JCS the greatest benefit of an alliance would be access to North Atlantic bases, and for the administration it would be far easier to obtain if there were a collective security arrangement including all involved parties rather than the existing situation in which the U.S. had to ask Denmark, Iceland and Portugal to provide bases for assistance in defending North America. It would also be possible to persuade Congress that it was not a "one way street" in which the U.S. received nothing in return for assistance.

As a result of the internecine warfare between the Navy and Air Force in late 1948 Truman asked Eisenhower, then president of

Columbia University, to serve as an unofficial "presiding officer" of the JCS beginning in January 1949. Eisenhower, keenly aware all along of the need to work with the British to secure Western Europe, became a powerful advocate of the new strategic concept. The guidance he gave the Joint Chiefs on 25 February 1949 for their future planning efforts affirmed that "the security of the United States required the pursuance of a definite policy to insure, at the earliest possible moment, the holding of a line containing the Western European complex preferably no farther to the west than the Rhine."[31] The end result of this planning effort was the emergency plan Offtackle, approved in November 1949, which, while taking cognizance of the inadequacy of American resources, included for the first time in American planning documents the objective of "retarding" Soviet advances in Western Europe.[32] In time, this mission would inevitably be translated into much larger ground forces, although it took the beginning of the Korean War to put an end to the efforts by Forrestal's successor as secretary of defense, Louis A. Johnson, to continue cutting the defense budget.

The establishment of NATO did not in itself create a viable military force, but it provided the necessary framework on which rearmament could be focused. At the time of the Korean War and the general strengthening of U.S. defense capabilities, plans were made to send an additional four divisions to Europe, provoking the so-called Great Debate over U.S. defense strategy. It was in actuality the final spasm of a dying isolationsim, and opposition to increased numbers of American ground forces in Europe was easily overcome.[33]

In the years after 1949 considerable progress was made in training and equipping North American and West European forces, including eventually West Germans, in accordance with plans and programs agreed upon by the NATO governments. Inevitably there were considerable differences between the requirements established by defense officials and spending levels which the separate legislatures would approve. Such tensions persist. NATO's effectiveness in combat conditions has been continuously questioned, and could only be demonstrated if war were to occur. The North Atlantic alliance has, nonetheless, had a vast influence on world politics in the past three and a half decades, and has served to maintain the close ties between North American and West European security policy which the British worked so hard to establish in the four years after V-E Day.

NOTES

1. JSPG 496/4, 18 December 1947, RG 218, CCS 381 USSR (3-2-46), section 8.

2. "Discussions on Policy for Western Europe," 27 January 1948, J.P. (48) 16 (Final), DEFE 4/10.

3. Montgomery, *Memoirs*, p. 449; the original document is "The Problem of Future War and the Strategy of War with Russia," 30 January 1948, COS (48) 26 (0), DEFE 5/10.

4. COS (48) 26 (O), DEFE 4/10.

5. As was reflected in the British position in the Western European Union talks, a follow-on to the signing of the Brussels Treaty, which were held in London at the end of April 1948; COS (48) 64th, 10 May 1948, DEFE 4/13. See Baylis, "Britain, the Brussels Pact and the Continental Commitment," p. 623 n. 49.

6. Montgomery, *Memoirs*, p. 450.

7. See Condit, *History of the Joint Chiefs of Staff*, pp. 288-93; also RG 218, JSPC 877, "Planners Conferences," 22 April 1948, CCS 381 USSR (3-2-46), section 13.

8. See Condit, *History of the Joint Chiefs of Staff*, p. 292.

9. See COS (48) 64th, 10 May 1948, DEFE 4/13.

10. Douglas to Marshall, 14 May 1948, *FRUS* 1948, 3: 125-26.

11. Wedemeyer to Marshall, 20 March 1948, RG 59, 840.00 B/3-2048; see also Rearden, *Formative Years*, pp. 461-62.

12. Timberman to Wedemeyer, 12 January 1948, Part 2, Appendix A, "Position of U.S. with Respect to France." RG 319, P & O 091 TS France (Section I) Case 7.

13. JCS 1844/2, Denfeld to JCS, 6 April 1948, RG 218, CCS 381 USSR (3-2-46), section 13, quoted in Condit, *History of the Joint Chiefs of Staff*, p. 287. See also Condit, *History of the Joint Chiefs of Staff*, pp. 313-15; David Alan Rosenberg, "American Atomic Strategy and the Hydrogen Bomb Decision," *Journal of American History* 66 (June 1979): 69-70.

14. JSPC 876, "United States Military Alliances with Nations of Western Europe," 21 April 1948, RG 218, CCS 092 W Eur (3-12-48), section 2.

15. "The Position of the United States with Respect to Support for

Western Union and Other Related Free Countries," 22 April 1948, RG 218, CCS 092 W EUR (3-12-48), section 2.

16. Marshall to Douglas, 16 July 1948, *FRUS* 1948, 3: 188; Gruenther to Hickerson, 16 July 1948, *FRUS* 1948, 3: 188-93; see also NSC 9/3, 28 June 1948, *FRUS* 1948, 3: 141.

17. See Clay to Bradley, 16 June 1948, Clay, *Papers*, 2: 679-80; Clay to Bradley, 16 July 1948, RG 218, CCS 092 W EUR (3-12-48), section 4; Memorandum of conversation between the U.S. Chiefs of Staff and Representatives of the British Chiefs of Staff, 16 June 1948, RG 218, "U.S.-British Chiefs of Staff Conversation 1948," Leahy File #107, Leahy Papers. Resultant planning undertaken by the staffs of Clay and Robertson is reflected in Clay, *Papers*, 2: 772-73, 828-29.

18. United States, *Public Papers of the Presidents, Harry S. Truman, 1948* (Washington: Government Printing Office, 1964), p. 185.

19. Memorandum of the Ninth Working Group Participating in the Washington Exploratory Talks on Security, 9 August 1948, *FRUS* 1948, 3: 210. Kennan had earlier argued against the need for a public alliance since "the very presence of our troops between Western Europe and the Russians is an adequate guarantee that we will be at war if they are attacked." Kennan to Lovett, 29 April 1948, *FRUS* 1948, 3: 109.

20. Shortly after the signature of the North Atlantic Treaty, the administration requested a $1.4 billion appropriation for military assistance, the bulk of which was designated for European allies. The aid was advocated as a means by which sending additional U.S. ground forces to Europe might be avoided. Congress approved this program in October 1949. See Timothy P. Ireland, *Creating the Entangling Alliance: The Origins of the North Atlantic Treaty Organization* (Westport, Conn.: Greenwood Press, 1981), pp. 153-58; Rearden, *Formative Years*, pp. 489-519; Lawrence S. Kaplan, *A Community of Interests: NATO and the Military Assistance Program, 1948-1957* (Washington: Office of the Secretary of Defense, Historical Office, 1980), pp. 16-49.

21. For an extended discussion of JCS thinking as to how this might be made to work, see Robert G. Joseph, "Commitments and Capabilities: United States Foreign and Defense Policy Coordination, 1945 to the Korean War" (Ph.D. dissertation, Columbia University, 1978). In the State Department, resistance to the enlarged role of American combat forces in Europe came from Kennan's Policy Planning Staff. In the fall of 1948—and again in 1949 after the end of the Berlin blockade—the PPS argued in favor of a German settlement which would involve the withdrawal of the occupying forces of the four powers to "specified garrison areas" along German borders. The plan did not gain support for a variety of technical and diplomatic reasons. The West Europeans, and no doubt the Soviets, still desired to have their forces present in Germany in order to

preclude any untoward remilitarization. The JCS also saw major logistical difficulties in moving U.S. occupation forces to a seaport garrison and perceived no compensating advantages. In the end, even Kennan backed off from the proposal. See PPS 37/1, "Position to Be Taken by the U.S. at a CFM Meeting," 15 November 1948, *FRUS* 1948, 2: 1320-38; Kennan, *Memoirs, 1925-1950*, pp. 423-26, 442-45; Acheson, *Present at the Creation*, pp. 291-92; Bullock, *Bevin*, p. 693. For JCS views, see Johnson to Acheson, 14 May 1949, *FRUS* 1949, 3: 875-76; Testimony of General Bradley, 10 August 1949, United States, Congress, Senate, *Military Assistance Program, 1949, Joint Hearings Held in Executive Session before the Committee on Foreign Relations and Committee on Armed Services*, 81st Cong., 1st sess., Historical Series (Washington: Government Printing Office, 1974), pp. 122-23.

22. JSPC 877/8, 14 July 1948, RG 218, CCS 092 Western Europe (3-12-48), section 4; Coleridge to Gruenther, 9/RG 218, Leahy#18, July 1948, Leahy Papers.

23. *FRUS* 1948, 3: 222 n. 5.

24. Telecon DATT 1084, 25 August 1948, RG 218, CCS 092 Western Europe (3-12-48), section 6. Kenneth C. Royall was Secretary of the Army. See also Bradley to Kibler et al., 6 October 1948, RG 218, CCS 092 Western Europe (3-12-48), section 9; Clay to Bradley and Wedemeyer, 6 November 1948, Clay, *Papers*, 2: 917-18; Bradley to Clay et al., 23 November 1948, RG 218, Europe, Western European Union, Nov.-Dec. 1948, Leahy File #24, Leahy Papers. Bradley to Clay et al., 27 January 1949, RG 218, Europe, Western European Union, Nov.-Dec. 1948, Leahy File #24, Leahy Papers. Bradley to Clay et al., 27 January 1949, RG 218, Europe, Western European Union, Nov.-Dec. 1948, Leahy File #23, Leahy Papers.

25. Later in the year, Clay's deputy, Lt. General Clarence Huebner, was directed to meet with the Western European Union's Commanders in Chief's Committee on a "non-membership" basis, but the command problem remained ambiguous until after the NATO command structure was established in 1949. See Rearden, *Formative Years*, p. 469.

26. Memorandum of Conversation by Marshall, 17 August 1948, *FRUS* 1948, 3: 643-44.

27. As reflected, for instance, in the text of the "Agreement reached by the U.S. Chiefs of Staff and Representatives of the British Chiefs of Staff, 13 August 1948," 21 August 1948, RG 218, CCS 092 Western Europe (3-12-48), section 5. Later thinking of the JCS on the question is described by Hickerson in a memorandum to Acheson (who had succeeded Marshall as secretary of state in January 1949), *FRUS* 1949, 4: 120-21.

28. Report of the Working Group on Organization of the North Atlantic Council , [17 September 1949], *FRUS* 1949, 4: 330-37; Condit, *History of the Joint Chiefs of Staff*, pp. 382-98.

29. See Condit, *History of the Joint Chiefs of Staff*, pp. 213-18.

30. See Walter S. Poole, *The History of the Joint Chiefs of Staff: The Joint Chiefs of Staff and National Policy*, 4, *1950-1952* (Wilmington, Del.: Michael Glazier, 1980), pp. 82-101. John Lewis Gaddis argues cogently that the willingness to increase military spending derived in large measure from "a group of liberal civilian advisers eager to apply Keynesian techniques to the management of the domestic economy"; *Strategies of Containment*, p. 93. However, the perceived need for increased defense spending (as opposed to the capability to sustain increased spending) derived primarily from the requirements of defense policy as established by the State and Defense Departments. In addition, an increased defense budget also served to alleviate the bureaucratic infighting between the Air Force and the Navy. Another factor was a desire by political strategists within the Truman administration to defuse the potentially damaging assertion that budgetary restrictions on defense spending had encouraged Communist aggression in Korea; see Elmer Staats, "The Truman Budget," in *Portraits of American Presidents*, 2, *The Truman Presidency: Intimate Perspectives*, ed. Kenneth W. Thompson (Lanham, Md.: University Press of America, 1984), p. 89.

31. Gruenther to Wedemeyer et al., 25 February 1949, RG 218, CCS 381 USSR (3-2-46), section 30, quoted in Eisenhower, *Papers,* 10: 515-16 n.2.

32. Offtackle is reprinted in *Containment: Documents on American Policy and Strategy, 1945-1950*, ed. Thomas H. Etzold and John Lewis Gaddis (New York: Columbia University Press, 1978), pp. 324-34; see also Condit, *History of the Joint Chiefs of Staff*, pp. 294-304; Eisenhower, *Papers*, 10: 515-19.

33. See Acheson, *Present at the Creation*, pp. 491-93; Poole, *History of the Joint Chiefs of Staff*, pp. 221-24; David R. Kepley, "The Senate and the Great Debate of 1951," *Prologue* 14 (Winter 1982): 213-26. Previously the Constabulary had been reorganized into a modified armored cavalry division and in November 1950 it was subsumed into the newly established Seventh Army. See Frederiksen, *American Military Occupation of Germany*, pp. 148-61.

AFTERWORD

In laying the North Atlantic Treaty before the House of Commons, Bevin claimed that he was convinced

> that in it we have taken one of the greatest steps for peace. In co-operation with like-minded peoples, we shall act as custodians of peace and as determined opponents of aggression, and shall combine our great resources and great scientific and organisational ability, and use them to raise the standard of life for the masses of the people all over the world.[1]

The emphasis on improving living standards was characteristic of the man who had devoted his life to the betterment of the British working classes. So also was the emphasis on the cooperation of like-minded peoples. Although the Canadians, the French and others played important roles, the North Atlantic Treaty was, as has been seen, primarily a product of Anglo-American cooperative endeavor. It has met its aim of restoring the European balance of power. In the late 1940s, as in the mid-1980s, the stationing of large numbers of American troops on European soil was not an ideal solution, but it was, and remains, far preferable to other options. By any measure, it has led to remarkably greater security in Europe than prevailed in the nineteen twenties and thirties.

The British, who were profoundly weakened by the war, had the motivation to see the United States deeply involved in the security of Western Europe. They efficiently used their access to American decisionmakers to good effect. But if it is fallacious to assert that Washington imposed the alliance on dependent and unwilling Europeans, it would also be wrong to suggest that it was a uniquely British program. NATO arose out of the shared perspectives of British and American officials, representatives of "like-minded peoples," who had drawn similar conclusions about the nature of the Soviet challenge and the need for a consolidated Western response.

The basis of American defense policy in the five years after the conclusion of World War II shifted from a regionalistic focus on the Western Hemisphere and the Pacific to a formal, constitutional commitment to resist aggression in Europe. Despite all the vicissitudes that have beset America's defense establishment in subsequent years, the United States has stood by this commitment. It remains the bedrock of American defense policy. The U.S. government did not build its defenses around some sort of Fortress America concept, buttressed only by technological superiority. Rather, the United States became committed to defending Western Europe, and, subsequently, other key areas. This policy has required massive expenditures and involvement in entangling alliances, but it has ensured that the United States is not isolated in a hostile, impoverished world.

In the last analysis, the most important impetus for the Atlantic alliance was the simple fact that leaders on both sides of the Atlantic had seen what global war could do. In the vast panorama of death and destruction that lay before them at the end of World War II, all had realized that the policies followed by their interwar predecessors had led to disaster. The British, who had spurned the French and attempted to appease Hitler, had been matched by Americans who had tried to isolate themselves in an age of dictators behind an army smaller than Bulgaria's. Both failed and both suffered enormous losses. After the end of the second global war, leaders in both countries felt themselves obligated to create a defense policy which would effectively deter aggression. Today the British Empire is at one with Nineveh and Tyre and London's voice has blended into that of the European Community, but the principle of cooperation among like-minded peoples remains a central component of the Western democracies' determined efforts to avoid another world war.

NOTE

1. 464 H.C. Deb. 5s. 2022 (12 May 1949).

SELECTED BIBLIOGRAPHY

Of the vast literature relevant to the history of defense policy in this period, the following materials were of the greatest use in the preparation of this study.

MANUSCRIPT COLLECTIONS

Library of Congress, Washington

Joseph E. Davies Papers
Ira C. Eaker Papers
William D. Leahy Papers
Robert P. Patterson Papers
Carl A. Spaatz Papers
Hoyt S. Vandenberg Papers

Naval Historical Center, Washington

Command History Files
James V. Forrestal Papers
William D. Leahy Papers
Records of the Strategic Plans Division

Harry S. Truman Library, Independence, Missouri

Eben A. Ayers Papers
Clark M. Clifford Papers

George M. Elsey Papers
President's Secretary's Files
White House Central Files

United Kingdom, Public Record Office, Kew

Cabinet Papers
Defence Papers
Foreign Office Papers
Prime Minister's Office Papers

United States, National Archives, Washington

Record Group 59, Records of the Department of State
Record Group 80, Records of the Department of the Navy
Record Group 218, Records of the Joint Chiefs of Staff
Record Group 273, Records of the National Security Council
Record Group 319, Records of the Army Staff
Record Group 330, Records of the Office of the Secretary of Defense
Record Group 341, Records of the Headquarters, U.S. Air Force
Record Group 353, Records of Interdepartmental and Intradepartmental
    Committees (State Department), Records of the State-War-Navy
    Coordinating Committee

GOVERNMENT DOCUMENTS

Butler, Rohan, and M. E. Pelly, eds. *Documents on British Policy Over-seas.* Series 1, Vol. 1. London: Her Majesty's Stationery Office, 1984.
Great Britain. Foreign Office. *British Foreign Office United States Corres-pondence, 1938-1948.* Wilmington, Del.: Scholarly Resources, 1979-1981. Microfilm.
_____. Parliament. *Parliamentary Debates*, 5th series, 1945-1949.
Map Room Messages of President Truman (1945-1946): The Presidential Documents Series. Frederick, Md.: University Publications of America, 1980. Microfilm.
Records of the Joint Chiefs of Staff, Part 2: 1946-53: Europe and NATO. Washington: University Publications of America, 1980. Microfilm.
Records of the Joint Chiefs of Staff, Part 2: 1946-53: The Soviet Union. Washington: University Publications of America, 1979. Microfilm.
U.S. Congress. House. Committee on Appropriations. *Navy Department Appropriation Bill for 1946. Hearings before the Subcommittee on the Navy Department, House Committee on Appropriations*, 79th Cong., 1st sess., 1945.

_____. *Navy Appropriation Bill for 1947. Hearings before the Subcommittee on the Navy Department, House Committee on Appropriations,* 79th Cong., 2d sess., 1946.

_____. *Navy Department Appropriation Bill for 1948. Hearings before the Subcommittee on the Navy Department, House Committee on Appropriations,* 80th Cong., 1st sess., 1947.

U.S. Congress. House. Committee on Naval Affairs. *Hearings on Sundry Legislation Affecting the Naval Establishment, 1945,* 79th Cong., 1st sess., 1946.

U.S. Congress. Senate. Committee on Armed Services. *Universal Military Training, Hearings.* 80th Cong., 2d sess., 1948.

U.S. Congress. Senate. Committee on Appropriatons. *Navy Department Appropriation Bill for 1946, H.R. 2907. Hearings before the Senate Committee on Appropriations,* 79th Cong., 1st sess., 1945.

_____. *Navy Department Appropriation Bill for 1947, H.R. 6496. Hearings before the Senate Committee on Appropriations,* 79th Cong., 2d sess., 1946.

_____. *Navy Department Appropriation Bill for 1948, H.R. 3493. Hearings before the Senate Committee on Appropriations,* 80th Cong., 1st sess., 1947.

U.S. Congress. Senate. *Military Assistance Program, 1949, Joint Hearing held in Executive Session before the Committee on Foreign Relations and Committee on Armed Services,* 81st Cong., 1st sess., Historical Series. Washington: Government Printing Office, 1974.

U.S. Department of State. *Foreign Relations of the United States.* Annual volumes, 1945-1949. Washington: Government Printing Office, 1967-1976.

_____. *Foreign Relations of the United States. The Conference of Berlin (The Potsdam Conference), 1945.* 2 vols. Washington: Government Printing Office, 1960.

_____. *Foreign Relations of the United States. The Conferences at Cairo and Tehran, 1943.* Washington: Government Printing Office, 1961.

_____. *Foreign Relations of the United States. The Conferences at Malta and Yalta, 1945.* Washington: Government Printing Office, 1955.

_____. *Foreign Relations of the United States. The Conferences at Washington and Quebec.* Washington: Government Printing Office, 1970.

UNPUBLISHED DISSERTATIONS AND STUDIES

Best, Richard A., Jr. "Approach to Alliance: British and American Defense Strategies, 1945-1948." Ph.D. dissertation, Georgetown University, 1983.

Cane, Guy. "The Build-Up of U.S. Naval Force in the Mediterranean as an Instrument of Cold War Policy." Individual Research Paper. Washington: National War College, 1975.

Converse, Elliott Vanveltner, III. "United States Plans for a Postwar Overseas Military Base System, 1942-1948." Ph.D. dissertation, Princeton University, 1984.

A Five Year Summary of USAFE History, 1945-1950. Wiesbaden, Germany: Headquarters, United States Air Forces in Europe, Historical Division, 1952.

Hedlund, Richard P. "Congress and the British Loan, 1945-1946: A Congressional Study." Ph.D. dissertation, University of Kentucky, 1976.

Jasse, Richard Leonard. "Zion Abandoned: Great Britain's Withdrawal from the Palestine Mandate, 1945-1948." Ph.D. dissertation, Catholic University, 1980.

Joseph, Robert G. "Commitments and Capabilities: United States Foreign and Defense Policy Coordination, 1945 to the Korean War." Ph.D. dissertation, Columbia University, 1978.

Libby, Brian Arthur. "Policing Germany: The United States Constabulary, 1946-1952." Ph.D. dissertation, Purdue University, 1977.

Miller, John Andrew. "Air Diplomacy: The Chicago Civil Aviation Conference of 1944 in Anglo-American Wartime Relations and Postwar Planning." Ph.D. dissertation, Yale University, 1971.

O'Brien, Larry Dean. "National Security and the New Warfare: Defense Policy, War Planning, and Nuclear Weapons, 1945-1950." Ph.D. dissertation, Ohio State University, 1981.

Parker, Sally Lister. "Attendant Lords: A Study of the British Joint Staff Mission in Washington, 1941-1945." Ph.D. dissertation, University of Maryland, 1984.

Pricolo, Dennis M. "Naval Presence and Cold War Foreign Policy: A Study of the Decision to Station the Sixth Fleet in the Mediterranean, 1945-1958." Trident Scholar Project Report No. 95. Annapolis, Md.: U.S. Naval Academy, 1978.

Rosenberg, David A., and Floyd D. Kennedy, Jr. "History of the Strategic Arms Competition, 1945-1972, Supporting Study: U.S. Aircraft Carriers in the Strategic Role, Part I—Naval Strategy in a Period of Change: Interservice Rivalry, Strategic Interaction, and the Development of a Nuclear Attack Capability, 1945-1951." Falls Church, Va.: Lulejian and Associates, Inc., 1975 [Deposited at NHC].

Sheehy, Edward John. "The United States Navy in the Mediterranean, 1945-1947." Ph.D. dissertation, George Washington University, 1983.

Wix, William M. "The Army's Plans for its Postwar Role, 1943-1945."
   Ph.D. dissertation, Columbia University, 1976.

BOOKS

Acheson, Dean G. *Present at the Creation: My Years at the State Depart-
   ment.* New York: W. W. Norton, 1969.
_____. *Sketches from Life of Men I Have Known.* New York: Harper
   and Brothers, 1961.
Albion, Robert G., and Robert H. Connery. *Forrestal and the Navy.*
   New York: Columbia University Press, 1962.
Alvarez, David J. *Bureaucracy and Cold War Diplomacy: The United
   States and Turkey, 1943-1946.* Thessaloniki: Institute for Balkan
   Studies, 1980.
Ambrose, Stephen E. *Eisenhower.* Vol. 1, *Soldier, General of the Army,
   President-Elect, 1890-1952.* New York: Simon and Schuster, 1983.
Anderson, Terry H. *The United States, Great Britain, and the Cold War,
   1944-1947.* Columbia, Mo.: University of Missouri Press, 1981.
Anderton, David A. *Strategic Air Command: Two-thirds of the Triad.*
   London: Ian Allan, 1975.
Attlee, Clement R. *As It Happened.* London: Heinemann, 1954.
Barclay, Roderick. *Ernest Bevin and the Foreign Office, 1932-1969.* Lon-
   don: published by the author, 1975.
Barker, Elisabeth. *The British between the Superpowers, 1945-50.* Toron-
   to: University of Toronto Press, 1983.
Baylis, John. *Anglo-American Defence Relations, 1939-1980: The Special
   Relationship.* New York: St. Martin's Press, 1981.
Blair, Leon Borden. *Western Window in the Arab World.* Austin, Tex.:
   University of Texas Press, 1970.
Bohlen, Charles E. *The Transformation of American Foreign Policy.*
   New York: W. W. Norton, 1969.
_____. *Witness to History, 1929-1969.* New York: W. W. Norton, 1973.
Borowski, Harry R. *A Hollow Threat: Strategic Air Power and Contain-
   ment Before Korea.* Westport, Conn.: Greenwood Press, 1982.
Bullock, Alan. *Ernest Bevin: Foreign Secretary, 1945-1951.* London:
   Heinemann, 1983.
Byrnes, James F. *All in One Lifetime.* New York: Harper, 1958.
_____. *Speaking Frankly.* New York: Harper, 1947.
Churchill, Winston S. *The Second World War.* Vol. 6, *Triumph and Trag-
   edy.* Boston: Houghton Mifflin Co., 1953.
Clay, Lucius D. *Decision in Germany.* Garden City, N.Y.: Doubleday,
   1950.
_____. *The Papers of General Lucius D. Clay: Germany, 1945-1949.*

Edited by Jean Edward Smith. 2 vols. Bloomington, Ind.: Indiana University Press, 1974.

Coletta, Paolo E., ed. *American Secretaries of the Navy*. Vol. 2, *1913-1972*. Annapolis, Md.: Naval Institute Press, 1980.

Condit, Kenneth W. *The History of the Joint Chiefs of Staff: The Joint Chiefs of Staff and National Policy*. Vol. 2, *1947-1949*. Wilmington, Del.: Michael Glazier, 1979.

Cooper, Alfred Duff, Viscount Norwich. *Old Men Forget: The Autobiography of Duff Cooper, Viscount Norwich*. London: Readers Union, Rupert Hart-Davis, 1955.

Dalton, Hugh. *High Tide and After: Memoirs, 1945-1960*. London: Frederick Muller, 1962.

Darby, Phillip. *British Defence Policy East of Suez, 1947-1968*. London: Oxford University Press for the Royal Institute of International Affairs, 1973.

Davis, Vincent. *Postwar Defense Policy and the U.S. Navy, 1943-1946*. Chapel Hill, N.C.: University of North Carolina Press, 1966.

Divine, Robert A. *Foreign Policy and U.S. Presidential Elections, 1940-1948*. New York: New Viewpoints, A Division of Franklin Watts, 1974.

―――. *Roosevelt and World War II*. Baltimore, Md.: Johns Hopkins University Press, 1969.

―――. *Second Chance: The Triumph of Internationalism in America during World War II*. New York: Atheneum, 1967.

Dixon, Piers. *Double Diploma: The Life of Sir Pierson Dixon, Don and Diplomat*. London: Hutchinson, 1968.

Doenecke, Justus D. *Not to the Swift: The Old Isolationists in the Cold War Era*. Lewisburg, Pa.: Bucknell University Press, 1979.

Donovan, Robert J. *Conflict and Crisis: The Presidency of Harry S Truman, 1945-1948*. New York: W. W. Norton, 1977.

―――. *Tumultuous Years: The Presidency of Harry S Truman, 1949-1953*. New York: W. W. Norton, 1982.

Douglas, Roy. *From War to Cold War, 1942-1948*. New York: St. Martin's Press, 1981.

Eden, Anthony. *The Memoirs of Anthony Eden, Earl of Avon: The Reckoning*. Boston: Houghton Mifflin Co., 1965.

Eisenhower, Dwight David. *The Papers of Dwight David Eisenhower*. Edited by Louis Galambos. Vols. 6-11. Baltimore, Md.: Johns Hopkins University Press, 1978-1984.

Etzold, Thomas H., and John Lewis Gaddis, eds. *Containment: Documents on American Policy and Strategy, 1945-1950*. New York: Columbia University Press, 1978.

Feis, Herbert. *Between War and Peace: The Potsdam Conference*. Princeton, N.J.: Princeton University Press, 1960.

_____. *Churchill, Roosevelt, Stalin: The War They Waged and the Peace They Sought.* Princeton, N.J.: Princeton University Press, 1957.

_____. *From Trust to Terror: The Onset of the Cold War, 1945-1950.* New York: W. W. Norton, 1970.

Forrestal, James V. *The Forrestal Diaries.* Edited by Walter Millis. New York: Viking Press, 1951.

Frederiksen, Oliver J. *The American Military Occupation of Germany, 1945-1953.* N.p.: Historical Division, Headquarters, United States Army, Europe, 1953.

Futrell, Robert Frank. *Ideas, Concepts, Doctrine: A History of Basic Thinking in the United States Air Force, 1907-1964.* Maxwell Air Force Base, Ala.: Air University, 1974.

Gaddis, John Lewis. *Strategies of Containment: A Critical Appraisal of Postwar American National Security Policy.* New York: Oxford University Press, 1982.

_____. *The United States and the Origins of the Cold War, 1941-1947.* New York: Columbia University Press, 1972.

Gardner, Richard N. *Sterling-Dollar Diplomacy: The Origins and the Prospects of Our International Economic Order.* New expanded ed. New York: McGraw-Hill, 1969.

Gimbel, John. *The Origins of the Marshall Plan.* Stanford, Calif.: Stanford University Press, 1976.

Gladwyn, Hubert Miles Gladwyn Jebb, Baron. *The Memoirs of Lord Gladwyn.* London: Weidenfeld and Nicolson, 1972.

Gordon, Michael R. *Conflict and Consensus in Labour's Foreign Policy, 1914-1965.* Stanford, Calif.: Stanford University Press, 1969.

Gowing, Margaret M. *Independence and Deterrence: Britain and Atomic Energy, 1945-1952.* Vol. 1, *Policy Making.* London: Macmillan, 1974.

Hahn, Werner G. *Postwar Soviet Politics: The Fall of Zhdanov and the Defeat of Moderation, 1946-53.* Ithaca, N.Y.: Cornell University Press, 1982.

Hammond, Paul Y. "Super Carriers and B-36 Bombers: Appropriations, Strategy and Politics." In *American Civil-Military Decisions*, edited by Harold Stein. [University, Al.]: University of Alabama Press: A Twentieth Century Fund Study, 1963.

Hammond, Thomas T., ed. *Witnesses to the Origins of the Cold War.* Seattle, Wash.: University of Washington Press, 1982.

Harris, Kenneth. *Attlee.* London: Weidenfeld and Nicolson, 1982.

Hartmann, Susan M. *Truman and the 80th Congress.* Columbia, Mo.: University of Missouri Press, 1971.

Hathaway, Robert M. *Ambiguous Partnership: Britain and America, 1944-1947.* New York: Columbia University Press, 1981.

Haynes, Richard F. *The Awesome Power: Harry S. Truman as Com-

mander in Chief. Baton Rouge, La.: Louisiana State University Press, 1973.

Henderson, Sir Nicholas. *The Birth of NATO.* Boulder, Colo.: Westview Press, 1983.

Henrikson, Alan K. "The Creation of the North Atlantic Alliance." In *American Defense Policy,* edited by John F. Reichart and Steven R. Sturm. 5th ed. Baltimore, Md.: The Johns Hopkins University Press, 1982.

Herken, Gregg. *The Winning Weapon: The Atomic Bomb in the Cold War, 1945-1950.* New York: Alfred A. Knopf, 1980.

Hewlett, Richard G., Oscar E. Anderson and Francis Duncan. *A History of the Atomic Energy Commission.* 2 vols. University Park, Pa.: Pennsylvania State University Press, 1962, 1969.

Hollis, Leslie C. *One Marine's Tale.* London: Andre Deutsch, 1956.

Huntington, Samuel P. *The Common Defense: Strategic Programs in National Politics.* New York: Columbia University Press, 1961.

Hurley, Alfred F., and Robert C. Ehrhart, eds. *Air Power and Warfare: The Proceedings of the Eighth Military History Symposium, United States Air Force Academy, 18-20 October 1978.* Washington: Office of Air Force History, Headquarters USAF and United States Air Force Academy, 1979.

Huzar, Elias. *The Purse and the Sword: Control of the Army by Congress through Military Appropriations, 1933-1950.* Ithaca, N.Y.: Cornell University Press, 1950.

Ireland, Timothy P. *Creating the Entangling Alliance: The Origins of the North Atlantic Treaty Organization.* Westport, Conn.: Greenwood Press, 1981.

Ismay, Hastings Lionel. *Memoirs.* New York: Viking Press, 1960.

_____. *NATO: The First Five Years, 1949-1954.* N.p.,n.d. [Paris, 1954].

Jones, Bill. *The Russia Complex: The British Labour Party and the Soviet Union.* Manchester, England: Manchester University Press, 1977.

Jones, Joseph M. *The Fifteen Weeks (February 21-June 5, 1947).* New York: Harcourt, Brace and World: A Harbinger Book, 1964, originally published 1955.

Kaiser, Robert G. *Cold Winter, Cold War.* New York: Stein and Day, 1974.

Kaplan, Lawrence S. *A Community of Interests: NATO and the Military Assistance Program, 1948-1951.* Washington: Office of the Secretary of Defense, Historical Office, 1980.

_____. *The United States and NATO: The Formative Years.* Lexington, Ky.: University Press of Kentucky, 1984.

Kennan, George F. *Memoirs, 1925-1950.* Boston: Little, Brown, 1967.

Kuniholm, Bruce Robellet. *The Origins of the Cold War in the Near East:*

Great Power Conflict and Diplomacy in Iran, Turkey, and Greece. Princeton, N.J.: Princeton University Press, 1980.

Leahy, William D. *I Was There: The Personal Story of the Chief of Staff to Presidents Roosevelt and Truman Based on His Notes and Diaries Made at the Time.* New York: Whittlesey House, McGraw-Hill, 1950.

LeMay, Curtis E., with MacKinlay Kantor. *Mission with LeMay: My Story.* Garden City, N.Y.: Doubleday, 1965.

Lipgens, Walter. *A History of European Integration.* Translated by P. S. Falla and A. J. Ryder. Vol. 1. Oxford: Clarendon Press, 1982.

Louis, William Roger. *The British Empire in the Middle East, 1945-1951: Arab Nationalism, the United States, and Postwar Imperialism.* Oxford: Clarendon Press, 1984.

_____. *Imperialism at Bay: The United States and the Decolonization of the British Empire, 1941-1945.* New York: Oxford University Press, 1978.

Love, Robert William, Jr., ed. *The Chiefs of Naval Operations.* Annapolis, Md.: Naval Institute Press, 1980.

Lundestad, Geir. *America, Scandinavia, and the Cold War, 1945-1959.* New York: Columbia University Press, 1980.

McCagg, William O. *Stalin Embattled, 1943-1948.* Detroit, Mich.: Wayne State University Press, 1978.

Macmillan, Harold. *Tides of Fortune, 1945-1955.* London: Macmillan, 1969.

McNeill, William H. *America, Britain and Russia: Their Co-operation and Conflict, 1941-1946.* In *Survey of International Affairs, 1939-1946,* edited by Arnold Toynbee. London: Oxford University Press under the auspices of the Royal Institute of International Affairs, 1953.

Mallaby, George. *Each in His Office: Studies of Men in Power.* London: Leo Cooper, 1972.

_____. *From My Level: Unwritten Minutes.* London: Hutchinson, 1965.

Mastny, Vojtech. *Russia's Road to the Cold War: Diplomacy, Warfare, and the Politics of Communism, 1941-1945.* New York: Columbia University Press, 1979.

May, Ernest R., ed. *The Ultimate Decision: The President as Commander in Chief.* New York: George Braziller, 1960.

Messer, Robert L. *The End of an Alliance: James F. Byrnes, Roosevelt, Truman and the Origins of the Cold War.* Chapel Hill, N.C.: University of North Carolina Press, 1982.

Montgomery, Bernard L. *The Memoirs of Field-Marshal Montgomery.* Cleveland: World Publishing Co., 1958.

Morgan, Kenneth O. *Labour in Power, 1945-1951.* Oxford: Clarendon Press, 1984.

Nicholas, Herbert George. *The United States and Britain*. Chicago: University of Chicago Press, 1975.

Northedge, F. S. *British Foreign Policy: The Process of Readjustment, 1945-1961*. New York: Praeger, 1962.

Notter, Harley. *Postwar Foreign Policy Preparation, 1939-1945*. Washington: Department of State, 1949.

Osgood, Robert E. *NATO: The Entangling Alliance*. Chicago: University of Chicago Press, 1962.

Parrish, Noel Francis. *Behind the Sheltering Bomb*. New York: Arno, 1979.

Poole, Walter S. *The History of the Joint Chiefs of Staff: The Joint Chiefs of Staff and National Policy*. Vol. 4, *1950-1952*. Wilmington, Del.: Michael Glazier, 1980.

Potter, E. B. *Nimitz*. Annapolis, Md.: Naval Institute Press, 1976.

Radford, Arthur W. *From Pearl Harbor to Vietnam: The Memoirs of Admiral Arthur W. Radford*. Edited by Stephen Jurika, Jr. Stanford, Calif.: Hoover Institution Press, 1980.

Radosh, Ronald. *Prophets on the Right: Profiles of Conservative Critics of American Globalism*. New York: Simon and Schuster, 1975.

Range, Willard. *Franklin D. Roosevelt's World Order*. Athens, Ga.: University of Georgia Press, 1959.

Rearden, Steven L. *The Formative Years, 1947-1950*. Vol. 1 of *History of the Office of the Secretary of Defense*. Edited by Alfred Goldberg. Washington: Historical Office of the Secretary of Defense, 1984.

Reid, Escott. *Time of Fear and Hope: The Making of the North Atlantic Treaty, 1947-1949*. Toronto: McClelland and Stewart, 1977.

Rogow, Arnold A. *Victim of Duty: A Study of James Forrestal*. London: Hart-Davis, 1966.

Rosecrance, R. N. *Defense of the Realm: British Security in the Nuclear Epoch*. New York: Columbia University Press, 1968.

Ross, Graham, ed. *The Foreign Office and the Kremlin: British Documents on Anglo-Soviet Relations, 1941-45*. Cambridge, England: Cambridge University Press, 1984.

Rothwell, Victor. *Britain and the Cold War, 1941-1947*. London: Jonathan Cape, 1982.

Russell, Ruth B., assisted by Jeanette E. Multher. *A History of the United Nations Charter: The Role of the United States, 1940-1945*. Washington: The Brookings Institution, 1958.

Schilling, Warner R., Paul Y. Hammond and Glenn H. Snyder. *Strategy, Politics, and Defense Budgets*. New York: Columbia University Press, 1962.

Schnabel, James F. *The History of the Joint Chiefs of Staff: The Joint Chiefs of Staff and National Policy.* Vol. 1, *1945-1947.* Wilmington, Del.: Michael Glazier, 1979.

Sherry, Michael S. *Preparing for the Next War: American Plans for Postwar Defense, 1941-45.* New Haven, Conn.: Yale University Press, 1977.

Sherwin, Martin J. *A World Destroyed: The Atomic Bomb and the Grand Alliance.* New York: Alfred A. Knopf, 1975.

Shinwell, Emanuel. *I've Lived Through It All.* London: Victor Gollancz, 1973.

Shlaim, Avi. *The United States and the Berlin Blockade, 1948-1949.* Berkeley and Los Angeles: University of California Press, 1983.

Shlaim, Avi, Peter Jones and Keith Sainsbury. *British Foreign Secretaries Since 1945.* Newton Abbot, England: David and Charles, 1977.

Sissons, Michael, and Philip French, eds. *Age of Austerity.* London: Hodder and Stoughton, 1963.

Smith, Perry McCoy. *The Air Force Plans for Peace, 1943-1945.* Baltimore, Md.: Johns Hopkins University Press, 1970.

Sparrow, John C. *History of Personnel Demobilization in the United States Army.* [Washington]: U.S. Department of the Army, Office of the Chief of Military History, 1951.

Swetzer, R. L. *Wheelus Field: The Story of the U.S. Air Force in Libya: The Early Days, 1944-1952.* N.p.: Historical Division, Office of Information, United States Air Forces in Europe, 1965.

Thompson, Kenneth W., ed. *Portraits of American Presidents.* Vol. 2, *The Truman Presidency: Intimate Perspectives.* Lanham, Md.: University Press of America, 1984.

Truman, Harry S. *Memoirs.* Vol. 1, *Year of Decision.* Garden City, N.Y.: Doubleday, 1955.

————. *Memoirs.* Vol. 2, *Years of Trial and Hope.* Garden City, N.Y.: Doubleday, 1956.

United States. President's Air Policy Commission. *Survival in the Air Age: A Report by the President's Air Policy Commission.* Washington: Government Printing Office, 1948.

Vandenberg, Arthur H. *The Private Papers of Senator Vandenberg.* Edited by Arthur H. Vandenberg, Jr. Boston: Houghton Mifflin Co., 1952.

Walker, J. Samuel. *Henry A. Wallace and American Foreign Policy.* Westport, Conn.: Greenwood Press, 1976.

Wallace, Henry A. *The Price of Vision: The Diary of Henry A. Wallace, 1942-1946.* Edited by John Morton Blum. Boston: Houghton Mifflin Co., 1973.

Walton, Richard J. *Henry Wallace, Harry Truman, and the Cold War.* New York: Viking, 1976.

Ward, Patricia Dawson. *The Threat of Peace: James F. Byrnes and the Council of Foreign Ministers, 1945-1946.* Kent, Ohio: Kent State University Press, 1979.

Warner, Geoffrey. "The Reconstruction and Defence of Western Europe after 1945." In *Troubled Neighbours: Franco-British Relations in the Twentieth Century,* edited by Neville Waites. London: Weidenfeld and Nicolson, 1971.

Watt, Donald Cameron. "Britain and the Cold War in the Far East." In *The Origins of the Cold War in Asia,* edited by Yonosuke Nagai and Akira Iriye. New York: Columbia University Press, 1977.

_____. *Britain Looks to Germany: British Opinion and Policy Towards Germany Since 1945.* London: Oswald Wolff, 1965.

_____. *Succeeding John Bull: America in Britain's Place, 1900-1975.* Cambridge, England: Cambridge University Press, 1984.

Willard, Richard H. *Location of United States Military Units in United Kingdom, 16 July 1948-31 December 1967.* N.p.: United States Air Forces in Europe, Historical Division, Office of Information, Third Air Force, 1968.

Williams, Francis. *A Prime Minister Remembers: The War and Post-War Memoirs of the Rt. Hon. Earl Attlee.* London: Heinemann, 1961.

Wilson, Henry Maitland. *Eight Years Overseas, 1939-1947.* Foreword by Dwight David Eisenhower. London: Hutchinson, [1950].

Wittner, Lawrence S. *American Intervention in Greece, 1943-1949.* New York: Columbia University Press, 1982.

Wolk, Herman S. *Planning and Organizing the Postwar Air Force, 1943-1947.* Washington: Office of Air Force History, United States Air Force, 1984.

Woodward, Llewellyn. *British Foreign Policy in the Second World War.* 5 vols. London: Her Majesty's Stationery Office, 1970-1976.

Xydis, Stephen G. *Greece and the Great Powers, 1944-1947: Prelude to the Truman Doctrine.* Thessaloniki: Institute for Balkan Studies, 1963.

Yergin, Daniel. *Shattered Peace: The Origins of the Cold War and the National Security State.* Boston: Houghton Mifflin, Sentry Edition, 1978.

ORAL HISTORIES

Theodore C. Achilles (Independence, Mo.: HSTL, 1976).

Vice Admiral Bernard H. Bieri (Annapolis, Md.: U.S. Naval Institute, 1970).

General Lucius D. Clay (Independence, Mo.: HSTL, 1979).
Admiral Richard L. Conolly (New York: Columbia University, 1960).
Admiral Robert L. Dennison (Independence, Mo.: HSTL, 1972).
George M. Elsey (Independence, Mo.: HSTL, 1974).
John D. Hickerson (Independence, Mo.: HSTL, 1976).
Marx Leva (Independence, Mo.: HSTL, 1972).
H. Freeman Matthews (Independence, Mo.: HSTL, 1976).
J. Graham Parsons (Independence, Mo.: HSTL, 1978).

ARTICLES

Achilles, Theodore C. "U.S. Role in Negotiations that Led to Atlantic
    Alliance." *NATO Review* 27 (August 1979): 11-14; (October 1979):
    16-19.
Antsey, Caroline. "The Projection of British Socialism: Foreign Office
    Publicity and American Opinion, 1945-50." *Journal of Contem-
    porary History* 19 (July 1984): 417-51.
Baylis, John. "Britain and the Dunkirk Treaty: The Origins of NATO."
    Journal of Strategic Studies 5 (June 1982): 236-47.
_____. "Britain, the Brussels Pact and the Continental Commitment."
    International Affairs 60 (Autumn 1984): 615-29.
_____. "British Wartime Thinking About a Post-war European Security
    Group." *Review of International Studies* 9 (October 1983): 265-81.
Boyle, Peter G. "The British Foreign Office and American Foreign
    Policy, 1947-48." *Journal of American Studies* 16 (December 1982):
    373-89.
_____. "The British Foreign Office View of Soviet-American Relations,
    1945-46." *Diplomatic History* 3 (Summer 1979): 307-20.
Chambliss, W. C. "Base Nonsense." *United States Naval Institute Pro-
    ceedings* 71 (February 1945): 203-6.
Cunningham, Frank D. "Harry S. Truman and Universal Military Train-
    ing, 1945." *The Historian* 46 (May 1984): 397-415.
Davis, Forrest. "Roosevelt's World Blueprint." *Saturday Evening Post*
    215 (10 April 1943): 20+.
Evangelista, Matthew A. "Stalin's Postwar Army Reappraised." *Interna-
    tional Security* 7 (Winter 1982/1983): 110-38.
Goldberg, Alfred. "The Military Origins of the British Nuclear Deterrent."
    International Affairs 40 (October 1964): 600-618.
Gormly, James L. "Keeping the Door Open in Saudi Arabia: The United
    States and the Dhahran Airfield, 1945-46." *Diplomatic History* 4
    (Spring 1980): 189-205.
Greenwood, Sean. "Ernest Bevin, France and 'Western Union': August

1945-February 1946." *European History Quarterly* 14 (July 1984): 319-38.

_____. "Return to Dunkirk: The Origins of the Anglo-French Treaty of March 1947." *Journal of Strategic Studies* 6 (December 1983): 49-65.

Harbutt, Fraser. "American Challenge, Soviet Response: The Beginning of the Cold War, February-May, 1946." *Political Science Quarterly* 96 (Winter 1981-1982): 623-39.

Hogan, Michael J. "The Search for a 'Creative Peace': The United States, European Unity, and the Origins of the Marshall Plan." *Diplomatic History* 6 (Summer 1982): 267-85.

Hudson, Daryl J. "Vandenberg Reconsidered: Senate Resolution 239 and American Foreign Policy." *Diplomatic History* 1 (Winter 1977): 46-63.

Huntington, Samuel P. "National Policy and the Transoceanic Navy." *United States Naval Institute Proceedings* 80 (May 1954): 483-93.

Jackson, Scott. "Prologue to the Marshall Plan: The Origins of the American Commitment for a European Recovery Program." *Journal of American History* 65 (March 1979): 1043-68.

Kaplan, Lawrence S. "Toward the Brussels Pact." *Prologue* 12 (Summer 1980): 73-86.

Kepley, David R. "The Senate and the Great Debate of 1951." *Prologue* 14 (Winter 1982): 213-26.

Knight, Jonathan. "American Statecraft and the 1946 Black Sea Straits Controversy." *Political Science Quarterly* 90 (Fall 1975): 451-75.

_____. "America's International Guarantees for the Straits: Prelude to the Truman Doctrine." *Middle Eastern Studies* 13 (May 1977): 241-50.

Kousoulas, D. G. "The Truman Doctrine and the Stalin-Tito Rift: A Reappraisal." *South Atlantic Quarterly* 72 (Summer 1973): 427-39.

Krieger, Wolfgang. "Was General Clay a Revisionist? Strategic Aspects of the United States Occupation of Germany." *Journal of Contemporary History* 18 (April 1983): 165-84.

Leffler, Melvyn P. "The American Conception of National Security and the Beginnings of the Cold War, 1945-1948." *American Historical Review* 89 (April 1984): 346-81.

_____. "Strategy, Diplomacy, and the Cold War: The United States, Turkey, and NATO, 1945-1952." *Journal of American History* 71 (March 1985): 807-25.

Mark, Eduard. "American Policy toward Eastern Europe and the Origins of the Cold War, 1941-1946: An Alternative Interpretation." *Journal of American History* 68 (September 1981): 313-36.

_____. "Charles E. Bohlen and the Acceptable Limits of Soviet Hegemony in Eastern Europe: A Memorandum of 18 October 1945." *Diplomatic History* 3 (Spring 1979): 201-13.

Miscamble, Wilson D. "Anthony Eden and the Truman-Molotov Conversations, April 1945." *Diplomatic History* 2 (Spring 1978): 167-80.
_____. "The Evolution of an Internationalist: Harry S. Truman and American Foreign Policy." *The Australian Journal of Politics and History* 23 (August 1977): 268-83.
Moody, Walton S. "United States Air Forces in Europe and the Beginning of the Cold War." *Aerospace Historian* 23 (Summer/June 1976): 75-85.
Myers, Frank. "Conscription and the Politics of Military Strategy in the Attlee Government." *Journal of Strategic Studies* 7 (March 1984): 55-73.
Nitze, Paul. "The Development of NSC 68." *International Security* 4 (Spring 1980): 170-76.
Ovendale, R. "Britain, the U.S.A. and the European Cold War, 1945-8." *History* 67 (June 1982): 217-35.
Petersen, Nikolaj. "Britain, Scandinavia, and the North Atlantic Treaty, 1948-49." *Review of International Studies* 8 (October 1982): 251-68.
_____. "Who Pulled Whom and How Much? Britain, the United States and the Making of the North Atlantic Treaty." *Millenium: Journal of International Studies* 11 (Summer 1982): 93-114.
Pollard, Robert A. "Economic Security and the Origins of the Cold War: Bretton Woods, the Marshall Plan, and American Rearmament, 1944-50." *Diplomatic History* 9 (Summer 1985): 271-89.
Poole, Walter S. "From Conciliation to Containment: The Joint Chiefs of Staff and the Coming of the Cold War, 1945-1946." *Military Affairs* 42 (February 1978): 12-16.
Reid, Escott. "The Miraculous Birth of the North Atlantic Alliance," *NATO Review* 28 (December 1980): 12-18.
Resis, Albert. "The Churchill-Stalin Secret 'Percentages' Agreement on the Balkans, Moscow, October 1944." *American Historical Review* 83 (April 1978): 368-87.
Rosenberg, David Alan. "American Atomic Strategy and the Hydrogen Bomb Decision." *Journal of American History* 66 (June 1979): 62-87.
_____. "The Origins of Overkill: Nuclear Weapons and American Strategy, 1945-1960." *International Security* 7 (Spring 1983): 3-71.
_____. "The U.S. Navy and the Problem of Oil in a Future War: The Outline of a Strategic Dilemma, 1945-1950." *Naval War College Review* 29 (Summer 1976): 53-64.
_____. "U.S. Nuclear Stockpile, 1945 to 1950." *Bulletin of the Atomic Scientists* 38 (May 1982): 25-30.
Ross, Graham. "Foreign Office Attitudes and the Soviet Union, 1941-45." *Journal of Contemporary History* 16 (July 1981): 521-40.

Ryan, Henry B. "A New Look at Churchill's 'Iron Curtain' Speech."
    Historical Journal 22 (December 1979): 895-920.
Schlesinger, Arthur, Jr. "The Cold War Revisited." *New York Review of
    Books* 26 (25 October 1979): 46-52.
Selser, James C., Jr. "The Bomber's Role in Diplomacy." *Air Force*
    39 (April 1956): 52-56.
Singh, Anita Inder. "Imperial Defence and the Transfer of Power in
    India, 1946-1947." *International History Review* 4 (November
    1982): 568-88.
Siracusa, Joseph M. "The Night Stalin and Churchill Divided Europe:
    The View from Washington." *Review of Politics* 43 (July 1981):
    381-409.
Smith, Raymond, and John Zametica. "The Cold Warrior: Clement
    Attlee Reconsidered, 1945-7." *International Affairs* 61 (Spring
    1985): 237-52.
Stoler, Mark A. "From Continentalism to Globalism: General Stanley D.
    Embick, the Joint Strategic Survey Committee, and the Military
    View of American National Policy during the Second World War."
    Diplomatic History 6 (Summer 1982): 303-21.
Watt, Donald Cameron. "The British Cold War." *The Listener*, 1 June
    1978, 711-12.
Wiebes, Cees, and Bert Zeeman. "Baylis on Post-war Planning." *Review
    of International Studies* 10 (July 1984): 247-50.
————. "The Pentagon Negotiations March 1948: The Launching of the
    North Atlantic Treaty." *International Affairs* 59 (Summer 1983):
    351-63.
Xydis, Stephen G. "The Genesis of the Sixth Fleet." *United States Naval
    Institute Proceedings* 84 (August 1958): 41-50.
Young, John Wilson. "The Foreign Office and the Departure of General
    de Gaulle, June 1945-January 1946." *Historical Journal* 25 (March
    1982): 209-16.
Young, Lowell T. "Franklin D. Roosevelt and America's Islets: Acquisi-
    tion of Territory in the Caribbean and in the Pacific." *The Historian*
    35 (February 1973): 205-220.

INDEX

About the Author

RICHARD A. BEST, JR., is a research consultant in the areas of international relations and U.S. defense policy. He previously served as an analyst in the Office of Naval Intelligence and as a legislative assistant in the U.S. House of Representatives. He has contributed articles to *U.S. Naval Institute Proceedings* and the *Naval War College Review.*